"A Saint Joseph Edition"

COMPANION TO THE MISSAL

An Easy-to-Understand Explanation of the Mass Themes and Scripture Readings for All Sundays and Holydays

(Years A, B, C)

By

REV. JOHN KERSTEN, S.V.D.

Dedicated to ST. JOSEPH
Patron of the Universal Church

CATHOLIC BOOK PUBLISHING CO.
New York

NIHIL OBSTAT: Daniel V. Flynn, J.C.D.
Censor Librorum

IMPRIMATUR: ✠ Joseph T. O'Keefe, D.D.
Vicar General, Archdiocese of New York

The Mass themes and Scriptural commentaries found herein are a revised form of those originally printed in the *St. Joseph Sunday Missal and Hymnal*.

The Nihil obstat and imprimatur are official declarations that a book or pamphlet is free of doctrinal or moral error. No implication is contained therein that those who have granted the nihil obstat and imprimatur agree with the contents, opinions or statements expressed.

The Bible quotations contained herein are reproduced with permission from *The New American Bible*, Copyright © 1970 by the Confraternity of Christian Doctrine, Washington, D.C. All rights reserved.

(T-824)

© 1985 by *Catholic Book Publishing Co., N.Y.*
Printed in U.S.A.

PREFACE

IN Brazil there are thousands upon thousands of Biblical circles–base communities, each of which is composed of groups of families and their friends who come together to discuss their life in the light of Scripture. The groups are schooled to "see, judge, act," keeping in mind, though, that the conscious distinction between original meaning and contemporary significance has to be maintained. The leaders of these groups, trained lay persons, are called "ministros da Palavra—ministers of the Word."

A Third World Country is leading! We in this country should catch up.

This book may help both individuals and groups who come together to prepare the Sunday Liturgy. Together they may "see, judge, act," discuss their life in Biblical perspective, and pray over it. Since the themes of the first and third readings are always related, they may be read privately or discussed in one session. If deemed feasible, the second readings may be the topic of reflection another time.

After Vatican II, we have done away with so many paradigms, which kept us together. Let Bible and meaningful celebration of the Sunday Liturgy fill the vacuum!

This text is mostly a reprint of the Introductions originally written for the "St. Joseph Sunday Missal." They were and still are well accepted all over the English-speaking world. One legitimate complaint by some, though, is the small print in the Missal which was mandatory to keep manageable a book that embraces the three cycles A, B, and C in one volume. The large print in this edition will correct this.

John C. Kersten, S.V.D.

CONTENTS

1985—B	1988—B	1991—B	1994—B	1997—B
1986—C	1989—C	1992—C	1995—C	1998—C
1987—A	1990—A	1993—A	1996—A	1999—A

	Year A	Year B	Year C
ADVENT SEASON	7	7	7
1st Sunday of Advent	8	127	227
2nd Sunday of Advent	9	129	229
3rd Sunday of Advent	11	130	231
4th Sunday of Advent	12	132	232
CHRISTMAS SEASON	14	14	14
Dec. 25: Christmas (Mass of Vigil)	15	15	15
Dec. 25: Christmas (Mass at Midnight)	16	16	16
Dec. 25: Christmas (Mass at Dawn) ...	18	18	18
Dec. 25: Christmas (During the Day) ..	19	19	19
Holy Family	21	134	234
Octave of Christmas	23	23	23
2nd Sunday after Christmas	24	24	24
Epiphany	26	26	26
Baptism of the Lord	27	137	236
ORDINARY TIME	29	29	29
2nd Sunday in Ordinary Time	30	138	238
3rd Sunday in Ordinary Time	31	140	240
4th Sunday in Ordinary Time	33	142	242
5th Sunday in Ordinary Time	35	144	244
6th Sunday in Ordinary Time	37	145	246
7th Sunday in Ordinary Time	38	148	248
8th Sunday in Ordinary Time	40	150	250
9th Sunday in Ordinary Time	41	151	251
LENTEN SEASON	43	43	43
1st Sunday of Lent	44	153	253
2nd Sunday of Lent	45	155	255
3rd Sunday of Lent	47	157	256
4th Sunday of Lent	48	159	258

Contents

	Year A	Year B	Year C
5th Sunday of Lent	50	161	260
Passion Sunday [Palm Sunday]	52	162	262
EASTER SEASON	55	55	55
Easter Vigil Midnight Mass	56	56	56
Easter Sunday	57	57	57
2nd Sundy of Easter	60	166	265
3rd Sunday of Easter	62	168	267
4th Sunday of Easter	64	170	269
5th Sundy of Easter	66	171	271
6th Sunday of Easter	67	173	272
Ascension	69	175	275
7th Sunday of Easter	72	177	277
Pentecost (Vigil Mass)	73	73	73
Pentecost (Mass During the Day)	76	76	76
ORDINARY TIME (cont'd)	79	79	79
Trinity Sunday	80	179	279
Corpus Christi	81	181	280
10th Sunday in Ordinary Time	83	183	282
11th Sunday in Ordinary Time	85	184	284
12th Sunday in Ordinary Time	87	186	286
13th Sunday in Ordinary Time	88	188	288
14th Sunday in Ordinary Time	90	190	290
15th Sunday in Ordinary Time	92	191	292
16th Sunday in Ordinary Time	93	193	294
17th Sunday in Ordinary Time	95	195	295
18th Sunday in Ordinary Time	97	196	297
19th Sunday in Ordinary Time	99	198	299
20th Sunday in Ordinary Time	100	200	300
21st Sunday in Ordinary Time	102	202	302
22nd Sunday in Ordinary Time	104	204	304
23rd Sunday in Ordinary Time	106	205	306
24th Sunday in Ordinary Time	107	207	307
25th Sunday in Ordinary Time	109	209	309

Contents

	Year A	Year B	Year C
26th Sunday in Ordinary Time	111	210	311
27th Sunday in Ordinary Time	112	212	312
28th Sunday in Ordinary Time	114	214	314
29th Sunday in Ordinary Time	116	216	316
30th Sunday in Ordinary Time	118	218	318
31st Sunday in Ordinary Time	119	219	320
32nd Sunday in Ordinary Time	121	221	321
33rd Sunday in Ordinary Time	123	223	323
Christ the King	125	225	325

HOLYDAYS AND MAJOR FEASTS

Feb. 2: Presentation of the Lord 327
Mar. 19: St. Joseph 329
Mar. 25: Annunciation 330
June 24: Birth of St. John (Vigil) 332
June 24: Birth of St John (Day) 334
June 29: Sts. Peter and Paul (Vigil) 335
June 29: Sts. Peter and Paul (Day) 336
Aug. 6: Transfiguration 338
Aug. 15: Assumption (Vigil) 339
Aug. 15: Assumption (Day) 341
Sept. 14: Triumph of the Cross 342
Nov. 1: All Saints 343
Nov. 2: All Souls (1st Mass) 345
Nov. 2: All Souls (2nd Mass) 347
Nov. 2: All Souls (3rd Mass) 347
Nov. 9: Dedication of St. John Lateran 348
Dec. 8: Immaculate Conception 350

YEAR A
ADVENT SEASON

THE word "Advent" (Coming) indicates how Christians view the four-week period preceding the Nativity of our Lord. It is a time of preparation for an ever more intimate coming of the Lord to you and all of us.

When I come to visit a friend, I am present to him/her. Coming results in presence. Of course, the Lord is already present to his people. Therefore, his coming at Christmas should result in a more intimate presence. People (friends, lovers) who get to know and love one another better are becoming more intimately, more personally, present to one another. It is a question of opening up and sharing one another's personality. Our preparation for Christ's coming should consist in an ever more opening up to him who wants to share our human condition in loving care.

By preparing for the Lord's coming time and again at Christmas, Christians prepare for his final coming, which will be decisive for you and all human beings. "Now we watch for the day hoping that the salvation promised us will be ours when Christ our Lord will come again in his glory" (Preface of Advent).

1st SUNDAY OF ADVENT
Be Watchful!

WITH God revealing himself in the Lord Jesus, we Christians believe that there is a future for human beings. Life is not an absurdity. Death is not "a transition from being into nothingness," as some contemporary "sages" allege. Life has meaning.

In the confusion of daily life, the Lord Jesus comes to save us from apparent absurdity, from dangerous inertia and the numbness which the sedatives of modern life can bring about. The only prerequisite is that we be watchful and open up to him and his message found in the Scriptures. "When he [the Lord Jesus] comes may he find us watching in prayer, our hearts filled with wonder and praise" (Preface of Advent).

Reading I   Is 2, 1-5
Working for the Messiah's Peace

Inspired by God, the prophet Isaiah sees a bright future in the Messianic era—the time when God will appear in his Messiah, his anointed vicegerent on earth. The setting is Zion, the holy mountain of Jerusalem with the temple, God's dwelling place.

"They shall beat their swords into plowshares . . . , nor shall they ever train for war again." Wishful thinking? We Christians see Isaiah's vision fulfilled in Jesus, God's anointed one, the Christ. Therefore, "O house of Jacob [God's people], come, let us walk in the light of the Lord."

With God, present in Christ Jesus, we should keep working for this seemingly impossible dream. Start in your family, in your school, at your job, making them places of Shalom—peace.

Reading II   Rom 13, 11-14
"Put on the Lord Jesus"

Be watchful! Wake up! Carousing, drunkenness, sexual excess, lust, quarreling and jealousy are part of the human condition. The deeds of darkness can make us numb and insensitive to the beauty of life.

"Put on the Lord Jesus," i.e., be ever more intimately united to him and what he stands for, and a bright future of Shalom—peace will be yours.

Gospel — The Lord's Coming — Mt 24, 37-44

The coming of the Lord requires a decision. It is "either-or"! Matthew the evangelist is quite serious about this. It should be a decision of "conversion" to Jesus right now, as you are preparing for his coming on Christmas.

Again, be watchful! The moment you least expect it could be the final coming of the Lord to you. Do not become so engrossed in the daily routine of life that you forget that the Day of the Son of Man may come at any time.

2nd SUNDAY OF ADVENT
Christ's Leadership

CHRIST is the answer to the frightening questions of life. When the leaders of a nation are corrupt, its people usually suffer. The human family on this planet is afflicted with many maladies resulting from lack of leadership. The Hebrews of Isaiah's time (800 B.C.) yearned for a leader, an ideal king, who would be capable of restoring the nation and endowing it once again with the peace and prosperity of King David's time.

Jesus Christ is the God-given Leader, who came to establish God's kingdom on earth, "a kingdom of truth and life, a kingdom of justice, love and peace" (Preface of Christ the King). The Spirit of the Lord—a Spirit of wisdom, understanding, counsel, strength, knowledge and fear (filial respect) of the Lord—rests upon him (Reading I).

"Justice shall flourish in his time, and fullness of peace for ever" (Responsorial Psalm). Are you accepting Jesus Christ and the outlines he gives for a better society? We know that the ideal society as envisioned by Jesus will never be fully realized on this planet. Neither do we state that the Bible has all the answers. But society would be much better if all would heed the guiding principles of Jesus of Nazareth. Let us Christians give the example!

A — 2nd Sunday of Advent

Reading I   Is 11, 1-10
The Messiah's Kingdom

The setting of this reading is Jerusalem of Isaiah's time, the eighth century B.C. The king is Ahaz, a weak young man. Though a ne'er-do-well, he is of the royal family of David, whose father was Jesse. Ahaz has brought the royal family and his country to such ruin that Isaiah compares the left-overs with the stump of a tree.

But from the root of that stump a bud shall blossom. From this seemingly dead stock God will bring out a shoot, a prince, who will prove himself an ideal king. It is the yearning of a people that walk in darkness for an ideal king (leader) to come!

Christians see all of this yearning fulfilled in God's Anointed One, Jesus of Nazareth. The Spirit of the Lord rests upon him. He has established an ideal kingdom (reign) of peace and justice which is already partially realized now on earth and will be fully realized in the world to come.

Reading II   Rom 15, 4-9
Yearning for Christ

Paul tells us that Scripture was written for our instruction, that we might derive hope from it. In Christ is the yearning of people fulfilled.

Accept Jesus Christ as your leader, and heed his great commandment to accept one another! Like Christ, become one another's servants! Then you will be working toward the realization of that seemingly impossible dream of Isaiah and Jesus: A society where "the wolf is the guest of the lamb" (Reading I).

Gospel   Mt 3, 1-12
Change of Life-style

Preparing for the Lord's coming and fully accepting him may require a change in life-style. John the Baptizer speaks clear language not just to the Jews of his time but to all of us. You should not delay a decision.

"His [Jesus Christ's] winnowing-fan is in his hand. He will clear his threshing floor." Make sure you do not end up with the chaff that will be burned up in "unquenchable fire."

3rd SUNDAY OF ADVENT
Joyful in Hope

THE BIBLE readings for today tell us again about a bright future, seemingly a utopia. "Joyful in hope" is a Christian's theme of life.

Christian hope opposes despair, which often results in suicide or just "copping out." It opposes escaping from reality through the use of drugs, abuse of alcohol, or excessive addiction to the pleasures of modern life. Christian hope knows how to handle depression: You get on your knees, knowing that "over the world of the stars, a loving Father must reside" (Ode to Joy" in 9th Symphony of Beethoven).

What would you tell a friend who knows that he is a terminal cancer patient? A man without faith or hope might say: "Face it! We all have to die sooner or later!" What would you say? A Christian knows about "More to come. Stay tuned in!"

Reading I   Is 35, 1-6. 10
Christ, Light of the World

This beautiful poem is attributed to the so-called "Second Isaiah," a prophet who stayed with the Hebrews in Babylonian exile. This prophet saw the Babylonian rule about to be toppled by the mighty King Cyrus of Syria, who would free the captives and let them go home.

This is a poem of joyful hope. "Say to those whose hearts are frightened: Be strong, fear not! Here is your God, he comes with vindication."

Christians apply this vision to the future brought about by Jesus, the Messiah, God's Anointed One. "Then will the eyes of the blind be opened. The Lord gives sight to the blind." This is our Christmas theme of joyful hope: Our Lord, who comes to be a light to the world. The lights of Christmas symbolize this idea.

Reading II   Jas 5, 7-10
Patience in Affliction

James reminds us not to be overly optimistic. The bright future of the Messianic era will not be fully realized on this side of the grave. We must not be patient! "But steady your hearts, because the coming of the Lord is at hand."

The prophets should be our models. If you are suffering, this reading could be an inspiring starting point for a personal prayer to God!

Gospel   Mt 11, 2-11
The Beauty of Life

Matthew takes up the theme of the first Bible reading. "In reply, Jesus said: 'The blind recover their sight.' " Jesus is the one-to-come who will give hope to those who suffer.

This "hope" can be finding a way out of trouble through the aid of a loving human being; it can be resignation and acceptance of the unavoidable, founded in faith in a future to come hereafter. Every Christmas, the Lord Jesus should open our eyes to the beauty of life, and its extension, the life to come.

———◆———

4th SUNDAY OF ADVENT
Faith

KING Ahaz had more faith in a treaty with the Assyrians than in God, who approached him in the prophet Isaiah (Reading I). It is faith in God, who approaches us in the Lord Jesus, that saves us from a meaningless existence. God is willing to step into the darkness of our confusion, if we "let the Lord enter" (Responsorial Psalm).

Loneliness is the greatest threat to happiness. A person alone has no answers. A loner is an unhappy person, depressed, facing absurdity. "Emmanuel—God with us" in Jesus Christ saves us from ourselves.

Time and again, Christmas reminds Christians that God came to share our human situation on this planet. Looked at in this way, Christmas will become a happy and meaningful day for us. "Lord, as Christmas draws near make us grow in faith and love to celebrate the coming of Christ our Savior" (Prayer after Communion).

A — 4th Sunday of Advent

Reading I
Is 7, 10-14
God Willing To Step In

Just as at the Second Sunday of Advent, the setting of Isaiah's oracle is Jerusalem of 735-715 B.C., the reign of King Ahaz. God's people is in deep trouble mainly through the mismanagement of the king, who has rejected the offer of a "sign," which in the Bible is usually some event assuring human beings of divine intervention. Nevertheless, a "sign" is given. The virgin (young maiden) who will bear a son is probably Abi, the young wife of King Ahaz. "Immanuel" (with us is God) is his son.

The point (God's word to us) seems to be: When we are in trouble, going through the semi-darkness of the human situation, God is willing to step in, if in faith we let him do so. (For further explanation of this oracle, see the Gospel.)

Reading II
Rom 1, 1-7
Obedient Faith

Paul explains who the Savior, Jesus Christ, is. He is fully man, a descendant of King David, but made Son of God in power. Paul's task is to bring to obedient faith all the Gentiles.

It is through our "obedient faith" in the Lord Jesus, sent by God to enlighten all who go through the darkness of the human condition, that we will be saved.

Gospel
Mt 1, 18-24
God with Us

Matthew quotes Isaiah's oracle of today's first Bible reading. Both Matthew and the Church have seen in the birth of Christ from the Virgin Mother the perfect fulfillment of Isaiah's prophecy. It is in and through Jesus Christ that God steps in to save us, who pass through the twilight of human existence.

In the Lord Jesus, God is "Emmanuel—God with us." And this tremendous mystery ("God is with us—you do not have to go it alone") is what we are going to celebrate at Christmas. "Let the Lord enter; he is the king of glory" (Responsorial Psalm).

CHRISTMAS SEASON

CHRISTMAS is not just a commemoration of our Lord's birth, but the celebration of the great "Emmanuel" (God-is-with-us) mystery. A wealth of symbolism is used in the prayers and Bible readings of this season to shed some light on this tremendous fact that God wants to share our human condition. The light versus darkness theme is perhaps the most primitive one.

We have no evidence of Christmas earlier than approximately 330 A.D., and it appears to have been determined not primarily by our Lord's birth date, which is unknown, but rather by the pagan festivals of the winter solstice, when worshipers of the Sun celebrated the return of light after the shortest day. At Christmas, Christians celebrate the dawn of God's light shining upon human beings, who go through a valley of darkness.

Over the centuries, popular piety has sentimentalized Christmas into the well-known "baby Jesus" cult. This kind of piety is not reflected in the liturgical prayers and Bible readings of the Church. The four Christmas Masses, the feast of the Holy Family, the Solemnity of Mary, Mother of God, the Epiphany (Manifestation) of the Lord, and his Baptism elucidate the various aspects of God's self-disclosure in the Lord Jesus, in whom he is really "Emmanuel—God with us." "In him [Jesus] we see our God made visible and so are caught up in love of the God we cannot see" (Preface to the Eucharistic Prayer at Christmas).

December 25 — CHRISTMAS

MASS OF THE VIGIL

God Cares

TOURIST bureaus, which organize guided tours, usually show the better parts of the city. If you want to see the slums and misery of a large part of the population, you must explore a city on your own. Evil is something one wants to hide from visitors. But if you are honest, you cannot deny its existence.

Evil exists in and around us. We feel that often we fail to be the kind of persons we should be. When we have shown our ugly selves in an outburst of impatience or spell of selfishness, we should apologize and heal the wound we have made. There is even more evil around us, and it enslaves us more than we want to admit. We need redemption from selfishness, apathy and complacency in the kind of happiness which the mass media and society are constantly imposing on us.

"Tomorrow [Christmas, present to you!] the wickedness of the earth will be destroyed" (Gospel Acclamation). "May we celebrate this eucharist with greater joy than ever since it marks the beginning of our redemption" (Prayer over the Gifts).

Reading I   Is 62, 1-5

Have Hope!

The unknown prophet, called "Third Isaiah," addresses the Jews who have come from Babylonian exile. The reconstruction of their homeland is not working too well. There is widespread disappointment. The prophet encourages his fellow citizens. "Have hope! Better times are at hand. God cares."

The writer uses the model of marital love to describe God's care for his people. Through the incarnation, becoming "one flesh" (Mt 19, 6) with the human race, God espouses you and me. He sets us free, and "as a bridegroom rejoices in his bride, so shall your God rejoice in you." Let us "for ever sing the goodness of the Lord" (Responsorial Psalm).

16   A-B-C — Christmas (Midnight Mass)

Reading II   Acts 13, 16-17. 22-25
A Savior for You and Me

Paul explains the mystery of "Emmanuel—God with us" to the Jews in the synagogue of Antioch. These people know their history: their bondage in Egypt and their great King David.

God saved in the past. He continues to do so but now on a much broader scale through Jesus, "a savior for Israel," i.e., today, a savior for you and me.

Gospel   Mt 1, 1-25 or 1, 18-25
Called Emmanuel

Matthew wants to introduce Jesus as a very important person, and as customary in Biblical culture, he does so by mentioning his impressive ancestry. Although he was born of the family of David, Jesus' list of ancestors has been fashioned by Matthew into a set of three times fourteen generations for reasons that suggest perfection. The virginal birth of our Lord too brings out his importance as Son of God. He was conceived through the power of the Holy Spirit.

We learn from this that Jesus is indeed a very important person, the most important person of all history. He is the human being in whom God became man, Emmanuel—God with us.

MASS AT MIDNIGHT
Good News and Great Joy

WHERE politicians and their leadership fail and disappoint us, it is "good news and great joy" that reliable leadership is available. It has been said that a philosophy of science must be created in the near future, otherwise mankind is going to make this planet uninhabitable for the next generations, the lifetime of our children and grandchildren.

This philosophy must lay the foundation for ecology, the global use of the planet's resources, the function of money, international law, and the solution of other vital problems. Emmanuel (God with us in the Lord Jesus) offers such a philosophy of science. "Upon us, who dwell in the land of gloom, a light has shone."

A-B-C — Christmas (Midnight Mass)

Tonight, we should more than ever be aware of the wealth of our Christian heritage. And though we cannot claim to have ready-made answers for all the details, the Bible and the great social encyclicals of recent Popes give outlines which the human race can safely follow. "Today is born our Savior. He shall rule the world with justice and the peoples with his constancy" (Responsorial Psalm).

Reading I   Is 9, 1-6
His Dominion Vast and Peaceful

This enthronement anthem, to be sung when a new king ascended the throne, expresses faith in the new king. He will do better than his predecessors. "For a child is born to us" refers to the fact that the enthronement of the king was conceived as God's adoption of the king as his son.

Christians have reinterpreted this. Now these words suggest the birth at Bethlehem and explain what the Lord Jesus means to all of us. "His dominion is vast and forever peaceful." Hence, "sing to the Lord, bless his name, tell his glory among the nations" (Responsorial Psalm).

Reading II   A Philosophy of Life   Ti 2, 11-14

In the introduction to today's Mass it was mentioned that we need a philosophy of science in order to survive. Paul offers some Christian philosophy of life: "Reject godless ways, live temperately, justly and devoutly."

This is the way Christians try to live between the two comings of Christ: his first coming (the grace of God appearing—Bethlehem) and his final coming (awaiting the blessed hope).

Gospel   Lk 2, 1-14
Salvation for All

The narratives concerning Christ's infancy, as we find them in Matthew and Luke, pose difficult problems for those who would use them to reconstruct actual history. "The details and style of the narratives are symbolic and biblical; they communicate the mystery of redemption, not a diary of early events" (Jerome Commentary).

We should not romanticize the shepherds. They were the lowest strata of Jewish society and very poor. Luke shows that salvation is for them, just as it was for prostitutes and tax collectors later to be found in Jesus' company. Likewise the angelic announcement should be seen as a biblical way of bringing out the meaning of the Christ event.

Learn from Luke that divine salvation, initiated with Christ's birth, is for all, but especially for the lowly, the poor, the disadvantaged.

MASS AT DAWN
A Light Will Shine on Us

ANCIENT peoples, living before the electronic age, feared darkness more than we do. Darkness stands for isolation, uncertainty, evil, and also ignorance. We still speak of actions that shun daylight, and of the dark Middle Ages, a time of ignorance and decay. Light, especially bright daylight, changes a dark situation.

This contrast of light and darkness is used in today's Liturgy to explain the mystery of Christmas. "A light will shine on us this day, the Lord is born for us" (Responsorial Psalm). "Father, we are filled with the new light. . . . May the light of faith shine in our words and actions" (Opening Prayer).

The birth of our Lord marks the dawn of the Christian era. Christianity—Christians, you and I, filled with the light of faith—should shed light on dark human situations in our words and actions. The lights of your Christmas tree should symbolize this Christian concern.

Reading I   Is 62, 11-12
Your Savior Comes!

Salvation is promised to "daughter Zion," the holy mountain of Jerusalem, which stands for God's people. They shall be called "the redeemed of the Lord."

The Church reapplies this to the birth of Christ, which marks the dawn of our redemption from darkness and ignorance. "Light dawns for the just [you and me]; and gladness, for the upright of heart" (Responsorial Psalm).

A-B-C — Christmas (Day)

Reading II — Ti 3, 4-7
God Our Savior Appeared

The kindness and love of God was formerly hidden from human beings to a certain extent. If human beings follow the candlelight of their own insight, they live in semi-darkness. They are not aware of the overwhelming presence of a loving God. A television show is there right in your room, but you are not aware of it unless you are able to tune in.

Since God's love "appeared" in the Lord Jesus, we are aware of it and it saves us. Paul reminds us that this is a free gift of God, for which we should be grateful.

Gospel — Lk 2, 15-20
Go and See!

Luke associates Jesus with shepherds, poor people, members of a despised trade, just as he will do later with prostitutes and other kinds of sinners. These disadvantaged people have seen the light. "The glory of the Lord shone around them" (Lk 2, 9). Hence their conclusion: "Let us go over and see!"

Luke wants you and me to do the same today: go and see and try to understand what has been told to you concerning this child. Mary should be your example. "She treasured all these things and reflected on them in her heart."

MASS DURING THE DAY
God's Word Made Flesh

IF we are not able to meet famous persons, we can get to know them through pictures and the recording of their voice. We get even a better idea, if we have the opportunity to talk repeatedly with one of their children. This Christmas Mass sees the birth of Christ as "God's Word made flesh" so that we humans can hear it. God has an announcement to make! We should listen attentively and try to understand it.

Whatever God has to tell us has been made "flesh" in the words, actions, and loving personality of the Lord Jesus, born in Bethlehem, reared in Nazareth, put to death in Jerusalem.

The second Bible reading sees in the Christ-event God's final revelation to the human race.

However, we Christians should beware of triumphalism. Although in fragmentary and varied ways, God reveals himself (speaks) in all of creation, in the Jewish religion and in other religions as well. Each religion has its own distinctive insight. "They often reflect a ray of that truth which enlightens all" (Vatican II: *Relationship of the Church to Non-Christian Religions*, no. 2). As for the culmination of God's self-disclosure, we believe it took place in the Lord Jesus.

The point (God's word to you and me) is: Grow in awareness of God anywhere, but especially by careful study of Jesus Christ, "the exact representation of the Father's being" (Reading II).

Reading I — Is 52, 7-10
"Your God Is King"

God leads his people back from the exile in Babylon to Zion (site of the Jerusalem temple), from whose ruined walls watchmen shout for joy. The Church reapplies this passage to the Christmas event.

"Your God is king" in his Messiah, on whose shoulders dominion is laid and who shall be called Wonderful-Counselor (Entrance Antiphon). This represents "glad tidings," "euangelion" (Gospel), indeed, for the Lord comforts his people, leading us back from exile to our abode with him.

Reading II — Heb 1, 1-6
Reflection of the Father's Glory

God has spoken to us through his Son, his Word "made flesh." "This Son is the reflection of the Father's glory." It is true that we Christians can—like all human beings find God in his creation, daily life, and any religious statement through which he speaks "in fragmentary and varied ways." However, we also possess "the exact representation of the Father's being," his Word made flesh, in the Lord Jesus, given to us in Bethlehem of Judah.

Gospel Jn 1, 1-18 or 1, 1-5. 9-14
God's Word Made Flesh

The Gospel uses both the "Word" model (God's Word made flesh) and the symbolism of light to elucidate what the Lord Jesus is supposed to mean to us Christians. The light can shine in darkness and not overcome it. (The lights of the Christmas tree shining on sophisticated unbelievers and party-goers!) "The Word became flesh and made his dwelling among us."

Are you opening up and accepting it? Only then will your Christmas be real and your Christmas joy not be gone with your tree on the garbage heap! "God of love, make us faithful to your Word" (Opening Prayer).

Sunday in the Octave of Christmas
HOLY FAMILY
Family Life

WE are witnessing a breakdown of the traditional family and its values—filial respect for authority, exercised responsibly by parents—and a rising juvenile delinquency. Hence, our society can learn a few things from today's Bible readings.

There is no easy remedy available for today's family crisis. The Christian family is part of a culture in which human beings participate—neighborhood, school, television, friends and recreation patterns. But in stormy weather a ship may get at least some guidance from a beacon! And although authority from the earliest infancy on should be exercised perhaps in a different way, it should not be done away with. Parents could discuss this with their children. A substitute for sound family life has not yet been offered by any of the behavioral sciences.

Today's readings on the family necessarily reflect the patriarchal family pattern, hence the subordinationist family ethic, of the Biblical culture. We should distinguish between the core of the Christian ethic and the cloth in which it is wrapped. This cloth is conditioned by time and culture and not necessarily part of the divine message. But the message on family life as such is timeless.

A — Holy Family

Reading I   Sir 3, 2-6. 12-14
Filial Respect

By keeping in mind that the point of this passage (God's word to us) is conditioned by time and culture, a modern Christian can succeed in learning from it.

Respect, reverence, and love are values that should be cherished. Take care of your parents when they are old. Show love and care, even if you soothe your conscience with the fact that he/she is well taken care of in an old people's home far away! "Happy are those who fear [show filial respect to] the Lord and walk in his ways" (Responsorial Psalm). Nature, hence God, wants the family!

Reading II   Col 3, 12-21
Family Bible Reading?

The holy family, Jesus, Mary, Joseph, must have cherished the values brought out in this Bible passage. "Let the word of Christ dwell in you." Why not try regular family Bible reading, with a discussion afterward and an improvised prayer by one member of the family at the end?

The idea of wives being "submissive to your husbands" may not appeal to "women's lib"; however, where there is genuine love, constantly fostered, a mutual pattern of "doing the loving thing" spontaneously originates. Love and bitterness are incompatible.

Gospel   Mt 2, 13-15. 19-23
A Family Man's Care

Writing as a Jew for Christians of Jewish background, Matthew wants to present Jesus as recapitulating the history of Israel in his life. Israel was in Egypt. Matthew sees Jesus as a second Moses and the true Israel, God's chosen one. In order to bring this out, he uses this symbolic narrative.

Leaving evangelical explanations up to Bible scholars, we ask: What is the point, God's word to me? Today it may be Joseph's (hence any family man's) care for his wife and child, related to a firm faith in God. "Eternal Father, we want to live as Jesus, Mary and Joseph, in peace with you and one another" (Prayer after Communion).

January 1

OCTAVE OF CHRISTMAS
SOLEMNITY OF MARY, MOTHER OF GOD

Mary, Mother of God

PREGNANCY, birth, choosing a name, and baptism (in the Jewish faith, circumcision) are great events for a young mother who goes through this experience for the first time. Only mothers can witness this wonderful time in their lives. Outsiders can only marvel about the beautiful miracle God works in a woman, time and again.

In the second reading, Paul states that Jesus was "born of a woman, born under the law"; in other words, thoroughly human, greatly determined by the love, care, education, example and personality of his mother. This indicates the greatness of Mary. She is the mother of Jesus as man, but since Jesus is both God and man, Mary deserves the title of "Mother of God," just as any woman deserves the title of "mother of a medical doctor" if her son is one.

Notice that Mary did not understand clearly all the ramifications of her vocation right away from the beginning (Lk 1, 45). Yet, in faith, her whole life was a repeated "Let it be done to me as you say."

Reading I   Nm 6, 22-27
The Lord Bless You!

Israel, God's chosen people, knew God from what he did for them. By calling upon his name and power, the liturgical prayer of this reading implores God's graciousness for all of us.

"May God let his face shine upon us!" (Responsorial Psalm). God's face became visible to us in the face of the Lord Jesus.

Reading II   Gal 4, 4-7
Born of a Woman

In Jesus, God has given us all. Once we were slaves, subjected to evil, but in the Lord Jesus God adopted us as his children. Mary played an important role in God's self-disclosure as Father. She is the Mother of God's Son, in whose spirit we can cry out "Abba!" ("Father!").

Gospel   Lk 2, 16-21
Mary Reflecting

Whoever receives Jesus Christ receives the message of salvation. Luke relates the shepherds, poor and despised, as the first ones to receive Jesus as a Savior.

"Mary treasured all these things and reflected on them in her heart." As such Mary is an example to all praying people! "Father, may Mary's prayer, born of a humble heart, draw your Spirit to rest on your people" (Opening Prayer).

2nd SUNDAY AFTER CHRISTMAS
The Word Made His Dwelling Among Us

EVERY serious person desires a meaningful life. Wanting to be a playboy implies wanting to be and remain a boy, i.e., immature! We need a philosophy of life. As Christians, we believe that the wisdom (word, light) of God was dwelling in Jesus Christ. We look to the philosophy of life of the Lord Jesus as an example to be followed. We study the values he stood for.

The Hebrew Bible, the Old Testament, knows various ways of God's dwelling with human beings. A bright cloud is often a sign of God's mysterious presence. Divine wisdom dwells in Israel: "In Zion [the holy Temple mountain] I fixed my abode. I [God's wisdom] have struck root among the glorious people" (Reading I). God's wisdom as personified in this passage is still a figure of speech, perhaps a forerunner of the New Testament insight, where the wisdom (word) of God is seen as incarnated in the Lord Jesus.

A-B-C — 2nd Sunday After Christmas

In faith, Christians accept this hidden presence of God and by doing so are empowered to become children of God. Did God's wisdom (word, light) strike root in you? Others should notice it! "God of power and life, fill the world with your splendor and show the nations the light of your truth" (Opening Prayer).

Reading I   Sir 24, 1-4. 8-12
In Zion I Fixed My Abode

"A pillar of cloud" refers to the pillar in the desert manifesting God's "mist-like" presence. Clouds are often used as symbols of God's self-manifestation.

The Hebrews were proud of possessing God's wisdom, as incorporated in the Law of Moses. "He has not done thus for any other nation; his ordinances he has not made known to them" (Responsorial Psalm).

Reading II   Eph 1, 3-6. 15-18
Your Innermost Vision Enlightened

The Hebrews were proud to have God's wisdom as incarnated in the Torah, the Law of Moses. Paul explains that God has bestowed his blessings on us Christians, in Jesus Christ, the Word (wisdom, light) made flesh.

"May he [God] enlighten your innermost vision" that you may be aware of what we possess in the Lord Jesus.

Gospel   Jn 1, 1-18 or 1, 1-5. 9-14
His Dwelling Among Us

In beautiful poetical language, the evangelist meditates on our riches in Jesus Christ. Although covered by the humanity of Jesus, the wisdom (word, light) of God dwells with us. "For while the law was a gift through Moses (Reading I: God's wisdom incarnated in the Law of Moses), this enduring love came through Jesus Christ."

John warns us of our duty to appreciate God's gift. "To his own he came, yet his own did not accept him." We should accept in faith!

Sunday between January 2 and January 8
EPIPHANY
Jesus' Royal Messiahship of Both Jews and Gentiles

OFTEN people travel and pay $25.00 or $100.00 a plate to attend a dinner party where a famous politician makes an appearance. Today we celebrate the appearance of the Lord Jesus on the human scene. For the Greeks, the word "Epiphany" was used to describe the appearance or manifestation of a god among human beings. The Greek Fathers used it for the Incarnation of the Son of God.

As the feast is celebrated now in the Western Church, it brings out a prominent aspect of the Christmas Mystery, namely, the manifestation (epiphany) of the universal dominion of the newborn King, as dramatized in the Lord Jesus' manifestation to the Magi (wise men from the East).

Again the symbolism of light is lavishly used. "This day Christ appeared to the world as a light shining in the darkness. May you follow him in faith and be a light to others" (Solemn Blessing).

Reading I   Is 60, 1-6
Nations Walking by Your Light

Returning from exile in Babylon, the Jews make a pilgrimage to Jerusalem. The poet envisages all nations joining this pilgrimage to the light. God manifesting himself in Jesus Christ is a light shining in the darkness of the human condition. The Gentiles (non-Jews) responding to this revelation of God in Christ are symbolized by the Magi.

The Responsorial Psalm (72) describes the bliss of God's reign, if fully accepted. Pray that all may see the light!

Reading II   Eph 3, 2-3. 5-6
All Sharers of the Promise!

Paul stresses that God manifested himself in the Lord Jesus not only to the Jews but to all nations. The Gentiles (non-Jews) are now co-heirs with the Jews, members of Christ's body and sharers of the divine promise.

"God has called you out of darkness, with his wonderful light: May you be strong in faith, hope and love" (Solemn Blessing).

Gospel
We Observed His Star — Mt 2, 1-12

Yearning for self-determination, the Jews were constantly expecting a Messiah (Anointed King), freedom fighter, and redeemer from oppression. There was even a horoscope circulating, telling about his star, and we can readily understand that a superstitious Herod might be upset by astrologers.

But rather than searching for the background material of this story we ask: Inspired by God, what does Matthew try to bring out by adding this legend to his Gospel, because that is God's word to you and me? Quoting Scripture, Matthew teaches Jesus is the ruler who is to shepherd God's people. God's Epiphany (self-manifestation) in Jesus Christ is for all! All should join mankind's search for the Light of the World!

Sunday after the Epiphany
BAPTISM OF THE LORD
The Servant of Yahweh

EVERY time we discover a new aspect in the person we love, we stop in wonderment. "I did not know him/her as such!" And this deeper insight and sharing in a person's self results in greater appreciation, intimacy, and love.

Today we celebrate the Lord's baptism by John in the Jordan. Matthew relates Jesus' baptism as another epiphany (manifestation), declaring that the Lord Jesus is the servant (Son) of Yahweh. His call in life is that of the Servant as depicted in today's first reading. This is an aspect of Jesus' personality which gives us a deeper insight into who our Lord is. He is "the man for others." He is there for you and me.

Experiencing this in prayer, we should appreciate and love our Lord more for it. We each have our own calling in life. We must respond to it in the framework of our personal capabilities and the circumstances of time and milieu. Serious and mature people understand that only a life of service is a meaningful life.

A — Baptism of the Lord

What do you consider your main calling in life, and how do you fulfill it?

"Almighty, eternal God, keep us, your children born of water and the Spirit, faithful to our calling" (Opening Prayer). Today's feast marks the end of the Christmas season.

Reading I   A Call to Service   Is 42, 1-4. 6-7

It is not clear what kind of person the inspired poet had in mind, when he depicted an ideal servant of God in the four "Servant Songs," as we have them in Isaiah. Is it the whole nation of Israel? Is it some prophet or king of the past? Is it a Messiah (Anointed King) to come?

Reapplied by the evangelists and the Church, the Servant is identified with Jesus, who is manifested as God's beloved Servant (Son) in his baptism. The song depicts what the Lord Jesus' mission is to all of us. Reapplied by the Church, the psalm refers to the voice of God "over the waters," when Jesus was baptized in the Jordan.

Reading II   Doing Good Works   Acts 10, 34-38

Peter sees Jesus as in his baptism "anointed with the Holy Spirit and power" and so equipped for his calling: doing good works and healing all who were in the grip of the devil.

A similar calling is ours as baptized Christians. Being a Christian does not mean just avoiding sin. We are anointed to do good and to be concerned about other human beings who are in the grip of evil. And God will be with you!

Gospel   Jesus' Mission   Mt 3, 13-17

Jesus himself did not need a baptism of repentance, but by going to John he set an example for others. The voice from heaven confirms Jesus' mission. Matthew's wording is very close to that of the first Bible reading. He tells in his way that Jesus is in fact that "Servant of Yahweh," as depicted there.

Relate the Gospel and first Bible reading to your calling as a baptized Christian!

ORDINARY TIME

THE Sundays of the major seasons of the year are distinguished by their relationship to the Solemnities of Christmas (Advent, Christmas) and Easter (Lent, Easter). On the other hand, Ordinary Time refers to all the other Sundays of the year under the all-embracing heading of celebrations of the "Day of the Lord." These weeks number thirty-three or thirty-four according to the particular character of each year and are assigned to two parts of the liturgical year.

The first part begins with the Sunday after Epiphany (although this First Sunday is perpetually impeded by the Feast of the Baptism of the Lord) and continues until Ash Wednesday. Since the date of Easter varies each year, this part may include as few as four and as many as nine weeks.

The second part of Ordinary Time begins with the day after Pentecost and runs to the Saturday before the First Sunday of Advent. (See p. 79).

On these "Days of the Lord," Christians continue to celebrate the resurrection of Jesus. First, they listen to what Scripture has to say about him in the Liturgy of the Word. The Gospels for this Time are a semi-continuous reading of the three Synoptic Gospels providing a presentation of each Gospel's distinctive doctrine as well as a development of the Lord's life and preaching. Those after Epiphany are concerned with the beginning of the Lord's preaching and are related to his baptism and first manifestation.

Secondly, Christians commemorate Christ's death and resurrection in the signs of bread and wine. The setting for this memorial—the Lord's Passover Sacrifice—is the Eucharistic Prayer, the Great Prayer of Thanksgiving and Adoration.

◆

2nd SUNDAY IN ORDINARY TIME
Do We Know Jesus Christ?

WE may be acquainted with persons for a long time, have social or business contacts, and yet not know them as they really are, for our contacts are superficial. Then at a certain moment there is a real encounter. Behind that casual smile, we discover entirely different persons. Meeting beautiful persons, having the privilege of being their friends, enriches our lives.

How do you regard Jesus Christ? You have heard about him your whole life. You believe that he is alive, that he knows you, that he invites you to a person-to-person relationship. Yet you may know Jesus only superficially. John the Baptizer said: "I did not recognize him." But he (God) who sent him to baptize gave him insight, so that John could state: "Now I have seen for myself."

Pray that God may help you to recognize the Lord Jesus, to see him as a beautiful person, a friend.

Reading I   Is 49, 3. 5-6
A Light to the Nations

This Bible reading is from the second "Servant Song" in Isaiah. (See commentary at last Sunday's Mass, "The Baptism of the Lord.") The prophet speaks of the Servant's prophetical mission, namely, to raise up the tribes of Israel, who were downtrodden in Babylonian slavery.

The Church reapplies this poem to Jesus Christ, God's Servant, whose mission it is to raise up you and me when we are depressed. That is what a friend does for a friend!

The Responsorial Psalm is a prayer of thanksgiving for deliverance out of tribulation. The writer of the Letter to the Hebrews puts these words into the mouth of our suffering Savior. We should try to pray it with our Lord.

A — 3rd Sunday in Ordinary Time

Reading II — 1 Cor 1, 1-3
Consecrated in Christ Jesus

Paul sends his greetings to "the church of God which is in Corinth!" We are members of the universal Church, which is realized in our own congregation. We should not be narrow-minded and identify our own congregation with the universal Church. We are more than just members of "St. Jude's!"

Gospel — Jn 1, 29-34
The Lamb of God

This Gospel reading tells us about who the Lord Jesus is and about the process of getting to know him more intimately. Jesus is "the Lamb of God, who takes away the sin of the world": Christ, our passover sacrifice! He is great, greater than John the Baptizer himself: He is to baptize with the Holy Spirit.

Jesus is God's chosen one. Do you recognize the Lord as such in your life? Pray that you may see for yourself as John the Baptizer did with the help of God.

3rd SUNDAY IN ORDINARY TIME
Discipleship

DISCIPLESHIP and ministry are part and parcel of the Christian scene. All Christians are called to discipleship and service. The Lord continues his mission of service to humankind through the Church. And the Church is not just the ordained ministers! It is all of us.

The first Bible reading of today was also used on Christmas Eve. In that context it referred to Jesus Christ, a light that dawned in the darkness. Read now, it introduces the theme of the Gospel, namely, the beginning of Jesus' ministry, which Matthew puts in the land of Zebulun and Naphtali, Galilean territory in Jesus' time.

The very beginning of Jesus' ministry is marked by the calling of co-workers. Jesus said to the Galilean fishermen

Simon and Andrew: "Come after me and I will make you fishers of men." The co-workers of our Lord must forward this message, hand on the torch of faith!

We might ask: "How strong is that light of Christ shining in the darkness of the human condition?" If Christians leave it up to the ordained ministers to continue Christ's mission, then Christian impact on society is negligible. If all would be dedicated to Christian discipleship and ministry, a tremendous untapped source of energy would be activated for the benefit of "the people who walk in darkness."

What about your discipleship and ministry? Could it be a project of your parish council?

Reading I   Is 8, 23—9, 3
A Great Light

The setting is a civil war between the two kingdoms into which the Jewish nation was split after the death of Solomon: Judah (south) and Israel (north). Judah had called in Assyrians to come to her help. They invaded Israel and took many captives among the tribes of Zebulun and Naphtali (735-732 B.C.). Isaiah saw all this as a punishment for sin, especially the king's lack of faith in God. As descendants of the great King David, they should be the representatives of God on earth. They failed!

In his songs and poems, Isaiah dreams about an ideal king to come, a true king of peace, who will be Immanuel—God with us. Matthew sees Isaiah's aspirations fulfilled in Jesus Christ. (See the Gospel.) "Wait for the Lord with courage!" (Responsorial Psalm).

Reading II   1 Cor 1, 10-13. 17
Be United!

There is dissension in the congregation of Corinth. Paul points out that all members are called to be Christ's ministers and disciples. All share in the mission of Jesus, namely, to be a light to other human beings in darkness! But a house divided causes only misfortune and misery.

A — 4th Sunday in Ordinary Time 33

Accepting one another, human as we are, priests, members of the parish council, and ordinary parishioners, we should be one in the faith and in our dedication to Christian discipleship and service.

Gospel Mt 4, 12-23 or 4, 12-17
Come after Me

Matthew, a Jew writing for Christians of Jewish background, sees Isaiah's dreams (Reading I) fulfilled in Jesus Christ, who begins his missionary activity in the land of Zebulun and Naphtali. Jesus is a prophet like the ancient prophets of Israel. He is a teacher. He is the Servant of Yahweh. (See two previous Sundays!) He is the Son of God, not just adopted as Hebrew kings were at their enthronement, but in a very unique way.

Jesus is the great light, envisaged by Isaiah in the first Bible reading. Like the first disciples, all Christians share in Christ's mission of service.

◆

4th SUNDAY IN ORDINARY TIME
Humility

IT IS not easy to find a market for the value called humility. Humankind has achieved so much during the last few decades! Perhaps humility is misunderstood. Persons with an identity crisis and unsure of themselves are not necessarily humble in the Christian sense! Christians should develop themselves to their full potentiality, but always seeing themselves as God's partners. Covenant-partnership with God the Creator of the universe is an ancient Biblical concept. It is Hebrew wisdom, which Christians inherited from their Jewish brethren. With them they see it as divine wisdom.

God has designed human beings as his co-workers. He gave us the raw material. We mold it for our own and our neighbor's benefit. And whenever we achieve great things, we pray humbly! "Not to us, O Lord, not to us but to your name

A — 4th Sunday in Ordinary Time

give glory" (Ps 115), and in fairness we give credit to those who contributed to our success!

"The lowly" and "the poor in spirit" of today's Bible readings should be understood as Christians who are fully aware that they have no righteousness of their own. They see their talents and achievements as God-given, whether they are materially poor or not.

Reading I   Zep 2, 3; 3, 12-13
Seek Humility!

This reading from Zephaniah leads up to the theme of the Gospel, Jesus' sermon on the mountainside. In Judah, "a nation without shame," there is a remnant of faithful servants of Yahweh. They are called "the remnant of Israel."

In this remnant, the prophet addresses all of us: "All you humble of the earth, who have observed his law." Humility is a Christian virtue and a condition to be considered "blest," as explained in the Gospel.

Reading II   1 Cor 1, 26-31
No Boasting!

Paul addresses the slaves and "longshoremen" of Corinth: "God chose those whom the world considers absurd to shame the wise." Christ's special concern for the deprived implies a lesson for those who are going by the wisdom of this world, which is pride. Paul stresses: "God it is who has given you life in Christ Jesus."

See yourself as related to God in a sacred partnership (covenant) and then there will be "no boasting before God."

Gospel   Mt 5, 1-12
How Blest!

As mentioned earlier (see Feast of the Holy Family), Matthew was a Jew, writing for Christians of Jewish background. He compares Jesus often with the great lawmaker of Israel, Moses, with whom all Jews were familiar. In this Bible passage, Matthew states indirectly: Moses announced the laws (figuratively) from Mount Sinai. Jesus, greater than Moses, does (figuratively) the same "on the mountainside."

Notice that Luke has the Lord preach this sermon on the plain. Actually, Matthew combines various sayings of Jesus and has the Lord proclaim them in what is known now as the Sermon on the Mount. The beatitudes are ideals which we should pursue constantly, though humbly admitting that it is not easy to do so!

5th SUNDAY IN ORDINARY TIME
Who Are We?

IN daily life, we must be concerned about priorities. First things first! Prayer in the family and worship even in an expensive and luxurious church building are wonderful but not enough. A congregation as such must be socially concerned; otherwise it is not like salt in the community, not a city seen by all, not a light to those in town who walk in darkness. Two Sundays ago (3rd Sunday), the idea of discipleship and ministry by all was brought out. Today's Gospel suggests the same idea, but now by using metaphors: salt, a city set on a hill, and light.

The first Bible reading explains what our approach should be. Remove a few things out of your midst (oppression, malicious speech) and share whatever you have. "Then your light shall break forth like the dawn."

What are the priorities of your parish council? Is its first concern worship, some more expensive items for the sanctuary, and improvement of the parking lot? But are there poor and deprived in your community? What is done for the old and lonely?

Sharing time and yourself can be as important in our depersonalized society as sharing bread. It is the mark of Christians worth their salt, and their "generosity shall endure forever" (Responsorial Psalm). What can you do? If you are not a member of your parish council, you are a constituent!

A — 5th Sunday in Ordinary Time

Reading I
Is 58, 7-10

Satisfy the Afflicted!

The unknown prophet (composer of Is 56—66, called Third Isaiah) addresses Hebrews back from exile in Babylon. In their joy over newly found freedom, they have expected too much.

God's people must seek something deeper and more genuine than just the experiences of being free. The writer goes into details of sharing with the promise (also directed to us) that "then your wound shall quickly be healed."

Reading II
1 Cor 2, 1-5

Jesus Christ Crucified

The Christian philosophy of life is defined as a sharing (Reading I), especially of self, a sharing that hurts and can be a cross ("Jesus Christ and him crucified" as your example!). This is a kind of "wisdom" which many do not accept.

Paul is aware that there are members in the congregation of Corinth who do not accept it either. Hence, he emphasizes that "faith rests not on the wisdom of men but on the power of God." We should pray for it constantly.

Gospel
Mt 5, 13-16

Let Your Light Shine!

We are the new Israel (Reading I) and with our insight of faith (Reading II) we Christians are to be the "salt of the earth." But only by being dissolved in food does salt give its taste. "You are the light of the world." Only by diffusing itself in the darkness does light enlighten.

Only by losing ourselves (sharing of self!) can we give "taste" to the life of deprived persons and enlighten their path when they falter.

6th SUNDAY IN ORDINARY TIME
Law and Freedom

HUMAN beings are free but they encounter laws as well. It seems to be ever more difficult for modern persons to accept rules and regulations, which often are considered as handicaps for their full self-realization. Freedom is of paramount importance in the "land of the free and the home of the brave." Paul states that "it was for liberty that Christ freed us" (Gal 5, 1).

Comparing various sayings of Scripture may help us understand "freedom" better. Paul says also: "God sent his Son to deliver us from the law, so that we may receive our status as adopted sons" (Gal 4, 4-5). This gives us a clue. Paul sees freedom not just as "free from" but more as "free for," i.e., free to love God as his adopted children.

Love of God and neighbor is the great law from which there is never an exception. Other laws should be tested on that great law of love, of which they are supposed to be applications. There can be bad laws, hence conscientious objectors! We should respect others and always follow our own conscience.

Laws tell us how reasonable people have applied the law of love to situations which may be very similar to ours. Do not discard such wisdom too easily. Laws may be beacons in our often confused human condition.

Reading I Sir 15, 15-20
"You Can Keep the Commandments"

God's wisdom tells us that we must be careful with statements often made by contemporary psychologists who try to do away with human responsibility for evil committed. A breakdown of authority in the family, the Church, and the state, resulting in a high rate of juvenile delinquency, might have something to do with a certain kind of psychology, taught for several decades.

This Bible passage does not deny that human beings need the grace of God to be good; neither does it disclaim determining circumstances which can lessen their subjective guilt. But as a whole human freedom means that people can choose good and avoid evil. Certainly we cannot make God responsible for evil in the world! If this world is in a bad state, it is people who have made it so!

Pray with the psalmist: "[God] give me discernment, that I may observe your law and keep it with all my heart" (Responsorial Psalm 119, 34).

Reading II   1 Cor 2, 6-10
God's Wisdom

Nobody wants to be considered ignorant or lacking in understanding. Wisdom is a great asset. Paul speaks of a wisdom not of this age. It is a wisdom put on a higher level, since the wisdom of God is hidden in it. That wisdom, the insight of faith, may help us to make the right decisions in life.

We should pray that the Spirit may give us discernment in confused situations. And existing laws, reflecting what other people have done, could be guidelines to find out what the loving thing to do is in our life situations.

Gospel   Mt 5, 17-37 or 5, 20-22. 27-28. 33-34. 37
Fulfilling the Law

Jesus did not come to do away with the law, but to reinterpret it and raise it to a different level. Jesus stresses that we should pay attention not just to what is actually done, but also to the inner motive, which is known only to ourselves and to God.

It is principally this inner motive which constitutes our aversion from or conversion to God, and for which we will have to account. In strong Semitic language, Jesus draws a black-versus-white picture. The idea is clear. God claims our whole selves in the entirety of love.

7th SUNDAY IN ORDINARY TIME
Holiness

IT is the Hebrew genius, under divine guidance, that has related morality expressly to God and religion. Why should human beings be holy? Because God is holy (Reading I). "You

A — 7th Sunday in Ordinary Time

must be perfected as your heavenly Father is perfect" (Gospel). "You are the temple of God—the Spirit dwells in you—the temple of God is holy" (Reading II).

Of course, the nations surrounding Israel had morality too. But it was more related to an efficient understanding of what was good to keep society going than to their gods, who were often anything but holy!

Christians see their moral lives related to God. Hence, it is important to know what God thinks of morality. God's ideas on morality are best reflected in Jesus Christ and what he stands for. "He is the image of the invisible God" (Col 1, 15). Imitation of Christ is the best guide for a morally good life!

Reading I Lv 19, 1-2. 17-18
Be Holy!

God's people is called to be holy, "for I, the Lord, your God, am holy." The verses that follow explain what is most essential for holiness. It all revolves around love, mercy, kindness and compassion, as the Responsorial Psalm brings so beautifully. "The Lord is kind and merciful." Hence, we should be the same.

Reading II 1 Cor 3, 16-23
Wise in a Worldly Way?

There is dissension in the congregation of Corinth. How is this possible if you are aware that you are a temple of God and the Spirit dwells in you? Being smart, wise in a worldly way, and wanting to have it your way or no way is contrary to what Christians should be; they should be holy as depicted in Reading I and the Responsorial Psalm (103, 1-13).

Gospel Mt 5, 38-48
"Be Perfect as Your Heavenly Father Is Perfect"

The Gospel is a continuation of Jesus' sermon of last Sunday. "Love your enemies!" A civil rights leader who strove to follow this command till he was ultimately killed comments:

"I am not speaking of love in a sentimental or affectionate sense. It would be nonsense to urge people to love their oppressors in an affectionate sense. When I refer to love in this context, I mean understanding goodwill—we must in strength and humility meet hate with love."

◆

8th SUNDAY IN ORDINARY TIME
God's Providence

CHRISTIAN life requires a decision. "No [person] can serve two masters." The Gospel speaks in hyperbolic language: either-or. There is one thing we can learn from it, namely, that we Christians should be familiar with the whole Bible.

We should be like birds in the sky and wild flowers in the field: carefree. But the grocery bill and the car payments must be taken care of as well. The Bible speaks about human handiwork as often as it urges us to have trust in the providence of God.

The secret of the Christian life-style is to make the best of it without incurring the nervous breakdown and high blood pressure which afflict so many! After Christians have done what they reasonably can and must do, they can kneel down and pray with the psalmist: "He [God] only is my rock and my salvation, my stronghold; I shall not be disturbed at all" (Responsorial Psalm).

Reading I   Is 49, 14-15
"I Will Never Forget You"

The exile in Babylon was a test of the faith and patience of the Hebrews. It is understandable that Zion (the temple mountain in Jerusalem symbolizing Israel, the Hebrews) said: "My Lord has forgotten me."

The unknown wandering preacher whose sermons are preserved in Isaiah 40—55 (Second Isaiah) encourages his fellow exiles to have faith in the providence of God. This reading introduces the theme of the Gospel, where our Lord elaborates more extensively on this same theme.

A — 7th Sunday in Ordinary Time

Reading II 1 Cor 4, 1-5
A Trustworthy Administrator!

As far as doing his duty and preaching the Gospel is concerned, Paul states that he is not running a popularity contest. He wants to be "straight" with God, even if his message is not always accepted as well as it should be.

How do you accept the interpretation of Scripture in your church on Sunday? Your priest must preach the whole Gospel if he wants to be "straight" with God!

Gospel Mt 6, 24-34
"Stop Worrying"

"Your heavenly Father knows all that you need. Seek first his kingship over you, his way of holiness, and all these things will be given you besides."

Over-zealous pursuit of all the niceties of life is ultimately harmful. Too much work—"moonlighting" or urging one's partner to do so in order to keep up with one's neighbors—is damaging to family-life and inevitably leads to misery and trouble. Do we need all the gadgets possessed by the people next door in order to be happy? Where do you let your heavenly Father step in?

9th SUNDAY IN ORDINARY TIME
Honesty

ALL OF us know people who seem to be experts on the theory of life. They can explain beautifully what an ideal society, family, or work situation should be all about. High-ranking politicians, for example, may urge the people to practice frugality, but they are not credible if their own life-styles deviate widely from what they preach.

The Lord Jesus fought such hypocrisy in his lifetime: "Woe to you Pharisees! You pay tithes while neglecting justice and the love of God" (Lk 11, 42).

Parents who tell their children one thing while acting differently in their private lives are like those Pharisees. So are politicians, teachers, employers, who talk smoothly, but are involved in shady practices. Young people resent this. They want honesty, though often they themselves may be deficient in this regard.

Can we be honest with ourselves and our neighbor? "Lord, guide us with your Spirit that we may honor you not only with our lips, but also with the lives we lead" (Prayer after Communion).

Reading I — These Words of Mine — Dt 11, 18. 26-28

The Book of Deuteronomy (Second Law) is a series of sermons or meditations on the Law of Moses. It stresses honesty. "Take these words of mine into your heart and soul." We should heed honesty when we read the Bible. We know that Scripture never tells a story merely for a story's sake. It always wants to bring out a point, which is God's word to the reader.

In reading the Bible, we should search for that point and ask ourselves: "How does this apply to my life situation?" And then we should ask God for help to honestly realize his word in our daily lives.

Reading II — Through Faith in Jesus Christ — Rom 3, 21-25. 28

Paul teaches again about redemption and justification by faith rather than by the observance of the law. This seems to contradict the message of the previous reading where Moses said that we should be honest and obey God's commandments. There is no contradiction if we keep in mind what faith really is.

Faith, like love, is a total surrender of self to God. If you truly love and have real faith in God, you do not ask: "What must I do to avoid trouble?"; you are constantly concerned about what you can do to please the beloved, i.e., God. Paul explains beautifully: "Love is the fulfillment of the law" (Rom 13, 10). Keep this in mind also when you read the Gospel.

Gospel — My Words Put into Practice — Mt 7, 21-27

Jesus finishes the Sermon on the Mount by warning against hypocrisy. We find it everywhere and not least in religion. This does not mean that we can do without religion. It means that those who practice religion should constantly check whether they are being honest.

LENTEN SEASON

ACCORDING to Biblical tradition, Moses stayed on Mount Sinai forty days to receive the Law of the Covenant. Our Lord fasted forty days in the desert before he started his mission. Christians prepared themselves to celebrate the paschal mystery of our Lord's death and resurrection by a penitential season of forty days.

Penance is part of the Christian philosophy of life. The way it is done may change. The concept itself cannot be taken out of the Christian life. Penance has to do with sin and conversion. It is the inner aversion from evil in and around us and a generous conversion in love to God which are important.

The means to achieve this inner conversion, the traditional Lenten practices of prayer, charitable works, and even fasting, should not be considered outdated. However, it is true that the importance of "works" of penance (fasting, abstinence from meat, candy, shows, etc.) during Lent may have been overemphasized in the past. They have little value in themselves.

What you give up during Lent is a personal decision, but it should be related to that inner conversion to God. "More fervent in prayer, more generous in works of charity, more eager in celebrating the mysteries by which we are reborn may we come to the fullness of grace that belongs to the sons of God" (Preface of Lent).

1st SUNDAY OF LENT
Temptation and Sin

SINCE human beings are both God's masterpiece and fallen creatures, temptation and sin are daily realities which no psychology can talk away. It may be true that "temptation and sin" have been overemphasized in the past. Theologians were wont to offer long lists of sins, listed for the most part under the tag of "mortal" and "venial," whereas the reality is not quite so simple. However, this does not mean that temptation and sin are all of a sudden nonexistent either.

Sin is willfully breaking that beautiful love-relationship with God which is called grace. We do not accomplish this easily, although we are tempted daily not to live up to the ideal of love of God and neighbor as we should. Whether or not our daily failures should be called "sin" is not important. But we should not take them for granted.

One of the great temptations which ruin beautiful relationships (marriage, friendship) is the routine of daily failures. It is a kind of indifference which renders a love-relationship stale and trite. Finally, it gets boring and the next step is a breakup.

Today's Bible readings should make us take a realistic look at our relationship with our marriage partner, friends, children, and parents in whom God approaches us and our direct relationship with God in both private prayer and worship. Beware of the temptation of indifference!

Reading I   Gn 2, 7-9; 3, 1-7
Did God Really Tell You?

Who am I? Who am I supposed to be? I am dust (Ash Wednesday) but also related to God. Inspired by God, the sacred writer uses a beautiful allegory to teach us about the reality of temptation and sin in our lives.

Notice the woman (you and I) playing with temptation! The proposal is pleasing to her eyes! After some hesitation, the consent follows. Then the eyes of the man and woman are opened. Too late of course! You and I could do the same! The Responsorial Psalm is an act of contrition.

A — 2nd Sunday of Lent

Reading II
Rom 5, 12-19 or 5, 12. 17-19

Jesus Atoned for Our Sins

Paul draws up an analogy between the Adam of Genesis and Jesus Christ, the man to come. Adam began a history of fallen humanity, marked by sin and death. Jesus Christ began a new history of humanity, marked by forgiveness of sin and life everlasting.

Fallen human beings can pray hopefully: "Give me back the joy of your salvation" (Responsorial Psalm), since Jesus Christ atoned for our sins by his obedience even to the death on a cross.

Gospel
Mt 4, 1-11

The Tempter Approached

Pondering the words of Jesus in his heart, Matthew meditates on the meaning of three typical temptations which constantly threaten Christianity: (1) God may not be used for one's own gain or profit (turning stones into bread); (2) faith has nothing to do with the spectacular ("throw yourself down"); (3) and religion may not be mixed up with political power (kingdoms displayed in their magnificence).

Jesus answers with three quotations from Scripture. He will be faithful to his calling and not be swayed by these temptations. We who are the Church of this age and prone to these same temptations should keep in mind our Lord's example.

2nd SUNDAY OF LENT

God's Call and Our Response

IN THE Catholic tradition, the idea of vocation (calling) was very much restricted to priesthood and religious life. We should not forget that this special call rests upon the general call, which is basic to all Christians, namely, the call to a new existence. Today's Liturgy deals with the call of Abraham. Both Abraham's call and your own imply three elements.

The first is *God's free choice*. "Not because of any merit of ours, but according to his own design" (Reading II); "it was love of you" (Gn 7, 7-8). The second is a *mission*, which could entail leaving the safe, the familiar, the known, and accepting the new and untried. "Bear your share of the hardship which the gospel entails." As a Christian, you do have a mission to your family, your parish, your community, co-workers on your job, fellow students in school, friends. The third is a *promise*, which in Abraham's case consisted of a posterity—children: "I will make of you a great nation" (Reading I). In the case of Christians it consists of life and immortality (Reading II).

An appreciative fidelity to your calling requires faith. The promises are real but cannot yet be verified as the Gospel of the Transfiguration brings out: "When they looked up they did not see anyone but Jesus." "God our Father, enlighten us with your word, that we may find the way to your glory" (Opening Prayer).

Reading I Gn 12, 1-4

"Go Forth!"

Paul uses Abraham as the paradigm of Christian faith (Rom 4, 18-25). Abraham never questioned or doubted God's promise. He went as the Lord directed him. God calls you in the history of your life. All his works are trustworthy, as we sing in the Responsorial Psalm (33). Stanza two refers to the promise. (Fear means "filial respect.") Stanza three could be your answer.

Reading II 2 Tm 1, 8-10

Called to a Holy Life

God has saved you and called you to a holy life. Fidelity to this call may entail hardship especially when you have to be among people who live more or less unholy lives. Do you have the courage to be different? Think of the promises!

———◆———

Gospel
Not Anyone But Jesus — Mt 17, 1-9

"Fear" in the context of this Bible passage means "wholesome awe." For a brief moment the disciples experience the reality of the promise, "life and immortality." But the daily life experience of a Christian entails "not seeing anyone but Jesus."

When fidelity to your call to a holy life is tempted, pray for faith in the invisible but true reality of God's promise.

◆

3rd SUNDAY OF LENT
Is the Lord in Our Midst or Not?

PEOPLE will always be hungry and thirsty again. Besides a continued need for food and drink, human beings have many more wishes and desires, sometimes even conflicting ones. They may yearn for truth, freedom, justice, love, which require more perfect fulfillment time and again. The great bishop St. Augustine stated: "My heart is restless till it rests in God." God-with-us in the Lord Jesus is ready to satisfy human desires. The Bible uses a wealth of symbols to bring this out, among which are bread, wine, oil, and light.

Today's Bible readings use the symbolism of water. Water is life-giving. God's people lived in a land surrounded by barren deserts, and water constituted a question of life and death. The theme of this Sunday is: "Is the Lord with us or not?" He is.

The point (God's word to you and me) is that we should open up to this mysterious presence of God in our midst, which today's Bible readings present through the symbolism of water, so avidly experienced by our Biblical ancestors as life-giving. "Whoever drinks the water that I shall give him, says the Lord, will have a spring inside him, welling up for eternal life" (Communion Antiphon).

Reading I
Life-Giving Water — Ex 17, 3-7

"Is the Lord with us or not?" The authors of the Exodus traditions saw the wilderness period of their national history as a time to put security in God. Being thirsty, the Hebrews put God to a test. The water struck from the rock is the Biblical symbol for life, the life-giving presence of God. "Come, let us acclaim the Rock of our salvation. Let us greet him with thanksgiving" (Responsorial Psalm).

Reading II — Rom 5, 1-2. 5-8
God's Love Poured Out

The life-giving presence of God and "his love poured out in our hearts through the Holy Spirit" are Christian realities. But the water of baptism was life-giving to you because Christ died for us godless people who were powerless through sin. This should not fail to inspire gratitude in us.

Gospel — Jn 4, 5-42 or 4, 5-15. 19-26. 39. 40-42
"The Water I Give"

In this Gospel reading also, the symbol of water is used to describe God's life-giving presence. It is referred to as "God's gift," "living water," "the water which shall become a fountain within man, leaping up to provide eternal life." "Whoever drinks the water I give him will never be thirsty." Only God in our midst can ultimately saturate all our desires! The Samaritan woman stands for all of us.

We should cultivate our understanding of Biblical symbols. You were baptized with water. It gave you life everlasting. Making the sign of the cross with holy water when you enter church for worship is a reminder of your baptism. Make this symbolism meaningful!

———◆———

4th SUNDAY OF LENT
Faith and Unbelief

WE are often asked to take a stand, be it concerning politics, the education of the children, or the way work should be done. Taking a stand, especially one concerning a controversial issue, may involve opposition. Christians are asked to take a stand quite often.

In today's Gospel the writer of John brings out a wealth of suggestions. Let us consider one. How do people react to our Lord's message? Christianity offers beautiful and efficient outlines for a better society with promises for life to come. Christianity is not something one can sweep under the rug and ignore as nonexistent. It is there! One must take a stand.

The Gospel shows us the parents of the blind man (who do not want to be involved), the neighbors (who are indifferent), the Pharisees (who do not believe), and the blind man himself (a believer). Where do you stand? You are a baptized Christian. Does the Lord Jesus and the philosophy of life he stands for have real impact on your life-style?

Each of the four categories mentioned in the Gospel is found in today's society. Each promotes its own outlook by work and life-style. You must take a stand. Can you sincerely pray: "Father of peace, we are joyful in your Word, your Son Jesus Christ"? (Opening Prayer).

Reading I   1 Sm 16, 1. 6-7. 10-13
God's Choice

The readings of this Lenten season have a baptismal character as we are preparing for a renewal of our baptismal commitment to God at Easter. Two elements of this reading throw light on baptism: (1) *God's free choice:* God chose the youngest son of Jesse, not the others: "There—anoint him, for this is he!" (2) *The meaning of the baptismal anointing:* Priests, prophets and kings were anointed. Especially the kings were seen as the "Lord's Anointed"—Messiah—Christ. Anointed to royal dignity, the king was viewed as God's adopted son with "the spirit of the Lord . . . upon" him.

At baptism, the anointing with Chrism brings out our royal dignity as adopted children of God. God chose you! It is not the other way around. You share God's life and are filled with the Spirit through baptism. Be appreciative!

A — 5th Sunday of Lent

Reading II   Eph 5, 8-14
"Awake, O Sleeper!"

"You are light in the Lord" through faith sealed with baptism. It is a basic human symbol: light as good and darkness as evil. "Well, live as children of light." Take a stand, as suggested in the theme. It concerns the Christian life-style: "Goodness, justice, trust" as opposed to "the vain deeds done in darkness."

Lent should wake us up, make us aware of what we should be as Christians. "Awake, O sleeper!"

Gospel   Jn 9, 1-41 or 9, 1. 6-9. 13-17. 34-38
"I Do Believe, Lord"

The words "Rabbi [teacher], who sinned?" reveal that sickness and suffering were regarded by the Jews as punishment from God. Jesus does not agree. It is not that simple. Our Lord mentions only one possible reason for the sickness in question: that God's works may shine forth in the sick man. There are many others, and ultimately human suffering remains a mystery.

The main point of this reading (God's word) seems to be the need of faith to accept the rejection, suffering, death, and resurrection of Jesus and in it our own life cycle: suffering, death, life everlasting. Jesus' (and our) paschal mystery-passage through suffering and death to eternal life is one of the basics of Christian wisdom. "Lord, you enlighten all who come into the world; fill our hearts with the light of your gospel" (Prayer after Communion).

5th SUNDAY OF LENT
Newness of Life

EVERYONE wants to make the best of life. We love life, but we experience daily how brittle it is. There are people who try to live without restraints. They follow the epicurean philosophy of the pagan Romans: "Let us eat and drink, for tomorrow we may die."

But we could also look at life in the following way: In order to transcend life, I must die to my old, immature, egotistic self. If I want to become a mature and grown-up person, I must leave my youth behind me. Does this make sense? Is it meaningful to be generous and dedicated to ideals, to "mature in Christ," as the Bible puts it, if everything collapses with death anyway?

In the life, suffering, death, and resurrection of Jesus, we Christians discover the love of God who calls you and me to an everlasting life-sharing with him. The raising of Lazarus is a sign of Jesus' victory over death, and a sign of hope for all of us. In faith, we can regard a life of dedication to ideals as budding into the full blossoming of life everlasting.

Reading I Ez 37, 12-14
"That You May Live"

Using the language of vision (i.e., the famous vision of the "dry bones"), Ezekiel sees the Jews in exile to be as dead as the bones of dead men scattered on a battlefield. The Lord brings these bones back to life, and breathes a new spirit into them and resettles them upon their own land. The prophet refers to the exiles' return to the home country, where they will start a new life.

Reapplied to us today, the message, God's word, is: A Christian who is indifferent and/or disappointed by Church life, confused about changes, a person about to give up, is like those dry bones. God promises: "I will put my spirit in you that you may live." A Christian believes this and can pray: "With the Lord is kindness and with him is plenteous redemption" (Responsorial Psalm).

Reading II Rom 8, 8-11
The Spirit's Indwelling

Guided by God, Paul states that those who are "in the flesh," that is, those who look at life solely from the viewpoint of the flesh, get nowhere. But as a baptized Christian you are not "in the flesh," at least you should not be. If you act as if you are still "in the flesh," you are not your real self. You have not sufficiently died to your old self. The Spirit dwells in you. Let him animate you.

The main point is that as a Christian you should respond to this internal power in you. Only then will you really be alive. Note that Paul uses "Spirit of God," "Spirit of Christ," "Spirit," and even "Christ" interchangeably. In each case the point is the divine indwelling seen as a principle of life.

Gospel   Jn 11, 1-45 or 11, 3-7. 17. 20-27. 33-45
We Will Come to Life

John relates Jesus' miracles as "signs," earthly realities which indicate a full reality to come. Inspired by God, what does John wish to indicate by relating this miracle of Jesus? We notice that the evangelist places the Lazarus story just before the passion narrative. Significantly, he remarks: "From that day onward there was a plan afoot to kill Jesus!" (Jn 11, 53).

This passage teaches: Jesus, calling himself the resurrection and the life, will die to inaugurate the resurrection of human beings. "As the Father raises the dead and gives them life, so the Son gives life to anyone he chooses" (Jn 5, 21). John suggests that you should put your faith in Jesus as many Jews did when they witnessed the raising of Lazarus.

◆

PASSION SUNDAY [PALM SUNDAY]
Death and Life

GREAT people were often controversial figures during their lifetime. It is history, which can look on from a distance and see things in proper perspective, that rectifies the often limited judgment of contemporaries. Something like this has happened to the Lord Jesus. His contemporaries, even his closest co-workers, did not understand him, especially not his strange ideas on suffering and death as a necessary passage to a better life. Only later did all of this become clear to them.

Today Christians celebrate Passion (or Palm) Sunday. "Christ entered in triumph into his own city to complete his

A — Passion Sunday [Palm Sunday] 53

work as our Messiah: to suffer, to die, and to rise again" (Procession Rite). The triumphal entry, celebrated at the beginning of the passion-week, emphasizes that the three elements: suffering, death, and resurrection, belong together. Jesus' death was not a defeat. It was a victory.

It is the genuine insight of Christianity that the events of Jesus' earthly life were the execution of God's saving purpose. This genuine insight should be ours also concerning our own lives when suffering strikes us.

Gospel   "Who Is This?"   Mt 21, 1-11

Like King David and all kings in his culture, Jesus enters the capital riding on the traditional animal. In the midst of the people, he is the Son of David, a Messiah sent by God to give freedom and self-determination to his country. But Jesus is a humble and peaceful king, not in favor of worldly display. He enters Jerusalem, "meek and riding on an ass" (Zec 9, 9).

All four of the evangelists relate this tradition as an introduction to Jesus' passion and cruel death. Why? To teach us that Jesus is indeed the Messiah, though on a higher level than the people thought. Jesus is sent by God to establish his reign (kingdom) on earth. His impending suffering and death will not thwart this divine plan, but must be seen as the means to fulfill it, as will be clearly understood after the resurrection. "Did not the Messiah have to undergo all this so as to enter into his glory?" (Lk 24, 26).

Participating in the Liturgy of Holy Week, we should keep in mind that suffering, pain, and death are also mysteriously part of our passage to a glorious life with our Lord.

Reading I   Is 50, 4-7
"The Lord Is My Help"

This reading is taken from the third song of the Servant of Yahweh. As mentioned at the feast of the Baptism of our Lord, it is not clear whom the inspired writer had in mind when he composed these four songs describing the ideal Servant (Son) of God. Is he a collective person: Israel, God's people? Is he a king of the past or the Messiah (anointed king) to come?

In any case, the Christian community applied these hymns very early to Jesus and they are used throughout Holy Week as a beautiful commentary on the passion narratives. Indeed, "the Son of Man [Jesus] came not to be served but to serve, and to give his life for the ransom of many" (Mt 20, 28).

Read the Responsorial Psalm (22) meditatively, applying it to the Lord Jesus dying on the cross.

Reading II "Your Attitude" — Phil 2, 6-11

This text is actually a Christ hymn, sung in church. It beautifully describes our Lord's utmost humiliation which he suffered on the cross. By being obedient, he made up for our sinful disobedience. But this hymn also sings of Christ's exaltation by the Father.

Meditating on the Lord's suffering and death, as Christians do during Holy Week, we should keep both sides of the Christ event in mind. It is suffering and death which actually constitutes a passage to exaltation. Good Friday and Easter belong together even in our lives!

Gospel — Mt 26, 14—27, 66 or 27, 11-54
No Greater Love

Paul states: "For our sakes God made him who did not know sin, to be sin so that in him we might become the very holiness of God" (2 Cor 5, 21). Jesus identified himself entirely with sinful humankind, whom he freed from sin and death.

Each of the evangelists relates the narrative of Christ's passion with only a few different memories of the tragedy. In Matthew and Mark, Jesus' last words are: "My God, my God, why have you forsaken me?" Luke remembers that on the cross Jesus promised paradise to the criminal who repented and that Jesus said: "Father, into your hands I commend my spirit." All three relate the Lord's Supper, which Jesus gave us to celebrate as a memorial of his passion, death, and resurrection.

Prayerful meditation on Jesus' passion should make us grateful for what Jesus did. He has said: "There is no greater love than this: to lay down one's life for one's friend. You are my friends" (Jn 15, 13-14).

EASTER SEASON

IN PAUL'S first letter to the congregation of Corinth (56 or 57 A.D.) we have the oldest summary of Christian belief. Paul refers to his former preaching in Corinth in 51 A.D. and declares that he received this Gospel (Good News) as witnessed by the apostles and Palestinian disciples: "I [Paul] handed on to you first of all what I myself received, that Christ died for our sins in accordance with the Scriptures, that he was buried and, in accordance with the Scriptures, rose on the third day; that he was seen by Cephas, then by the Twelve. This is what we preach and this is what you believed" (1 Cor 15, 3-5).

Some thirty to fifty years later, the evangelists preached the same message, but often drew on local traditions which extensively elaborate on the theme of our Lord's resurrection. There are legendary details in those traditions which have nothing to do with the faith in the resurrection. Each of the Gospel traditions, as we will read them during the Easter Season, centers on an all-important appearance to the Twelve in which they are commissioned for their future task, namely, to be witnesses of the Lord, who is alive and will be with us until the end of the world (Mk 28, 16-20). (Cf. Jerome Commentary.) And this is the Paschal message to all Christians.

Following the example of the Bible, Christians celebrate the mystery of our Lord's Resurrection for fifty days. The Lord's Ascension and Pentecost are the final memorial days. "Christ has become our paschal sacrifice; let us feast with joy in the Lord" (1 Cor 5, 6-8). "God our Father, let our celebration today raise us up and renew our lives by the Spirit that is within us" (Opening Prayer for Easter).

EASTER VIGIL MIDNIGHT MASS
Christ Our Light

THIS evening's service draws on the symbolism of light versus darkness. The Liturgy identifies darkness with sin, ignorance, and insecurity. For people who walk in darkness, Christ shines as a bright light. The Easter Candle symbolizes "Christ our light." Tonight we are invited to revive in ourselves the grace of our baptism. New candidates will be baptized. All will renew their baptismal commitment.

Through baptism, we participate in the Lord's resurrection and are "children of the light." "Christ is the new lamb who took away the sins of the world. For us his death brings ransom from death, his rising brings new life in him" (Easter Preface). "Lord God, you have brightened this night with the radiance of the risen Christ. Renew us in mind and body" (Opening Prayer).

Epistle   Rom 6, 3-11
Dying with Christ

The baptismal ceremony Paul mentions is the baptism by immersion which was generally practiced in the early Church. The old self, with its egotism and sin, was buried in the baptismal water and a new person, a Christian, arose from it.

However, we should not forget that this "dying with Christ and rising up to a new life" is an ongoing process until it is fully realized in the life to come. For that reason we will renew our baptismal commitment tonight. Its meaning is a renewed dying to our sinful self and a new and more Christian life with the risen God. "In Christ," a Christian can say: "I shall not die, but live, and declare the works of the Lord" (Responsorial Psalm).

Gospel   Mt 28, 1-10
"Carry the News!"

The "angel of the Lord" in Matthew's version (cycle A) of the announcement of Christ's resurrection, the "young man" in Mark's version (cycle B) and the "two young men" in Luke's version (cycle C) are messenger-figures of the Old Testament. The authors want to bring out the message from God: "He [Christ] has been raised from the dead."

The legendary details (see General Introduction to the Easter Season, p. 55) belong to the tradition as such. The evangelists took this tradition at face value and used it to proclaim the risen Lord and what he means to you and me: "Peace! Do not be afraid!"

EASTER SUNDAY
The Lord Has Indeed Risen

A PERSON who is privileged to visit the tombs of the Pharaohs in Egypt or reads about them in pictorial books is struck by those people's concern about a hereafter. The hieroglyphics for "life everlasting" appear on the murals time and again. People want to live. Easter is the feast of life. "The Lord has indeed risen, Alleluia" (Entrance Antiphon). "Alleluia—Praise the Lord!" marks all prayers and songs of this festival season. It represents the joy of Christians: The Lord's death was not a defeat but a victory! And we share in the Lord's victory over suffering and death, knowing that life everlasting with Christ will be ours. "We look for the resurrection of the dead, and the life of the world to come" (Profession of Faith).

People want to know: What is the manner of my existence after death? "How are the dead raised up? What kind of body will they have?" (1 Cor 15, 35). Paul calls this a nonsensical question. And he adds: "The seed you sow does not germinate until it dies. When you sow, you do not sow the full-blown plant, but a kernel of wheat or some other grain. God gives body to it as he pleases—to each seed its fruition" (1 Cor 15, 36-38).

This seems to indicate that our lives now are the kernels from which "earthly human beings" must grow into the persons they will be for all eternity. "This corruptible body must be clothed with incorruptibility" (1 Cor 15, 53). The words found in 1 Corinthians 15, 35-38 offer some insight to the inquisitive reader, but ultimately we must leave the details up to God who promised that our reward will be hundredfold.

A — Easter Sunday

Reading I
Acts 10, 34. 37-43
"He Rose from the Dead"

In this speech of Peter, Luke wants to bring out the basic message of the early Church: The Lord's rejection ("they killed him"); God's vindication ("God raised him up"); and the apostles' witness to the Christ-event ("he commissioned us to preach").

Referring to the stone rejected and made the headstone of the corner, the Church applies Psalm 118 to the death and resurrection of Christ. Indeed, "this is the day the Lord has made; let us rejoice and be glad" (Responsorial Psalm: 118).

Reading II
Col 3, 1-4
Things Above!

The first reading proclaims the living Christ, his life, death, and resurrection. This second reading tells us about the implications of all of this for us. Through baptism you have died to your own sinful and egotistic self and you have been raised up to a new life with Christ. You are a Christian. This life is hidden. In its fullness, it will appear in the life to come.

The lesson is: "Be intent on things above rather than on things of earth." This is a strong Semitic saying with the obvious meaning: Do not be so captivated by the tinsel of life or so infected with the commercialism of the day that you lose sight of the things above!

OR

Reading II
1 Cor 5, 6-8
A Fresh Dough!

Jewish housewives used to bake their own bread. Yeast or leaven was a piece of the old (previous day's) dough which was exposed to decay and then mixed with the new batch. Hence, figuratively, yeast was seen as a principle of decay. It was part of the passover preparation to do away with the old dough (yeast) and eat the passover lamb with *unleavened* bread. The symbolism is obvious: Do away with the principle of moral decay and eat the passover with a clean heart.

A — Easter Sunday

Paul reinterprets this Jewish passover. The Christian passover lamb is the Lord himself, the Lamb of God, who takes away the sin of the world. "Christ our Passover has been sacrificed." Do away with moral decay. Celebrate the feast with the unleavened bread of sincerity and truth. Against this background, Christians see the Eucharist as a reinterpreted Jewish passover!

Gospel   Jn 20, 1-9
Faith Required

(For the resurrection narratives, see the General Introduction to the Easter Season p. 55). The point (God's word) seems to be: "He saw and believed." The disciples were slow in coming to a realization of the resurrection since the Holy Spirit had not yet come to enlighten the Church concerning all these divine mysteries. We need the Holy Spirit! "God our Father, let our celebration today raise us up and renew our lives by the Spirit that is within us" (Opening Prayer).

OR

Gospel   Mt 28, 1-10 (A); Mk 16, 1-8 (B); Lk 24, 1-12 (C)

Announcement of Christ's Resurrection

The "angel of the Lord" in Matthew's version (cycle A), the "young man" in Mark's version (cycle B) and the "two young men" in Luke's version (cycle C) are messenger-figures of the Old Testament. The authors want to bring out the message from God: "He [Christ] has been raised from the dead." The legendary details (see General Introduction to the Easter Season, p. 55) belong to the tradition as such.

The evangelists took this tradition at face value and used it to proclaim the risen Lord and what he means to you and me: "Peace! Do not be afraid!"

(FOR AN AFTERNOON OR EVENING MASS)

Gospel   Lk 24, 13-35

Coming To Know Him

This simple beautiful story refers to all of us. These two men are "down in the dumps." We might compare them with the campaigners for Robert Kennedy, who had worked for him in the primaries. We remember their hope and joy in the hotel lobby in Los Angeles, and then their utter dismay, after witnessing the tragic assassination. "We had hoped that he would be the next president of the United States!"

In a similar mood the two disciples are on their way back home. "We were hoping that he [Jesus] was the one [the Messiah—freedom fighter] who would set Israel free [from Roman occupation]." They do not understand that the Messiah had to undergo all this so as to enter into his glory. Do we understand suffering as a passage to a better future?

Before this tradition reached Luke, it had been modified by the Eucharistic Liturgy: "They came to know him [Jesus] in the breaking of bread!" "May the risen Lord breathe on our minds and open our eyes that we my know him in the breaking of bread" (Alternative Opening Prayer).

2nd SUNDAY OF EASTER
Faith and Fellowship

"BIRDS of a feather flock together." With respect to certain instincts, we humans are no different from cows in a pasture flocking together when a thunderstorm is threatening. We need one another's company and inspiration to keep going. Marital love can survive only if the partners daily foster togetherness with all the means nature and religion suggest. The survival of faith is subject to the same conditions. A Christianity lived "alone," all by oneself, does not last.

A — 2nd Sunday of Easter

The first reading describes the communal life of the early congregation in Jerusalem. "Koinonia" (fellowship, brotherhood, communion) should be an important element in the life of Christians of all ages. Faith, like love, is constantly exposed to the temptation of doubt and indifference. We need one another's support. You are blessed, if you have/belong to a family where Christian fellowship is part of family life, where the members pray/worship together, read the Bible together, practice the Christian values of love, justice, mutual respect, decency, and concern together. In such a case, the members of the family carry one another and that fellowship keeps faith alive.

Fellowship should also be part of every congregation though this poses a problem in a large parish. We need belonging! Parish Councils should discuss available options. Participate in some activity of your parish. Do not be a loner! Without being exclusive, have friends who feel the same as you do in matters of faith. And at meetings, contribute to the value of "belonging" for all. Listen, be open to others, exchange ideas and experiences, share time and talents. "The brethren devoted themselves to the apostles' instruction and the communal life." The above may suggest how to realize this in our time and culture.

Reading I   Acts 2, 42-47
Fellowship Needed

We learn from this reading that besides communal life the early Jerusalem Church devoted itself to the teachings of the apostles (the Hebrew Bible and the way Jesus had interpreted it by word and example), the breaking of the bread ("agape"—daily meal with a distinctly sacred character, the Eucharist in its earliest form), and the prayers (participating in the prayers of the Jewish temple).

"Sharing all things in common" was done in the Jerusalem Church for at least some time. This is not a universal law for all Christians. The point for us is their fellowship, which we should all practice.

Reading II   1 Pt 1, 3-9
Keep the Faith!

This reading is taken from the First Letter of Peter which is probably a homily (sermon) given on the occasion of a baptismal ceremony. Notice how the homilist relates our rebirth through baptism to the resurrection of Jesus Christ. Christian rebirth from water and Spirit is a birth to hope—to an imperishable inheritance. It is all for you "who are guarded with God's power through faith." Although you have never seen the Lord Jesus, you love him, and without seeing you believe in him.

A well-known Baptist preacher of Harlem used to say: "Keep the faith, baby!" This is a folksy way of saying it. But the underlying concern must be ours, and it should be done in fellowship with others!

Gospel   Jn 20, 19-31
Faith from Hearing

The second reading has made the point that "without seeing you [Christians] believe in him [Jesus]." By relating the well-known tradition concerning the unbelieving Thomas, the writer of John wants to shed further light on this point. He indicates that even seeing, as Thomas did, is no guarantee of faith. Faith comes by hearing the word of the risen Lord who addresses Thomas personally.

Christianity knows the golden rule: Faith comes from hearing. It is God, personally addressing you in an "I-Thou" situation! This intangible situation can never be fully explained just as we cannot explain what exactly happens when someone falls in love! Respond when the Lord says: "Shalom—peace" to you in any situation of your life and keep that faith alive!

———◆———

3rd SUNDAY OF EASTER
Word and Sacrament

IT CAN happen that communication through a symbolical action (burning an effigy, giving a present, honoring the flag)

A — 3rd Sunday of Easter 63

is more efficient than simple word-commiunciation. Actually, we need both words and signs to communicate with one another. In today's Gospel the disciples respond both to God's word: "Were not our hearts burning inside us . . . as he explained the Scriptures?" and to God's sign (sacrament): "They had come to know him in the breaking of bread."

Our growth in faith is made through the ministry of God's word (first part of Mass: Bible readings and the explanation in the homily) and comes to its fulfillment in the celebration of the Eucharist—a sacramental (signifying) meal. A Christian can know a great deal about our Lord without knowing him as a person! Make every Sunday worship service a personal encounter with the Lord Jesus in both Scripture and Sacrament (the Eucharist).

Reading I   Acts 2, 14. 22-28
God's Purpose

This passage is the first of six major sermons in Acts. All of these six sermons deal with the substance of the Christian message. It is: "Dying you destroyed our death, rising you restored our life. Lord Jesus, come in glory" (2nd Memorial Acclamation at Mass).

Peter's citation from Psalm 16 illustrates the freedom with which the early Church made use of the Hebrew Bible. The Psalm describes God as saving his chosen ones from destruction. Peter applies this to God's chosen one par excellence, Jesus Christ, and brings out his point: God raised up Jesus from the dead according to his "set purpose and plan."

Reading II   1 Pt 1, 17-21
Your Faith and Hope

The writer describes Christ's death and its salutary effect on us in terms of the Jewish passover: sojourn in a strange land and deliverance by the blood of a spotless passover lamb. We are still in a strange land, but we are delivered by Christ our Passover Sacrifice. For final deliverance from pain and evil, we have "faith and hope centered in God."

Gospel
Lk 24, 13-35

Meeting the Lord

(For commentary, see Easter Sunday and Introduction of today's Mass.) This story is one of the most beautifully written by Luke and it offers a wealth of theological (religious) insight. God's word should be "burning inside" us as often as we meditatively read it at home and listen to it in church.

Meeting the Lord Jesus in the breaking of bread (the Eucharistic celebration) should open our eyes ever more! "Lord Jesus, make your word plain to us, make our hearts burn with love when you speak" (Gospel Acclamation).

4th SUNDAY OF EASTER
The Good Shepherd

AT many moments of our lives, especially when we have to put up with suffering and unexpected problems, we feel that we are not self-sufficient. In such cases, modern people go to a psychiatrist, a marriage counselor, or a lawyer for guidance and advice. Where does God, visible in Jesus Christ, fit in your schedule? God's advice and wisdom is available in the words and example of the Lord Jesus.

The writers of the New Testament were concerned to bring out who the risen Lord is and how we are related to him. This Sunday we are invited to see the Lord as both the gate of a sheepfold, through which we should enter in security, and our Shepherd, whom we should follow. Though sheep and shepherds are not part of the contemporary American scene and we know them perhaps only from television, with a little goodwill we can understand what the inspired writer wants to say.

By prayerfully reading the Bible and diligently following the Lord Jesus who is "the shepherd, the guardian of your souls" (Reading II), modern Christians know how to integrate the guidelines of their religion with whatever science offers them for the solutions of their problems!

A — 4th Sunday of Easter 65

Reading I
Acts 2, 14. 36-41
Jesus Both Lord and Messiah

Last Sunday's first reading gave part of Peter's speech on Pentecost. Today we listen to the effect of that speech. Some three thousand people respond to Peter's call for reform and are baptized. What does the Bible want to teach you and me with this narrative?

One point may be that we should accept Jesus as "both Lord and Messiah." You have already done so at your baptism. But this acceptance is an on-going process. Is the Lord your guardian and shepherd in your daily life? Can you truly pray: "The Lord is my shepherd; there is nothing I shall want"? (Responsorial Psalm).

Reading II
1 Pt 2, 20-25
Shepherd and Guardian

The author of the First Letter of Peter applies the shepherd-theme to the situation of a man afflicted with pain and suffering in order to show us what is the right thing to do. What guidance does the Lord Jesus offer in such a case? The suggested answer is to accept the pain and suffering. Why? Because Jesus has done so!

This general suggestion is not an invitation to accept passively any and all suffering that may strike you. But there are situations in which we have no choice. Hence, is the Lord Jesus the shepherd and guardian of your soul? Do you get on your knees in faithful prayer and supplication?

Gospel
Jn 10, 1-10
Hearing His Voice

We have in this reading a fusion of two parables. The first is a picture of a sheepfold into which two parties seek to enter, a marauder and the shepherd himself. This parable refers to the false shepherd of Israel (vv. 1-3a). The second parable concerns the relationship between the sheep and the shepherd (vv. 3b-5). Oral tradition (preachers telling them for several decades) has fused these two parables together.

Jesus, as seen by the author of John's Gospel, identifies himself with both the gate and the shepherd. Both identifications make the same point. The allegorical interpretation of this combined parable is an addition of the evangelist.

◆

5th SUNDAY OF EASTER
Kairos—Time of Favor

EDUCATORS know that children have their particular sensitivity moments, which should be exploited for learning. Adults follow the same law of nature. There are times when we are more than usually sensitive to God's word. Sometimes these may be the result of a happy or sad event in life, such as a wedding, funeral, birth, success, failure, or even a deeply moving book, motion picture, or television program. At other times there is no apparent reason for them at all.

We speak of "disclosure moments," i.e., times when we are more than usually open to some transcending reality. The New Testament word for one such moment or time is "kairos." The Greek language has two words for time: "chronos," time measurable in years, and "kairos," time of opportunity, time of grace.

Jesus said: "The kairos (time of favor or fulfillment) is at hand. Be converted and believe in the good news" (Mk 1, 14-15). God is present to you in Christ, the Bible, the breaking of bread, any good person. The "kairos" (time of favor) for you is when you experience this mysterious presence. This "kairos" (time of favor) is a gift of God, which we should exploit.

Reading I Embracing the Faith Acts 6, 1-7

This reading shows that the word of God continues to spread in and through human beings. There is dissension between the Greek- and Hebrew-speaking members of the congregation—a very human occurrence. But the ministry of the word, service to one another, and the Spirit of Jesus combine to keep them together. Indeed, the eyes of the Lord are upon those who fear [have filial respect for] him" (Responsorial Psalm).

A — 6th Sunday of Easter   67

Reading II   1 Pt 2, 4-9
Jesus the Cornerstone

The first reading showed a congregation as it is at the grass-roots level: human beings kept together by the Spirit of Jesus. This reading tells baptismal candidates what the Church is at the level of faith: a temple (the place of God's presence), of which the members are the living stones, a people sharing in the royal priesthood of the Lord Jesus, a consecrated nation, a people God claims as his own.

The citations from the Old Testament bring out that it is the Lord Jesus who as a cornerstone keeps those "living stones" together. The Church is a community of believers who want to be the witnesses of God's presence in the midst of life.

Gospel   Jn 14, 1-12
Knowing the Way

It is through Jesus that we have access to the Father: "Jesus told him [Thomas]: 'I am the way.'" It is through the same Jesus that we can know the Father: "Jesus replied [to Philip]: 'Whoever has seen me has seen the Father.'" The Lord Jesus is God's word to us. The point is that we must open up to God's word. The "kairos" (time of favor) should be utilized. God's grace is freely offered, but it must be accepted and used well.

———◆———

6th SUNDAY OF EASTER
Diversity in Unity

THE founders of any endeavor cannot expect their work to be lasting and to continue unless their disciples accept the message wholeheartedly. Those disciples must be faithful to the traditions of the founder and have an open mind for the intuitive vision concerning the future of the particular work. Guided by the spirit of the founder, those who continue the work must operate creatively, constantly adapting themselves to new situations. This is what the early Church has tried to do as we see in the readings from the Acts of the Apostles on the Sundays of this Easter Season.

Jesus' disciples knew their mission to preach the Gospel to all nations (Mt 28, 19). Today we will read that Philip took the "Good News" to Samaria. The apostles in Jerusalem heard about this and were rather surprised. Jews and Samaritans did not socialize (Jn 4, 9). We notice the same surprise when the first Roman joined the Church (Acts 10, 65). Indeed, this going beyond the boundaries of traditional Judaism was a daring and creative step!

From that moment on the Church has had the task to accept diversity in its bosom and guard unity in the Spirit. That is why the apostles went to Samaria to impose hands on the converted Samaritans as a seal of approval. "And they received the Holy Spirit." We should accept this same situation in the Church of our time and culture. "There are different gifts but the same Spirit" (1 Cor 12, 4). There are charismatics, floating parishes, conservatives and liberals. We have young and old emotionally involved and more cerebral members in one congregation. Let us bear with one another, as long as the same Spirit breathes upon all under the guidance of our bishops.

Reading I   Acts 8, 5-8. 14-17

All Accepted

We read about the success of the disciples witnessing to the Lord Jesus. Their words and signs bring people of all walks of life, even "the despised Samaritans," to faith in the risen Lord Jesus. By imposing hands on them, the apostles receive them into the Christian fellowship whose headquarters are still in Jerusalem at this time.

Be on your guard to insure that diversity remains under the umbrella of unity in the Spirit. "Vae Soli!"—Do not be a loner! Opinions shared only by a very few or by no one else are suspicious, to say the least.

Reading II
1 Pt 3, 15-18
Ready To Reply

Peter addresses Christians who are defamed because of their way of life in Christ. He urges them to have hope and to be ready to reply when anyone asks them questions. The point (God's word to you and me) seems to be: This can happen to you as well.

Do your co-workers know that you are a Christian in the Catholic tradition? You have a hopeful, optimistic outlook on life. Can you reply when people ask questions? It requires reading. Are you up-to-date concerning the "daring and creative steps" the Church is taking nowadays, adapting itself to new situations? (See Introduction).

Gospel
Jn 14, 15-21
To Be with You Always

Jesus reminds his followers that he will not remain with them visibly. But in the Spirit he will! He will send a Paraclete (advocate), a counselor, a defender, to help them. Jesus calls him "the Spirit of Truth," and this Spirit is promised to all of us, "to be with you always." This is the reason for our hope (see Reading II) and optimistic outlook on life. Being different, let us remain one in the Spirit! In faith "you can recognize him, because he remains with you and will be within you."

◆

ASCENSION
Heaven and Earth

NOT ALL members of our species have the same outlook on life. There are people for whom this life means everything and "heaven" nothing. Naturally good people, they may cherish love as a great value, but they believe that when death comes, that is the end. There are others for whom "heaven" is all-important and this life almost completely unimportant. Save your soul! Many Christians have cherished this outlook, especially concerning others and as long as the self was not involved. Finally, we have those for whom "heaven" is realized already on earth in love!

If we understand Jesus' philosophy of life well, and try to understand the exaltation of his humanity as we celebrate it today, we could give it a try. We may live life, including marital sex and love, as an earthly reality. We may develop our potential as earthlings to its fullest. We may make use of the results of science (sociology, etc.) to achieve a better life on this planet. We may consult marriage counselors and psychiatrists and seek the best medical care available. Yet in our best moments ("disclosure situations"), we know that there must be something more than all of this, a transcending reality.

In faith, following Jesus of Nazareth, we see this "transcending reality" as a loving Father who is waiting for us. He (Jesus) is the beginning: "Where he, our head, has gone, we, his members, hope to follow him" (Preface). "God our Father, may we follow him [Jesus] into the new creation, for his ascension is our glory and our hope" (Opening Prayer).

Reading I   Acts 1, 1-11
Lifted Up

The wording of this tradition on the ascension of our Lord is clearly conditioned by the limited understanding of the universe during the writer's lifetime. This wording is not part of divine revelation. There is no absolute up or down. Heaven is not a place somewhere up in outer space. Heaven is a situation outside our concepts of time and space. What the evangelists have tried to do is describe the final appearance of Jesus and/or the fact that the Lord Jesus is "sitting at God's right hand," which is a Hebrew idiom for sharing power with God. (For both this reading and today's Gospel, see the General Introduction to the Easter Season, p. 55.)

Luke's message is: Christ has died ("in the time after his suffering"), Christ has risen ("he showed them that he was alive"), Christ will come again ("this Jesus . . . will return").

A — Ascension

That is the way we word it in our Memorial Acclamation at Mass.

Reading II — Eph 1, 17-23
In Heaven

Paul, a learned Jewish rabbi, relates the same message as Luke and Matthew do in the first and third readings, only he does it in difficult theological language. Paul relates the risen and ascended Christ to all that exists. Christ is supreme, above all creatures, seated at God's right hand (a Hebraism for "sharing power with God").

Paul prays for the Ephesians and for all of us: "May God grant you a spirit of wisdom and insight to know him [the Lord Jesus] clearly."

Gospel — Mt 28, 16-20
Falling Down in Homage

In Matthew's version of the ascension account, the appearance takes place on a mountain. As the great appearance of God to Moses took place on Mount Sinai (Ex 19), so Matthew has Jesus' great sermon delivered on a mountain (Mt 5, 1), and the transfiguration take place on a mountain as well (Mt 17, 1). This final appearance of Jesus on a mountain has theological significance for Matthew, who as a Jew writing for Christians of Jewish background constantly writes with concepts and allusions taken from the Hebrew Bible (Old Testament).

We should keep in mind that the primary significance of the Easter appearances is that they were revelations of the risen Lord Jesus. They could be doubted as well as believed. But once the disciples believed, they "fell down in homage," and with admirable dedication they heeded the Lord's mission and went out to all nations to preach the Gospel. "And know I am with you"—a great assurance to "the pilgrim Church" on its way to a great future!

◆

7th SUNDAY OF EASTER

Prayful Waiting

PEOPLE today, constantly on the go, are not easily convinced that they need some quiet time to have a look at themselves and ask hard questions, such as: Am I consistent with my past? have I changed values? how do I look at my future? Traditionally, a retreat or mission was the time to do this. Whatever our options are, we could join the ancient novena of the early Christians, their nine days of prayerful waiting for the celebration of Pentecost, the outpouring of the Spirit.

Meditatively reading the traditions concerning the resurrection and ascension of our Lord, we distinguish two modes in the mystery of the ascension: (1) our Lord's invisible exaltation in the resurrection, and (2) a visible manifestation of it on the Mount of Olives. The Lord sits at the right hand of the Father (i.e., shares power with him) and communicates the Spirit which we need so dearly.

The energy crisis keeps our minds busy. We are frightened to think of the fatal possibility of running out of energy. Our planet would soon be like the moon without any sign of life. But the spiritual energy, the source of Christian life, is there. It is the Spirit whom Jesus sends from the Father. In preparing for the feast of Pentecost open up for God and you will never die.

Reading I   Acts 1, 12-14
Constant Prayer

Luke's narrative, separately elucidating three aspects of the Easter event—resurrection, ascension, communication of the Spirit—reflects early Christian Liturgy. On the third day, Chrisitians celebrate the Lord's resurrection (he is alive), on the fortieth day his ascension (he shares power with God), on the fiftieth day the communication of the Spirit. The days between Ascension and Pentecost were dedicated to prayerful waiting for an ever more bounteous outpouring of the Spirit on all Christians.

A — Pentecost (Vigil Mass)

This is the last time Mary is mentioned in the New Testament as a member of a believing congregation engaged in prayerful waiting. We are in good company if we make this week a time of special prayer: "Come, Holy Spirit, and fill the hearts of your faithful!" "Hear, O Lord, the sound of my call; have pity on me, and answer me" (Responsorial Psalm).

Reading II — 1 Pt 4, 13-16
Sharing Christ's Suffering

Peter reminds Christians who have to suffer that they can be happy nevertheless, "for then God's Spirit in its glory has come to rest on you." If you suffer for being a Christian, do not be ashamed! Pray that God's Spirit may give all of us this insight!

Gospel — Jn 17, 1-11
"For These I Pray"

Today's Gospel is taken from Jesus' high priestly prayer, also called "prayer of consecration," because Jesus consecrates himself for his approaching redemptive death. Actually, this prayer reflects an elaborated meditation on the thoughts and aspirations of our Lord. Jesus begins his passion with prayer. Our Lord meditates on what he has to do. He recommends his disciples to his Father. He has made them know the Father. Now they must go out into the world and, filled with Jesus' Spirit, teach all nations.

The task of a Christian in the world is not an easy one. As the Lord prayed in the difficult hours of his life, we should do the same, especially during this week of prayerful preparation for Pentecost.

PENTECOST
VIGIL MASS
The Spirit at Work

WE know how difficult it would be to explain the intricacies of a computer or the complexity of ballistics used for space flights to a person without formal education. For such a person lacks the very concepts that would be needed to understand such things. We face somewhat the same problem when we apply our limited hearts and minds to the contemplation of the infinite God and outpouring of his Spirit. We should therefore realize that all the Bible can do is attempt to say some meaningful things about the Spirit of God in limited human terminology. Human speech cannot possibly express adequately who God is.

The Bible readings for both the Vigil and the Day of Pentecost bring out the function of the Holy Spirit. This evening, Old Testament images are used which have also inspired New Testament passages on the Spirit. First, the Spirit is seen as *a unifying force*. "It holds all things together" (Wis 1, 7: Entrance Antiphon of the Day Mass). Hence, the first reading concerns the confusion of speech at Babel, a reversal of the Pentecost narrative where the Spirit unites by overcoming division caused by misunderstanding (different tongues!). This is symbolism, of course, but entirely meaningful.

Secondly, the Spirit is seen as *the principle of love*. Hence, the symbolism of fire is used. In the second reading from Exodus, the Lord came down in fire, as on the disciples at Pentecost. "Come, Holy Spirit, . . . and kindle in them the fire of your love" (Gospel Acclamation). Thirdly, the Spirit is seen as *life-giving*, as the *"ruah* Yahweh"—the breath (spirit) of the God-Creator hovering over the water (Gn 1, 1). Hence, the third reading is the famous passage from Ezekiel where the spirit (breath) of the Lord reanimates dry bones, which stand for the house of Israel, God's people.

Fourthly, the Spirit is seen as *a strong driving wind* inspiring people to preach the Gospel. Hence, the fourth reading is from Joel: "I will pour out my spirit [breath] upon all mankind. Your sons and daughters shall prophesy," as the apostles did on Pentecost: "making bold proclamation as the Spirit prompted them." The point of all these readings (God's word) is that we should apply this to the Church of today, to ourselves! "Come, Holy Spirit, fill the hearts of your faithful" (Gospel Acclamation).

A — Pentecost (Vigil Mass)

Reading I   Gn 11, 1-9
The Lord Scattered Them

Using a folktale, the writer brings out that pride (making a name for oneself) results in confusion. This is the reversal of the Pentecost narrative which states that God's Spirit overcomes human divisiveness and confusion, caused by misunderstanding.

OR

Reading I   Ex 19, 3-8. 16-20
"The Lord Came Down"

This tradition uses the familiar Biblical imagery of smoke and fire to describe a theophany (appearance of God). It has influenced Luke's narrative about the tongues of fire coming to rest on each of the apostles. "All were filled with the Holy Spirit."

OR

Reading I   Ez 37, 1-14
The Spirit Gives Life

"From the four winds come, O spirit, and breathe into these slain [standing for God's people, dead from aversion to God] that they come to life." The Church reapplies Ezekiel's vision of the dry bones to the life-giving function of the Spirit.

OR

Reading I   Jl 3, 1-5
Pouring Out My Spirit

The spirit (breath) of God makes the sons and daughters of God's people prophesy. The imagery of smoke and fire is used as in Ex 19 (Reading I). Reapplied, it refers to the function of the Spirit, as related in the Pentecost narrative.

The Church also reapplies Psalm 104, making its wording a prayer to the Holy Spirit: "Lord, send out your Spirit, and renew the face of the earth" (Responsorial Psalm).

Reading II   Rom 8, 22-27
The Spirit Helping Us

Reapplied, the Responsorial Psalm says: "If you [God] take away their [creatures'] breath, they perish and return to their dust. When you send forth your spirit, they are created and you renew the face of the earth." Paul picks up this trend of thought. Without the Spirit, "all creation groans and is in agony." And even though we have the Spirit, we too groan, while we await full redemption in the hereafter.

God, the Holy Spirit, is the animating principle of all life. Without the help of the Holy Spirit we cannot even pray as we ought. So many Christians nowadays complain about the difficulty they have in praying! They should turn to the Holy Spirit!

Gospel   Jn 7, 37-39
Living Water

Jesus refers to himself as the source of life-giving water. This water is used here as a symbol of Jesus' Spirit to be poured out on all Christians through the life-giving water of baptism.

―――――◆―――――

MASS DURING THE DAY
The Holy Spirit, Gift of the Father

A FULL-RIGGED ship under an unfurled sail makes a beautiful picture, but it does not move without wind. Without "the breath of life," human beings cannot perform. An artist needs inspiration. The *"ruah* Yahweh"—the breath, animating Spirit, of God—was given to us at baptism. On the fiftieth day after Easter (Passover) the Jews celebrated the giving of the Mosaic Law at Sinai and the establishment of Israel as God's people. At Pentecost we celebrate the giving of the Spirit to God's people and related to it, the establishment of the new Israel, the Church.

A — Pentecost (During the Day)

The Spirit, whom the Lord Jesus sends from the Father, will remind us of all that the Lord has taught us. He will animate us and help us to know and understand our religion not just with our mind but also with our heart and soul (Jn 14, 26). "Father of light, send your Spirit into our lives with the power of a mighty wind, and by the flame of your wisdom open the horizons of our minds" (Alternative Opening Prayer).

For a more profound insight into the mystery of Pentecost, we should refer to the Introduction to both Easter and the Pentecost vigil. Pentecost marks the conclusion of the "great fifty days," the Easter Season.

Reading I — Acts 2, 1-11
The Spirit for All!

The Bible, especially the New Testament, should never be read in the past tense. It is God's word to you and me now! Jesus is alive. His Spirit is with every Christian. This is the meaning of the Christ event, meaningfully celebrated at Easter, Ascension and Pentecost, three aspects of the one mystery.

Luke follows the early Christian custom of celebrating the communication of the Spirit at the conclusion of the "great fifty days," our Pentecost. Hence, he relates the outpouring of the Spirit as we have it in the first reading. John puts the communication of the Spirit on Easter day (Gospel). The gift of the Spirit is one with the risen Lord Jesus. (See Introduction to the 7th Sunday of Easter.) Notice that both traditions stress that the Christian message is not just for the Jews but for all people.

Psalm 104 may refer to the renewal of nature at springtime, time and again, done by God's life-giving breath (spirit). In Christian use, it is reinterpreted and applied to the renewal of life through the Holy Spirit.

Reading II — 1 Cor 12, 3-7. 12-13
The Spirit for Common Good

Paul is concerned about his congregation in Corinth. In it, a charismatic group has originated and glossolalia (speaking in tongues) is practiced. Its effect on the congregation has not been good. Those who have failed to participate are looked upon as second-class Christians and divisiveness has ensued. Paul does not condemn the movement. He sees in it the Spirit at work. But on the other hand he stresses that the outpouring of the Spirit must build up the community (the body of Christ), not tear it apart.

To have the Spirit means, first of all, to confess: "Jesus is Lord." This is done in various ways, not just by speaking in tongues. Each gift, even the least spectacular one, must be used for the common good! This could be a reminder to contemporary movements and counter-movements in the Church.

Gospel — Jn 20, 19-23
A Life-Giving Spirit

Sometimes this reading is called "the Pentecost according to John." The theological background has been explained above. Notice that Jesus uses the symbolism of "breathing," when he communicates his Spirit to the disciples. Breath was the sign of life of the ancient Hebrews, and we ourselves still practice mouth to mouth resuscitation in a case of emergency.

This symbolism of "breathing" reminds us also of the first verse of the Bible, where the "*ruah* Yahweh" (breath-spirit of the Creator-God) is mentioned as the life-giving and animating principle of all creation. Jesus was a Jew and as such deeply steeped in Hebrew literature and culture.

―――――◆―――――

ORDINARY TIME (Cont'd)

THE second part of Ordinary Time (see p. 29 for the special character and make-up of this period) begins with the day after Pentecost and runs to the Saturday before the First Sunday of Advent.

If the number of ordinary weeks is thirty-four, the week after Pentecost is the one which follows immediately the last week celebrated before Lent. The Masses of Pentecost, Trinity and (in countries where Corpus Christi is not observed as a holyday of obligation and is therefore celebrated on the following Sunday) Corpus Christi replace the Sunday Masses in these weeks. If the number of ordinary weeks is thirty-three, the first week which would otherwise follow Pentecost is omitted.

The readings for these Sundays follow a carefully selected arrangement that enables the faithful to become acquainted with the most important passages of both the Old and the New Testaments. The Gospels are taken in almost continuous fashion from Matthew (A), Mark (B), and Luke (C). (The parts of John that have not been read before or after Easter are now read after Mark.)

The Old Testament readings have a specific relationship to the Gospel passages and illustrate the main themes of the Old Testament. Finally, there is also a semi-continuous reading of the letters of Paul and James, which provides practical application of the Gospel teachings.

TRINITY SUNDAY
The Ineffable Mystery of God

THE FIRST thing our parents taught us about our religion was most probably the sign of the cross. The last thing a priest will do at our graveside is make the sign of the cross over our body. A Christian's life is marked "in the name of the Father, and of the Son, and of the Holy Spirit." The Sunday Bible readings often speak to us about the Father (as originator of all life related to creation), sending his Son or Word (for our salvation), and communicating the Spirit (related to our rebirth from water and the Spirit).

The revelation of God as Father, Son, and Holy Spirit tells us first of all what God is for us. But as to the mysterious unity of Father, Son, and Holy Spirit, we can only stammer with inadequate human concepts, which are not able to express the ineffable mystery of God in himself. Human beings want to know. But we must realize that more important than knowing about God is knowing God, the way two beloved know one another!

An intimate person-to-person relationship gives a knowledge which cannot possibly be expressed in human terminology. It is that kind of knowledge of God which ultimately satisfies a human being. "How deep are the riches and the wisdom and the knowledge of God! How inscrutable his judgments, how unsearchable his ways" (Rom 11, 33).

Reading I His Name "Lord" Ex 34, 4-6. 8-9

The content of this reading concerns the infidelity of God's people at Sinai. They have made a golden calf to worship. Moses, coming down from the mountain, sees the infidelity, becomes angered, breaks the tablets of the law and destroys the calf. But Moses goes back to God, who appears to him again. Note how the author ascribes human characteristics to God, as is done often in the Bible (the eye of God, his punishing hand, his anger, etc.). Humans try to say something about God! Note also the cloud, a favored image (symbol) of God's presence.

A — Corpus Christi

The Old Testament does not reveal the Blessed Trinity. In retrospect we see some indications: God in himself—shares himself—creates a response in the heart of Moses. Our response: Bowing down in worship, as Moses did!

Reading II — The God of Love — 2 Cor 13, 11-13

In this reading we have Paul's fervent wish for the congregation in Corinth, Greece. He mentions the Father, the Son, and the Holy Spirit, God related to us and our salvation. "The grace of the Lord Jesus Christ [which he acquired for us by his death and resurrection], and the love of God [the Father, the origin of our salvation], and the fellowship of the Holy Spirit [keeping us together] be with you all!"

Gospel — God Loves the World — Jn 3, 16-18

"God so loved the world [us] that he gave his only Son [Word: a word is our brainchild!]." God, not far away, but closely present (Reading I), wants to be present to you. He wants to communicate with you. The condition is that you open up to him, for communication is a two-way street! You can do so since God has given you the Spirit of his Son to form your heart and make you cry out: Abba, Father! (See Communion Antiphon).

◆

Sunday After Trinity Sunday

CORPUS CHRISTI
Sharing Life with Christ

IN an affluent society basic food such as bread and water is no problem. However, for many people in the world it still is. Thus, they can understand better than we do that it is a real sign of love and care when God intervenes to feed his people. For them, water and bread are a question of life and death. But we are often hungry and thirsty for other values than sustenance of physical life. In a depersonalized society we suffer from absence where there should be presence. We hunger and thirst for companionship, love, concern, mercy, and respect which are no problems in the great family of primitive people. Whose need is greater?

Where we suffer from absence, the Lord Jesus wants to be present to us with all the concern and love of a friend for a friend. In the signs of plain daily food for Orientals—water, bread, wine—Jesus indicates what he intends by being present to us. He wants to share life. He wants to strengthen. He wants to mean something to you and me.

When we celebrate the Eucharist, we celebrate this mysterious presence of the Lord Jesus with the community. Open up to make "Communion" possible. "Whoever eats my flesh and drinks my blood will live in me and I in him, says the Lord" (Communion Antiphon).

Reading I Dt 8, 2-3. 14-16
Not by Bread Alone

During the time of affliction in the desert, God took care of his people and gave them the basics they needed, water and bread. But the writer of Deuteronomy, meditating on the desert experience of his people, lets Moses indicate that God intended more than just taking care of physical needs. "He [God] fed you with manna in order to show you that not by bread alone does man live, but by every word that comes forth from the mouth of God."

The psalmist, and we with him, thank God for his care: "With the best of wheat he fills you." He has proclaimed his word to Jacob (patriarch of God's chosen people, who stands for you and me). Praise the Lord, Jerusalem (capital of the chosen people, which again symbolizes you and me!).

Reading II 1 Cor 10, 16-17
Sharing

Paul does not want the Christians of Corinth to take part in pagan sacrifices to which relatives may invite them. We have our passover sacrifice, the body and blood of Christ. Notice that in Biblical language, "body and blood" do not indicate the things as such but the whole person and the event which they signify, namely, Jesus Christ giving himself in his meritorious death, in which we share when we partake in the Eucharist.

Moreover, Paul teaches that not only is such partaking communion with the Lord and a guarantee for salvation. It also means communion with the fellow members. God's word: Heed both aspects of Holy Communion!

Gospel   Jn 6, 51-58
Jesus, the Living Bread

Every time we take part in the Eucharistic celebration, we should enter a more intimate relationship with Jesus Christ. Notice again (as at Reading II) that the words "flesh, body, blood" stand for the person! "The man who feeds on my flesh and drinks my blood remains in me, and I in him," and through that continuous encounter with our Lord, such persons will have real life, life everlasting.

10th SUNDAY IN ORDINARY TIME
Love Rather Than Worship!

THE Bible readings stress the necessary connection of piety with daily life. They do so in strong language which we should understand in context. God does not want fine liturgy (worship services) but *fine lives*. Does this mean that we should not worship any longer and that all of us should become social workers in the ghettos of our inner cities? Of course not!

What God does not want is meaningless worship. Thus, well-to-do and middle-class Christians tend to isolate themselves and be cliquish even in their practice of worship. Their priorities go to a wealthy and well-furnished church building, and they experience little collective or individual concern for their deprived fellow humans.

We should be concerned as individuals for lonesome, old, poor, distressed people regardless of race or creed and we should be concerned collectively, as a congregation. If there is social injustice and deprivation in your community, what can the congregation do? You might start by collectively urging your representatives on the city, state, and national level to do something to solve social issues. You could also contact your parish council.

Reading I
Hos 6, 3-6
Love Desired

Hosea carried out his prophetic mission in the rather wealthy but corrupt society of the Northern Kingdom, before it was destroyed by the Assyrians (722 B.C.). The setting may have been the sanctuary in Bethel. With various shades of interpretation, sacrifices (livestock, produce of the land) are gifts of human beings to their gods/god in order to please them/him (thanking, atoning for sins, asking for favors.)

If sacrifices really stand for a person's affection for God, they are good and no prophet would condemn them. But Hosea had reasons for putting into God's mouth the statement: "For it is love that I desire, not sacrifice." He blames the worshipers: "Your piety is like a morning cloud, like the dew that early passes away." The point (God's word to us) is: Formal worship should symbolize a life of love and concern, otherwise it is meaningless. Actually, God does not need our favors! "Mine (God's) are the world and its fullness" anyway!

Reading II
Rom 4, 18-25
Abraham's Faith

Abraham provides the classical example of Christian faith. And "our faith will be credited to us also." Putting things in perspective, we realize that our good works cannot buy our sanctification. God does not need our favors. ("If I [God] would be hungry, I should not tell you, for mine are the world and its fullness"—Responsorial Psalm 50, 12.)

God loves us first, not the other way around, and it is he who made it possible for us to love him in return. Our faith, seen as love, and love seen as fulfillment of the law (Rom 13, 10), will be credited to us.

A — 11th Sunday in Ordinary Time

Gospel
Mt 9, 9-13

Mercy—Sacrifice—Worship

The Pharisees of Jesus' time stressed the external observance of the many human precepts of the law as a means for justification. The first two readings stress the fact that sacrifices and the observance of the law cannot buy salvation. It is love in return for God's love (faith) that will be credited.

Jesus quotes the first reading and tells the Pharisees and us: "Learn the meaning of the words, 'It is mercy [love] I desire and not sacrifice,' " and he practices it by eating with social outcasts, tax collectors, and those regarded as sinners.

◆

11th SUNDAY IN ORDINARY TIME
God's Kindness Endures Forever

WHEN human beings try to describe God, they are bound to do so with human concepts and limited terminology. We cannot adequately describe God, the "wholly Other." We simply do not have either the concepts or the words to do so. The Biblical writers were limited by the same human condition, though we view their message as inspired (guided) by God. Hence, in reading the Bible, we should first find out what the human word means (by analyzing its historical setting and literary form: history, poem, allegory, etc.); then through it we will discover what God has to say to us.

Today's Bible readings portray God as kind, good, loving, compassionate, even moved with pity. Can God be emotionally moved with compassion? We do not know. But he can be so in and through the heart of the Lord Jesus. The message of today is: We, you and I, are God's own, his special possession. Let us appreciate this invitation to intimacy with God! Love is a two-way street. A love relationship can easily lose its flavor through indifference and lack of constant care. Keep contact with God, especially through regular meditative Bible reading.

A — 11th Sunday in Ordinary Time

Reading I — Ex 19, 2-6
I Bore You Up

The theophanies (manifestations of God) on Mount Sinai are perhaps the best known of the Bible. Of course, a human imagery in vogue during Biblical times is used. Clouds, thunder, lightning—these are so many images to describe the awe-inspiring presence of God. (See Ex 19.)

The theophany of this Bible passage is an idyllic one. An eagle is said to gently bear her young on her wings. Hence meditating on God's loving care, the writer has God say: "I bore you up on the eagle wings." This is a tantamount to saying: " I brought you out of bondage in Egypt. You are now my special possession." God cares for you and me! indeed. "The Lord is good, his kindness endures forever. (Responsorial Psalm).

Reading II — Rom 5, 6-11
God Proves His Love

Again, God's love is suggested as a topic for meditative reading. "God proves his love for us." Paul brings out that God's love is not a sentimental love. He reasons: Someone may have the courage to die for a good man. But Christ died for us while we were still sinners. Hence, we should be all the more appreciative of God's love.

Gospel — Mt 9, 36-10, 8
Moved with Pity

"The heart of Jesus was moved with pity." In the Lord Jesus, God's loving care became a really human, emotional love, for all of us. He cares; and he shows it through compassion for deprived, sick, and unhappy people. Notice that in the mind of the ancients disease was caused by evil spirits or demons. Hence, a sick person did not go first of all to a doctor but to the holy man to ask him to pray and cast out the demon.

The healing activity of Jesus and his co-workers, seen as expelling the evil one, is a beautiful sign of the coming of God's reign in this world. "The reign of God is at hand! Cure the sick—expel demons!" All of this is another sign of God's kindness and compassionate love for ailing human beings.

12th SUNDAY IN ORDINARY TIME
Witness And Fear

THE mystery of God's kingdom on earth, a reign of justice, love, and truth, can only be known by the witness of those who are committed to a better society, as God envisions it. Witnessing for God's reign implies denouncing evil. Today's second Bible reading tells about the power of evil and all humanity's solidarity with it. Hence, witnessing for God's values can be risky when the Lord's disciple encounters that ominous power of evil and must oppose it. Like a wild and wounded animal evil can strike back. We know the evil that overtook great human beings. Think of Blessed Maximilian Kolbe who offered his life in exchange for that of a family man condemned to death in a Nazi concentration camp, and many unsung heroes!

In the Bible readings, the question is not fear in general; it is the particular fear which Christians feel at the moment they must witness to their faith in God, the Lord Jesus, and that mysterious reign of justice and love to be established in society. The temptation is to keep silent, not to rock the boat. But may we? Christianity has its long history of glorious martyrs.

When we have to witness and must oppose injustice, we too may fear. Then we should pray: "[God,] for your sake I bear insult, and shame covers my face. I pray to you, O Lord, for the time of your favor, O God!" (Responsorial Psalm)

Reading I   The Lord Is with Me   Jer 20, 10-13

Jeremiah is so appealing to us because he is very human. He knew what it means to be scared to death. When God called him, he tried to talk his way out of his prophetic vocation: "Ah, Lord God! I know not how to speak; I am too young" (Jer 1, 6). Yet though afflicted with fear and trembling, this humble man ultimately accepted his mission. Unlike the "professional prophets," who were careful not to oppose the king and public opinion, Jeremiah spoke up and condemned evil. Hence, he was constantly harassed and persecuted to such an extent that martyrdom, rejection, and persecution came to be regarded by later Israelites as inseparable from the prophetic vocation.

Jesus and later Paul referred to the prophets, and especially Jeremiah, when they had to suffer for their vocation of being witnesses for God's reign. Jeremiah was afraid but he drew strength out of prayer. Consider his statement: "But the Lord is with me, like a mighty champion".

Reading II Rom 5, 12-15
God's Gracious Gift

We mentioned the power of evil opposing those who witness for God's reign of justice, love, peace and truth on earth. Paul meditates extensively on evil and its threatening power in society. The sin of the world is a fact. All of mankind is born into this sinful situation, which is the root of all misery in this world. But Paul also speaks about evil's defeat by Jesus' meritorious death on the cross. Threatened by evil and tempted by sin, we Christians trust in the redeeming power of our Lord Jesus Christ.

Gospel Mt 10, 26-33
No Intimidation

When the Lord sent his disciples on their mission to announce that the reign of God was at hand, to cure the sick and expel demons (see last Sunday), he knew that they would run into opposition. He encourages them: "Do not let men intimidate you. . . . Whoever acknowledges me before men I will acknowledge before my Father in heaven." This is God's word to all Christians whenever their conscience tells them to witness.

───────◆───────

13th SUNDAY IN ORDINARY TIME
The Sermon

ONCE a week, millions of Christians are more or less a captive audience when the priest in the pulpit delivers the sermon. Both the first Bible reading, which usually introduces the theme of the Gospel, and the Gospel itself speak about receiving a holy man. "A holy man" in the Bible does not signalize a

A — 13th Sunday in Ordinary Time

mystical experiences with God, but simply refers to a bearer of God's word, in other words, a preacher. Of course, Christians have a right to expect that the minister of God's word is trained in Biblical exegesis (explanation of Scripture), so that he will not air just his own opinions from the pulpit but will declare God's word enshrined in Scripture.

On the other hand, the hearers also have a responsibility. They should be aware that they should not look primarily for an eloquent speech, but for a clear and honest explanation of the Bible. Neither should Christians in the pews expect the preacher to be always "the nice guy" who practices some gentle shoulder-patting.

The priest has the serious duty to apply the Biblical message to the life situation of the congregation. Paul said to Timothy, a young bishop: "I charge you to preach the word, to stay with this task whether convenient or inconvenient—correcting, reproving, appealing—constantly teaching and never losing patience" (2 Tm 4, 2). See your priest as a "holy man" in the Biblical sense, as a bearer of God's word to you!

Reading I   2 Kgs 4, 8-11. 14-16
Accepting of the Preacher

This reading stresses the reason why the woman received Elisha into her house: "I know that he is a holy man of God," a preacher, which means in the Bible "a bearer of God's word." (See Introduction.) Christians should accept their priests as such, especially when listening to the Sunday sermon. They should also keep in mind that the priest has to gear his sermon to all levels of the congregation. When you do not get enough out of the sermon, you could do some additional reading at home.

Reading II   Rom 6, 3-4. 8-11
Alive for God

In this passage, notice that references to our dying with Christ in baptism (best symbolized by baptism of immersion) are all in the past tense. No matter how much a Christian fails, baptism cannot be undone. References to our resurrection with

Christ, however, are future. Our new life with Christ must constantly grow, and working on it is a lifetime job.

Gospel — Welcoming — Mt 10, 37-42

Like the last two Sundays, this reading from Matthew's Gospel also deals with our Lord's missionary charge to his apostles. The first part brings out that Jesus requires total dedication to their calling. The second part tells how the Lord Jesus expects his envoys to be accepted. As in the first reading, the emphasis is on the motive why we should accept the prophet (a man who speaks for God), the holy man (the bearer of God's word).

14th SUNDAY IN ORDINARY TIME
God's Reign To Be Established

EARTHLY kingdoms and nations came into being usually through violence (war, revolution). Authoritarian rule keeps them together. Even necessary improvements in society (social justice and civil rights for all) are often carried out only after violent killing. The divine Master was sent to initiate God's kingdom of love and justice on our planet. But our Lord wants it to be done in his own way. Jesus, too, is a king, ruling a kingdom. But how different he is from the leaders of this world!

The Bible readings tell us about a king who is a Savior, who is meek (without the majestic pomp of royalty), and averse to chariots (war vehicles) and the warrior's bow, who enters his city not on horseback, as monarchs in wartime were wont to do, but riding on an ass (peacefully), who is gentle and humble of heart.

The Church, all of us, must continue our Lord's work of establishing God's kingdom on earth. The latest techniques of public relations, television, radio, pictorial books and magazines should be used to forward the message. But the most simple way to establish God's reign, which all of us can use, is that of gentle persuasion, especially the persuasion of a good example. Does your life-style invite others to even consider the values of God's reign?

A — 14th Sunday in Ordinary Time

Reading I — Zec 9, 9-10
Your King a Savior

Zechariah set down this prophecy during the time that his country was overrun by the mighty Greek Alexander the Great. The prophet visualizes a messianic king to come. After he has defeated the foreign invaders, he will enter Jerusalem peacefully, not on a warrior's horse but on riding an ass. The king will reunite the Northern and Southern Kingdoms of Palestine and his kingdom will comprise the entire civilized world.

The Church reapplies this vision to Jesus Christ, king of God's universal kingdom. The characteristics of this Messiah (see Introduction) introduce the theme of the Gospel. All who choose to live under the dominion of Christ the king should pray: "I will extol you, O my God and king, and I will bless your name forever and ever" (Responsorial Psalm).

Reading II — Rom 8, 9. 11-13
Not in the Flesh

In learned rabbinical language, Paul sketches the kind of persons that Christians who are dedicated to the reign of God should be. Note that "body" in the Biblical sense does not mean body as opposed to soul (as in Greek thought) but the whole person, subject to sin and death yet open to redemption. "Flesh" in Paul's thinking stands for "unredeemed nature."

Gospel — Mt 11, 25-30
My Burden Is Light

The first part of this Gospel tells us that it is Jesus Christ who reveals the Father. "The learned and the clever " are obviously the wise according to this world, self-sufficient and unwilling to listen; "the merest children" are the humble and simple of heart who feel the need for a transcendent message, hence listen.

The second part, introduced by the first reading, characterizes Jesus and his rule over all who choose to live under his dominion. If you are weary, submit to our Lord's dominion and you will find rest!

15th SUNDAY IN ORDINARY TIME
The Word of God

A WORD, be it spoken or written, always has something to do with the person who speaks or writes. There is power and inspiration in a human word and through it we feel contact with a living person. The same can be said of the word of God. As the great Hebrew poet Isaiah says, it never returns void but is always fertile. The power of God's word is like the germinal force of the seed, which makes us hope for fruit and harvest.

Today's Scripture readings tell us about God's word, what can and should happen to it when it is spoken to human beings, to you and to me. Various kinds of people hear God's word, but the harvest (the results of that living contact through his word) are not the same in all people. Where do you classify yourself? "The seed is the word of God, Christ is the sower; all who come to him will live forever" (Gospel Acclamation).

Reading I — Not Returning Void — Is 55, 10-11

This poem, clear in itself, introduces the theme of today's Gospel: The fate or final outcome of God's word when (poetically speaking) it comes down from heaven to water thirsty ground. The poet wants to emphasize that God's word can bear fruit only when it is soaked up in human life.

The point is, do we listen? We cannot blame God for lack of guidance. The Church reapplies Psalm 65 to stress this: "You [God] have visited the land and watered it [with your word]; greatly have you enriched it" (Responsorial Psalm).

Reading II — Not without Hope — Rom 8, 18-23

Paul offers his attitude toward the created world. God made the world, hence it must be good. Nevertheless, it is in slavery to corruption because Adam's [every human being's] sin. As part of the created world humans groan too. But there is hope of liberation. We expect a new heaven and a new world. Redeemed humanity will live in peace with God in a world transformed by his Spirit.

A — 16th Sunday in Ordinary Time 93

Gospel Mt 13, 1-23 or 13, 1-9
Hearing the Message

Before the parable of the sower finally ended up in the Gospel version of Matthew, it went through a long period of oral transmission. The first part (its short form) is substantially the parable as originally told by Jesus. The allegorical interpretation at the end was added later. The discussion on the purpose of teaching in parables in between is also a later insertion which refers to the kingdom of God, mysteriously present in the works of Jesus.

One may ask, if Jesus did not say all of this, is it nevertheless the word of God? Yes it is. There is much in the Gospels which was not said by Jesus verbatim. Much of the Gospels is meditative interpretation of Jesus' spirit and attitude toward life. Later the Church recognized herself in the four Gospels, as we have them now, and accepted them as God's word.

Since the point of the parable is offered by the Bible itself, we do not need to comment on it. Ask yourself this question: In reading your Bible and searching for the point (God's word to you), do you establish a living contact with God by meditative prayer? This is all that Christian Bible reading is about. (See Introduction.)

———◆———

16th SUNDAY IN ORDINARY TIME
God's Forbearing Patience

IN observing our fellow humans we should be careful not to think in just two categories: good and evil. No person is entirely good, neither is anyone entirely evil. Some people look harshly upon all who are not in perfect consonance with their opinions about what good people should be and do. They speak of "law and order" (which must be!) without considering the whole situation, i.e., people in their total environment, which determines their character to a very great extent.

Advocating and pleading for law and order without eliminating poverty and slum conditions, without promoting equal education and job opportunity (so that the poor can help themselves), without furthering constructive family life programs and facilities, without efficient rehabilitation programs for prisoners to be paroled is shameless hypocrisy. Better than any physician, social worker, or psychologist, God knows the case history of a person who has failed, and he is a patient!

What can a Christian do as an individual and what can a congregation do as a group to give persons who are considered a failure a chance to prove themselves? Perhaps a project by the parish council might be begun and a concerted attempt to contact responsible politicians!

Reading I Wis 12, 13. 16-19
Judging with Clemency

This reading, emphasizing the notion of God's forbearance, provides an introduction for the parable of the weeds in the Gospel. "Though you [God] are master of might, you judge with clemency. . . . And you taught your people, by these deeds, that those who are just must be kind." Can you honestly pray: "You, O Lord, are kind and forgiving" (Responsorial Psalm); "forgive us our trespasses, as we forgive those, who trespass against us"?

Reading II Rom 8, 26-27
The Spirit Helps Us

Weak and inclined to evil as people are, in prayer they should turn to the Spirit. We do not even know how to express ourselves in prayer. The Spirit must translate our inarticulate desires.

Gospel Mt 13, 24-43 or 13, 24-30
God's Patience

This parable of the weeds, its allegorical explanation, the remark on teaching in parables, and two other little parables (on the mustard seed and the yeast) require the same approach as the parable of the sower of last Sunday. The Short Form gives just the parable, which may be closest to the form in which Jesus spoke it. The allegorical explanation at the end has been added later. The remark on teaching in parables is also a later insertion. And in the final redaction of Matthew's text, somehow the two little parables on the mustard seed and the yeast ended up in between! Since the first reading on God's forbearance sets the tone, we concentrate on the parable of the weeds and its explanation. We should be patient with our failing fellow humans! (See Introduction.)

17th SUNDAY IN ORDINARY TIME
Priority of Values

DURING all the ages of human history, tribes and nations have had their sages, philosophers, friends of wisdom. Indeed, wisdom, insight, sound judgment is a precious possession. But human wisdom is not always adequately the same as truth. Often sages have narrowed their observation by working with their intellect alone. This resulted in all forms of rationalism which had no eye for the transcendent. In the Bible we find a type of wisdom which originates from both heart and intellect. It is an often intuitive wisdom of the total person. Moreover, Biblical wisdom is a special gift of God. That is why we pay attention to it.

In today's Bible readings, wisdom is considered the supreme value of human life, and the parables of the treasure and the pearl bring out that the kingdom of God is a value for which no sacrifice is too great. It is a question of priority of values! Wise and mature Christians have a sound judgment about what is more or less important in life, since they blend human insight with the God-inspired wisdom of the Bible. "[God,] the revelation of your words sheds light, giving understanding to the simple" (Responsorial Psalm).

Reading I 1 Kgs 3, 5. 7-12
An Understanding Heart

In this tradition, King Solomon is pictured as looking upon wisdom, understanding of heart to judge people and to distinguish right from wrong, as the greatest value of life. The point (God's word) for us is that we should do the same!

A — 17th Sunday in Ordinary Time

"God our Father, without you nothing has value. Guide us to everlasting life by helping us to use *wisely* the blessings you have given to the world" (Opening Prayer).

Reading II Rom 8, 28-30
God Foreknew Us

This passage teaches us that when we are depressed, we should be guided by the God-given understanding that God knows us from all eternity, that he loves us, that somehow he will make all things work together for good of those who love him. Certainty concerning this point requires faith, that blend of human and divine wisdom which today's other Bible readings deal with! Pray: "God, open our eyes to see your hand at work in the splendor of creation, in the beauty of human life" (Alternative Opening Prayer).

Gospel Mt 13, 44-52 or 13, 44-46
A Buried Treasure

Again, as on the last two Sundays, we have a Short and Long Form of Gospel reading. The Short Form, the two parables on the treasure and the pearl, suggests that the kingdom of God (reign of God) is the supreme value of life, well worth the sacrifice of everything else. This is the theme suggested by Solomon's appreciation of wisdom and understanding in the first reading. Understanding in the area of priority of values is precious.

In our country there is no persecution of the Church as in Matthew's time. We are not required to sacrifice our physical lives for the reign of God. But in a society which is ever more doing away with values sacred to Christians, sound judgment about a priority of values is of paramount importance and could require sacrifice especially from young Christians!

———◆———

18th SUNDAY IN ORDINARY TIME
The Messianic Banquet

IMPORTANT diplomatic activity is usually sealed with a banquet. A festive meal together or a joyous picnic is a symbol of human togetherness in love and happiness. What a salesman does when he stops on the road to eat lunch is entirely different from participating in a thanksgiving banquet. Parties, eating and drinking together, play an important role in our society and signify beautiful values. In Biblical times it was the same. Hence the Bible repeatedly evokes the banquet symbol to describe God's love and humankind's relationship of love with him.

The writers of the Bible were fully aware that human beings do not have the concepts and terminology to describe adequately who God is and what he does to us by adopting us as his children, or how all of this will be fully accomplished in the hereafter. So they utilized the banquet symbol as an apt sign to indicate the lines along which we should think when we meditate on God and what he has in store for those who love him (see 1 Cor 2, 9).

Rather than being too inquisitive about details, we should hope for a happy future with the spontaneous and simple excitement of a child who sees the packages around the Christmas tree but must wait. "The eyes of all look hopefully to you, [O God] . . .; you open your hand and satisfy the desire of every living thing" (Responsorial Psalm).

Reading I   Is 55, 1-3
Receive Grain and Eat!

The prophet known only as Second Isaiah addresses the captives in Babylonian exile. He gives them hope by referring to the eschatological banquet, i.e., the banquet of the end-time, when God's kingdom on earth (a kingdom of peace and prosperity for all Hebrews) will be established with an ideal Messiah (anointed king) to rule over them in the name of God. Then God will make a new and everlasting covenant (partnership) with his people.

A — 18th Sunday in Ordinary Time

Participation in the bliss of God's kingdom is a free gift of God granted to all on the sole condition that they thirst for God. The Church sees this oracle fulfilled in the reign of God which was initiated in this world by the Lord Jesus and will be fully accomplished in world to come. As such, we should read it meditatively.

Reading II   Rom 8, 35. 37-39
The Love of Christ

In rhetorical language, Paul brings out that we should have a firm hope of participating in the bliss of God's promise, the Messianic Banquet, as we have meditated upon in the first reading. We may be depressed and have to go through times of confusion, but nothing can separate a believing Christian from the love of God that comes to us in Christ Jesus.

Gospel   Mt 14, 13-21
They Ate Their Fill

Matthew sees this episode as taking place in a crucial time in Jesus' life. John the Baptizer was thrown into prison. Is it possible that Jesus felt called upon to take John's place to proclaim the Good News of the kingdom at hand? He initiated his ministry with the same message as John's, "Reform your lives! The kingdom of God is at hand!" (Mt 4, 11. 17). Ultimately, John the Baptizer was put to death. "When Jesus heard this, he withdrew by boat to a deserted place." Did Jesus see his own impending death in the beheading of John? To continue his mission was to risk death. Yet Jesus took this risk!

The event of this passage (feeding the people) is a messianic sign that will find its fulfillment in the true messianic banquet, the Eucharist, which contains the promise of everlasting life in God's kingdom. "Lord, you give us the strength of new life by the gift of the Eucharist. Protect us with your love and prepare us for eternal redemption" (Prayer after Communion).

19th SUNDAY IN ORDINARY TIME
Prayer in Days of Affliction

HUMAN life is a remarkable mixture of that famous "smile and a tear." We all have our ups and downs in life. We attend both weddings and funerals. Parents witness graduations and often the failures of their children as well. Married life can be like the smell of roses and turn into a nightmare. Young people are successful today and can be turned down tomorrow. Friends may disappoint us and we may witness infidelity not only in our government but even in our Church. All this may leave us confused and downcast. What are we to do? Are we to give up our faith in God?

Queen Jezebel threatened the life of Elijah. He went to a cave in search of God; he prayed and encountered God in "a tiny whispering sound," as the beautiful, idyllic tradition of the first Bible reading has it. Jesus' best friend, John the Baptizer, was beheaded in jail (see last Sunday's Gospel commentary) and "he went up on the mountain by himself to pray, remaining there alone as evening drew on" (Today's Gospel).

That night, Jesus' disciples were in serious trouble, their boat being tossed about in the waves. Lack of faith made them desperate and perhaps Peter, becoming frightened, would have drowned if he had not cried out: "Lord, save me!" God's word to everyone tossed about on the waves of life is: Find a quiet moment for yourself (Is your church open weekdays?), search for God, pray with faith: "Lord, save me!"

Reading I 1 Kgs 19, 9. 11-13
Finding God

This beautiful narrative tells about God's prophet in trouble. Elijah had confronted the prophets of Baal, the god Queen Jezebel worshiped. He took a stand which caused him to lose Jezebel's favor. She threatened the prophet's life. Elijah went to a cave where he met the Lord—not in a mighty wind, an earthquake, or fire, but rather in a tiny whispering sound. A lesson for the prophet so fond of the spectacular!

As Christians, we know that the Bible does not tell stories just to entertain us. Inspired by God, the sacred writer wants to teach by relating these ancient traditions to the believing reader. The point of the narrative is God's word to us. In this case, it could be a hint as to what we should do when evil besets us, and/or that we should find God not in the spectacular but in the simple events of daily life. In time of confusion, our prayer should be: "Lord, let us see your kindness, and grant us your salvation" (Responsorial Psalm).

Reading II — Rom 9, 1-5
A Lesson To Love

Paul expresses his love for his people in strong language which might scandalize if taken literally. His example could be a lesson to love, respect, and even care for others even if we cannot share their opinions!

Gospel — Mt 14, 22-33
Praying with Confidence

Matthew has molded this tradition in such a way that it is clearly a lesson for the harassed Church of his day and God's people of all times! The Church, the traditional bark of Peter, is tossed on the waves of affliction. It needs encouragement. It should have faith in Jesus, for he saves us if we have faith and pray with confidence. Jesus is able to still any storm and can bring us to safety.

───────◆───────

20th SUNDAY IN ORDINARY TIME
Universalism

THE "I am better than you" syndrome is part of the human condition. Collectively, it appears as triumphalism in religion. The evil of triumphalism has stained the Church for many centuries. Let us humbly admit it. If a certain kind of triumphalism would have been confined to "Jesus Christ and his abundant love for us is unsurpassed," it would have been all right. But often the beauty, truth, and riches of the Catholic

Faith were identified with its proud sharers, and resulted in that ominous "we are right and you are wrong" complex which has caused so much damaging alienation.

It is the great merit of Pope John XXIII that he "opened the windows" and of the Second Vatican Council that it strove to do away with all "ghetto mentality." Belonging to God's chosen people does not mean that we are necessarily better than people who following their own conscience seek God in different way.

Today's Bible readings suggests an openness in love and respect for others, as taught in the contemporary setting by the Council's Decree on Ecumenism. "Almighty God, your care extends beyond the boundaries of race and nation to the hearts of all who live. May the walls, which prejudice raises between us, crumble beneath the shadow of your outstretched arm."

Reading I   Is 56, 1. 6-7
A House for All Peoples

After the Hebrews returned from exile in Babylon, they found many foreigners not of the Jewish religion living there. The anonymous prophet called Third Isaiah had to face this changed situation. Ezekiel, "the father of Judaism," was opposed to uncircumcised foreigners in the temple precincts.

The composer of this poem is not so rigorous. He lists the conditions under which non-Jews may worship in the temple. "Their holocausts and sacrifices will be acceptable on my [God's]) altar." This passage has been chosen to introduce the idea of universalism found in today's Gospel reading. "May the peoples praise you, O God; may all the peoples praise you! (Responsorial Psalm).

Reading II   Rom 11, 13-15. 29-32
Jews Deserving Our Love

We must interpret this reading in the light of Paul's misconception that the end, that is, the second coming of Christ, would occur during his lifetime. Israel rejects the message of Christ; hence, Paul turns to the Gentiles (non-Jews). This will provoke Israel's jealousy and they will join before the end!

Matthew, who wrote some thirty years later, had to make a slight adjustment in Paul's vision of Salvation History. This adjustment should not shock us. The Bible itself suggests that the understanding of Salvation History should be adjusted constantly in the light of changing circumstances.

In dealing with the Jews and their religion, we should keep in mind Paul's statement: "God's gift and his call are irrevocable." Anti-Semitism is wrong. Israel's place in Salvation History is God's concern, not ours. The Jews deserve our love, respect, and gratitude! Christ, Mary, Joseph, and the apostles were all Jews and our Old Testament is the Hebrew Bible.

Gospel — Open-Minded Respect — Mt 15, 21-28

Matthew took this story from Mark. But he molded it to bring out a message for the Church of his day, which was beset with constant friction between Christians from Jewish background and pagan converts. We see therein classic Jewish exclusionism as opposed to God's universal will of salvation for all. Matthew wants to stress the fact that faith breaks down the barrier between Jews and Gentiles. "Jesus then said in reply: 'Woman, you have great faith. Your wish will come to pass.'"

God's word to the Church of today is clear: Do not condemn people! Have an open-minded respect for all who seriously follow their religious convictions, provided of course that they fulfill their obligation to find the truth. "He [God] wants all men to be saved and come to know the truth" (1 Tm 2, 4).

21st SUNDAY IN ORDINARY TIME
Support Your Bishop!

IT is clear that perseveringly living up to what Jesus Christ stands for cannot be done alone. We need one another's inspiration and encouragement. In accord with the will of our Lord himself and the oldest traditions, we live Christianity in groups or congregations. Consequently, wherever one establishes a group one needs institution, rules and regulations as an alternative to chaos. Hence, authority (one or another form of government) becomes a necessity.

A — 21st Sunday in Ordinary Time 103

As it is, authority in the Catholic tradition, exercised in Jesus' name and seen as brotherly service, is invested in our bishops and their head the bishop of Rome who holds "the office of Peter." Indeed, bishops receive their mission and authority in the name of God's people and as such they stand before God as any other "receiving" faithful.

On the other hand, authority is not given to the bishops as in a democracy. Christ gave authority to God's people by putting it into the hands of his apostles and their successors, the bishops: "I send you. . . ." Our bishops are human beings. Some are conservative, some progressive, and others just careful. We should responsibly think with our bishops and support them with "creative fidelity" and constant prayer!

Reading I — Vicarious Power — Is 22, 15. 19-23

This oracle of Isaiah announces the appointment of a new royal overseer, who will exercise authority in name of his master. The keys given to him are a symbol of his vicarious power. The tradition concerning the keys of the kingdom entrusted to Peter as we have it in today's Gospel refers to this oracle.

The Church knows that the human instruments of God's authority on earth can fail but they cannot undo the divine purpose. Hence, we pray with the words of Psalm 138: "Lord, your love is eternal; do not forsake the work of your hands" (Responsorial Psalm).

Reading II — God's Greatness — Rom 11, 33-36

After Paul has been trying to describe the bounteous love of God, visible in Jesus Christ sharing himself with sinful humanity, we might say he gives up and exclaims in sudden emotion and gratitude: "How deep are the riches and the wisdom and the knowledge of God! How inscrutable his judgments, how unsearchable his ways!"

In his own unsearchable way, God has planned a future for each and every one of us. In our best moments ("kairos"; see 5th Sunday of Easter) we should try to feel as Paul did, when we meditate on the greatness, love, and wisdom of God.

Gospel

Mt 16, 13-20

Authority

This Gospel tradition puts things in their right perspective. Jesus is the Son of the Living God. All authority has been given to him; hence he can delegate it. No longer visibly with his people, our Lord gives authority to the Church (Mt 18, 18), by puting it into the hands of Peter (Gospel), who rules over God's people together with his fellow apostles (Jn 21, 15-22).

◆

22nd SUNDAY IN ORDINARY TIME
Love Implies Sacrifice

THOSE who are dedicated to a once given commitment know that their dedication implies sacrifce. Married people may think of their mutual commitment in love; religious sisters, brothers, and priests may think of their vows; children and parents, if committed to mutual happiness in the family, may think of their daily living under one roof. Love means giving of self.

This self-giving is a source of happiness but it entails sacrifice as well. For Jeremiah, duped by the Lord into loving, it was "derision and reproach all the day" (Reading I). After Paul has described God's redemptive work in Christ (Rom I—11), he explains the human response in love: "Offer your bodies (selves) as a living sacrifice . . . to God (Reading II).

Christian life, although seen as a response to God's love for human beings, implies carrying a cross, as the Lord himself has done (Gospel). Is Christian life then a miserable life, a life of those trapped in a situation from which there is no escape? No, as long as "sacrifice" is seen in the perspective of love. The secret of a happy Christian life is not to avoid "the cross," but to keep love alive! "Lord God, place in our hearts a desire to please you and fill our minds with insight into love" (Alternative Opening Prayer).

A — 22nd Sunday in Ordinary Time

Reading I   Love—Fidelity   Jer 20, 7-9

"You duped me, O Lord." Jeremiah here uses the same word that the Law of Moses uses for the seduction of a virgin. This is daring language but it brings out clearly how Jeremiah sees himself in relation to God. And Jeremiah, most tender and loving, is so human. He would love to escape from that relationship of love with God. He would rather not be a prophet (spokesman for God) anymore. "I say to myself . . . I will speak in his [God's] name no more." But then he has to continue!

Love is like a burning fire. But it can be painful. It requires sacrifice. "O God, you are my God whom I seek; for you my flesh pines and my soul thirsts" (Responsorial Psalm). It is the prayer of a Christian who loves!

Reading II   Love—Denial of Self   Rom 12, 1-2

Paul has been describing at length God's great love for human beings shown in his sending his Son Jesus Christ (Rom 1—11). Now he starts explaining Christian ethics as a response to that love. A life of love, a life pleasing the beloved (God), implies denial of self. "Do not conform yourself to this age," i.e., the values advocated by a corrupt society and not compatible with the values of God!

Gospel   The Challenge of Love   Mt 16, 21-27

Our Lord speaks clear language. God's standards are not always the same as human standards. Love requires denial of self and by nature it is sometimes painful. Jeremiah was tempted to turn away from his mission in life: "I say to myself . . . I will speak in his name no more," and all of us can feel that same temptation in certain stages of our lives.

A life of lasting commitment (renouncing a selfish life for God's sake), though leading to lasting happiness, is not easy. It is a challenge! "May the Father of our Lord Jesus Christ enlighten the eyes of our hearts, that we might see how great is the hope to which we are called" (Gospel Acclamation).

23rd SUNDAY IN ORDINARY TIME
Fraternal Correction

IT seems that the set of values ("do's and don'ts") by which an adult is guided becomes fixed in early infancy. Hence, from the very beginning on, sound education is important—emphasizing its positive function (encouragement to do good) but not neglecting its negative function (correction of evil). If parents would be more concerned about correcting their children from early infancy on, if marriage partners and friends would be honest in their love and friendship, which demands fraternal correction once in a while, perhaps the government would not have to do it so frequently in its penal institutions. Children who are either spoiled or neglected are on their way to becoming the criminals of tomorrow. Always being patted on the back or feared, hence flattered constantly and never corrected, makes one blind to one's own faults till it is too late.

Many people would be less narrow and not so peculiar if they had friends who were honest with them. This applies as well to little children, who need playmates to correct them, as to grown-ups: bachelors, priests, and religious for whom a sound community life or fellowship with peers is a must for the same reason. Today's Bible readings share ancient, God-inspired, Hebrew wisdom concerning fraternal correction with believers of all ages. See it as God's word to you.

Reading I Ez 33, 7-9
Accepting Correction

Watchmen on the city walls or out on the hills formed part of the defense system in Biblical times. They had to sound a warning when undesired foreigners were spotted. Ezekiel sees the prophet, God's "mouthpiece" (Jer 15, 19), as such a watchman, in charge of the well-being of the community. He must do his duty.

The message (God's word) seems to be that we must be willing to accept correction first of all from those in charge of the community: children from parents; parishioners from priests; students from teachers; employees from the employer;

citizens from the law enforcer. Those who are not willing to accept fair and respectfully given correction are in a weak position when they have to correct others.

Reading II — Rom 13, 8-10
A Unifying Principle

As Jesus did, Paul quotes the Old Testament (Lv 19, 18) and sees love as the unifying principle behind all laws and commandments. "Love never does any wrong to the neighbor," even though an honest and respectful fraternal correction may cause some necessary pain (Reading I and Gospel).

Gospel — Mt 18, 15-20
Correction—Fairness—Love

As we have this tradition in Matthew, it brings out that fraternal correction is the concern not only of "the watchmen" (Reading I), but of all "the brethren." Genuine love for others implies the willingness to correct them, if necessary, and to accept correction from them as well!

Fraternal correction given with due respect and inspired by love is a favor for which we should be grateful, even if it hurts our pride. In strong language we are told that the well-being of the community should prevail over the questionable well-being of an individual if there is no other way.

24th SUNDAY IN ORDINARY TIME
Be Kind and Merciful!

THE lesson of today may run counter to certain opinions on what it means to be "a man," "a strong person," a person who stands for principles which are not for sale. Where do the values of the Lord Jesus fit into this traditional picture of strong and unyielding personhood? One thing is certain: our Lord did not come to destroy human nature; he came to elevate it, to preserve the best in us, to ennoble us to what a Christian man or woman should be.

A — 24th Sunday in Ordinary Time

Hatred, revenge, and anger are human vices. The law of talion, "an eye for an eye," is even Old Testament ethics, but it is not Christian. Jesus refers to Old Testament ethics, and states: "But I tell you . . ." Have a realistic look at yourself and check where your personality should be "Christianized." The "human" in us may be vengeful, but God, whom we should follow, is different: "The Lord is kind and merciful; slow to anger, and rich in compassion" (Responsorial Psalm).

Reading I Sir 27, 30—28, 7
Forgiveness

The Jews knew Sirach, Psalm 109 (today's Responsorial Psalm), and the challenge of Scripture to be holy as God is holy! "Wrath and anger are hateful things." But they also had the civil law of talion: "An eye for an eye." Many were selective. Soothing their consciences by selecting that civil law for personal behavior, they ignored the best in their Scriptures.

Christians are also tempted to be selective. We must realize that listening to this Scripture on Sunday and yet practicing any kind of vendetta is inconsistent and un-Christian.

Reading II Rom 14, 7-9
God's Partner

Paul offers the Biblical outlook on human beings. They are not autonomous. They are God's stewards living with him in a sacred partnership (covenant). It is a beautiful philosophy of life.

As God's partners, we can and must develop our potentialities, but we remain responsible to the Lord. Do we develop potential for love, as suggested in the first and third readings?

Gospel Mt 18, 21-35
Selective Ethics?

All Catholics in this country hear this same Gospel today, all Christians have it in their Bible, and all pray: "Our Father . . . , forgive us our trespasses, as we forgive those who trespass against us." Yet some favor violence and hatred to solve both social and personal issues. Can a real Christian be selective, ignore God's word whenever it is inconvenient, and practice what most do?

Christian commitment is total and not selective! Jesus states: "He who is not with me is against me" (Mt 12, 30), and during Mass we pray: "May he [Christ] make us an everlasting gift to you [God]."

―――――◆―――――

25th SUNDAY IN ORDINARY TIME
God's Generosity

THE dollar is a much cherished value in our culture. The person who makes an honest dollar in abundant numbers is thought to have succeeded in life. Students learn in school whatever can be cashed in dollars tomorrow. Doing something or not doing it depends largely on the amount of dollars that go with it. More effort, more recompense! There is truth and some good ethics in this attitude. No doubt about it. But we also find therein a few warped misconceptions.

Applied to God, such an attitude may result in the opinion that God owes us salvation after we have done our "good works." The Bible speaks of reward, but focusing all attention on this aspect alone may result in the immature attitude of the child who thinks his father "owes" him money for every little job he does. Then questions come up like: "Are you envious because God is generous?" (see Gospel).

The main reason for serving God should be love and gratitude, not merely reward, and certainly not a reward God owes us! The parable of today's Gospel on God's generosity challenges this "recompense only" attitude.

Reading I   Is 55, 6-9
God's Mercy

The exile in Babylon was experienced as God's punishment for Israel's sins. Israel had deserved to be abandoned by God. Now the prophet promises that freedom is at hand. Why?

Because of Israel's "good works" in exile? No, because of God's generosity only! "For my thoughts are not your thoughts, nor are your ways my ways, says the Lord."

God does not owe the repentant scoundrel a thing. A sinner must return to God for mercy, and God forgives because he is generous. "The Lord is gracious and merciful" (Responsorial Psalm) introduces the Gospel theme on God's generosity.

Reading II   Phil 1, 20-24. 27
Your Conduct

Paul wrote the Letter to the Philippians, from which this reading is taken, while he was in prison in Ephesus (Turkey), where he faced the possibility of a death penalty for preaching the Gospel. "For, to me, 'life' means Christ."

Let us listen to the advice of this great apostle: "Conduct yourselves, then, in a way worthy of the gospel of Christ."

Gospel   Mt 20, 1-16
Salvation a Free Gift

In the previous chapter Matthew has our Lord discussing the conditions for a person to be saved. It is difficult for rich people since they feel so easily self-sufficient. The same was true in Jesus' time. It was not the well-established who responded most willingly to Jesus' ministry but the outcasts, prostitutes, and collaborators with the Romans (tax-collectors). And Jesus paid more attention to them than to "respectable people" who thought that God owed them salvation because of their obedience to the Law of Moses.

The parable, definitely not a lesson in labor relations, challenges this "more effort—more recompense" conception in religion. God does not owe salvation to anyone, even though this same misconception may still be alive in our day. It is a generous free gift. Note that rewards are not denied, but they should not be wielded as a key to open the gate of the kingdom of heaven.

26th SUNDAY IN ORDINARY TIME
Responsibility

PROJECTION ("Not I, but he/she did it; he/she is responsible, not I") is as old as the story of Adam and Eve. With great psychological insight the author of Genesis has Adam reply: "The woman . . . gave me fruit from the tree, and I ate it." And the woman answers: "The serpent tricked me into it, so I ate it" (Gn 3, 12-13). Every teacher hears the same thing daily: "Not me! He did it!

No one who goes to jail can be said to bear the total guilt for his/her crime. Past family upbringing and society also contribute to making persons what they are, but only to a certain extent. In point of fact, free grown-up persons are responsible for what they do. Judges, lawyers, and psychologists wrangle daily with the tension between individual responsibility and the collective guilt of the environment.

Today's Bible readings discuss this problem of sinful human beings related to God, their judge. We should be careful in judging others since we do not know how much a failing brother or sister is determined by his or her past; but knowing ourselves we should be realistic and accept full responsibility for what we do and should do!

Reading I   Ez 18, 25-28
My Way Unfair?

Among the first group of Hebrews deported to Babylon there was a priest and prophet called Ezekiel. As a wandering preacher, he went from one Jewish settlement to another, encouraging his people to have faith in God, but also correcting them when he found them guilty.

Human freedom implies full responsibility for what we do and should do. Only when I do not project my guilt onto somebody else and honestly admit "that I have sinned through my own fault, in what I have done, and in what I have failed to do" (Penitential Rite of Mass), can God forgive and show the mercy besought by the Responsorial Psalm (125, 4-9).

A — 27th Sunday in Ordinary Time

Reading II   Phil 2, 1-11 or 2, 1-5
Unanimity

Notice that Paul writes from his "imprisonment in Christ's cause" (1, 12). He worries about dissension, an evil that besets many congregations. "United in spirit and ideals"—this should be the goal of all the members of your parish as well! Christ is the model, as described in the hymn Paul quotes in his letter.

Gospel   Mt 21, 28-32
Openness to Christian Values

Jesus was constantly refuting the legalism and void formalism of the religious establishment of his time. One of the two sons in this reading signifies the self-styled righteous people who criticize Jesus for paying so much attention to religious outcasts like tax-collectors and prostitutes. The other one represents the outcasts who first refused to join the kingdom (by their life-style), but then repented.

The message (God's word) may be: Avoid formalism, as a cover-up for genuine love and commitment. Have an open eye for the real Christian values! "Father, . . . continue to fill us with your gifts of love" (Opening Prayer).

27th SUNDAY IN ORDINARY TIME
Appreciation

PARENTS and teachers may sacrifice time and talents to give children the best they have to offer. Nevertheless their task is not always rewarding. They love their children and students, but they are frequently disappointed by them. Lack of response can hurt badly. Following Jesus of Nazareth, we call God "Father." In his infinite love and wisdom, he has bestowed his riches upon us. Hence, as all parents and educators do, God has his expectations. According to Biblical wisdom, he sees us as his co-workers, related to him in a sacred partnership (covenant).

Do we live up to what God expects from us? God has chosen you and me to go and bear fruit that will last. (See Gospel

A — 27th Sunday in Ordinary Time

Acclamation). "Why, when I [God] looked for the crop of grapes, did it [my vineyard, i.e. you and I] bring forth wild grapes?" (Reading I) There is much more to being a Christian than just avoiding big sins! We should do good and always be concerned that we do enough of it.

Reading I   Is 5, 1-7
God's Expectation

This is Isaiah's beautiful "song of the vineyard," written in the form of a ballad, a love song. Isaiah, calling God his friend, sees him in an affectionate relationship with his vineyard, the house of Israel, the chosen people, you and me. God has done whatever he could do. He cleared the vineyard of stones, made a wall around it (to keep the animals out), built a watchtower, and hewed out a winepress—and see what happened! Notice God's painful disappointment when people do not live up to what he expects them to be.

The Responsorial Psalm is the prayer of a person who has made a shambles of his life. " A vine from Egypt" is God's people led out of bondage in Egypt. Apply this beautiful poetry to your own life!

Reading II   Phil 4, 6-9
Your Thoughts Directed to Truth

Paul has restlessly traveled and preached the Gospel. He loved those who had accepted the message. He cares for his children in the faith as all parents do for theirs. He is disappointed when the congregations he has founded do not live up to his expectations. Now from jail he writes: "Live according to what you have heard me say and seen me do." Do you remember your religious instructors of the past? Can they be proud of you?

Gospel   Mt 21, 33-43
God's Disappointment

In this parable, the vineyard is Israel. The tenant farmers are the Jewish religious leaders. The son is Jesus Christ, sent by the property owner (God) to get his share of the grapes. This son, God's envoy, is thrown out of the vineyard (Jerusalem) and killed. The point is the presumption of the tenants. They want to act like owners of the vineyard though they are just stewards.

This parable marks the sharp dissension between the early Church and Judaism. Matthew's point is evident: Since Israel rejects Jesus as the Messiah, the Kingdom of God will be handed over to the Gentiles. God's word today may be: God's grace is offered to everyone. Do not disappoint this gracious giver. Make certain that God will not have to reject you.

28th SUNDAY IN ORDINARY TIME
The Banquet Is Ready

FOOD and drink are important at parties, but more important than food and drink are the host, the hostess, and the guests we hope to meet there. People to be met can even be the deciding factor as to whether or not we go to a certain party in the first place.

Parties/banquets can be the beginnings of beautiful friendships or they can seal and deepen existing human relations since such parties enrich us as human beings.

In the Bible, the invitation to a banquet is one of the favorite images of messianic times. Today's first and third Bible readings use it to describe the bliss of God's kingdom, once it has been established on earth. God rules through his vicegerent, the Messiah—Annointed King on earth. The people (you and I) are related to God in a sacred partnership called covenant.

Inspired by God, prophets give this covenant marital overtones. The banquet becomes a wedding in which God is the husband and his people the bride. And in the inspired awareness of the New Testament, this bridal relationship of human beings with God has a transcendent dimension, its full blossoming and realization in a life hereafter. In virtue of your baptism you have a standing invitation to God's eschatological (end-time) banquet.

A — 28th Sunday in Ordinary Time

Reading I
Is 25, 6-10
Rich Food

Eating or "breaking bread" with a person is a Biblical sign of intimate friendship. Isaiah locates the banquet of the endtime (the time of God's kingdom on earth) on Zion, the holy mountain of the Lord in Jerusalem. God will take away the veil that keeps us from seeing him. He will open the eyes of faith and we will recognize him as "our God." "Behold our God, to whom we looked to save us. This is the Lord for whom we looked."

The Responsorial Psalm (23, 1-6) describes the bliss of God's kingdom with the pastoral image of shepherd and sheep. It is a beautiful poem. Read it meditatively!

Reading II
Phil 4, 12-14. 19-20
Be Concerned

Paul in prison had received a gift of money from the congregation of Philippi. He is grateful and appreciative. "It was kind of you to share my hardships." And God will reward you: "My God in turn will supply your needs fully." God's message to us could be: Be concerned and help, when you know a fellow human enduring hardship.

Gospel
Mt 22, 1-14 or 22, 1-10
Appreciating the Invitation

The Long Form of this Bible reading may puzzle the reader. Why does the king cast out a guest for not being properly dressed for the occasion when the guests are "anyone you come upon" on the byroads? Maybe the poor fellow came from his field where he had been working all the day! The answer is that actually this passage consists of two parables that first went through the process of oral tradition and finally were fused together by Matthew.

When one takes the second parable on the wedding garment as such, the message (God's word) is clear: When you accept the invitation to God's banquet (the Holy Eucharist—God's companionship in heaven) you are supposed to be clean.

The first parable on the wedding feast also received some insertions along the way. The part about the king having the banquet ready and sending out his army to burn the city clearly refers to the destruction of Jerusalem in 70 A.D. Matthew has adapted the parable to the needs of his Church toward the end of the first century: The Jews were invited but refused; hence, the Gentiles come in! God's word to us may be: God invites you. Appreciate the invitation and join the banquet!

―――――♦―――――

29th SUNDAY IN ORDINARY TIME
The God of History

THE theme of "Fiddler on the Roof" is: "Play your little tune in life, but keep your balance and do not break your neck!" This is not always easy for Christians who are citizens of two cities: the earthly one (for example, the United States) and the heavenly one (the Church). We favor separation of the two, but there are areas which overlap. Christians are supposed to be good citizens, pay their taxes, exercise their voting rights. They must love their country, though in certain periods of national history politicians and leaders may turn out to be corrupt. As in all institutions, not even excluding the Church, the human element will always be there. Christians should be concerned about the cultural and social well-being of their community.

Today's Bible readings clearly pay tribute to the God of history. God makes use of an evil emperor (in Jesus' time the Roman Caesar!) as well as a good one (Cyrus, who freed the Jewish exiles in Babylon). We should recognize the God of history in both. "Give to Caesar what is Caesar's, but give to God what is God's" (Gospel). The state has its own sphere in promoting communal welfare and in maintainig law and order, but always under God to whom it is responsible. If it over-steps the mark, a Christian is absolved of obedience. We must obey God rather than humans. (Think of social justice, right to life, just war.) Pray for guidance to keep your balance.

A — 29th Sunday in Ordinary Time

Reading I
Is 45, 1. 4-6

"I Am the Lord"

After Cyrus had defeated Babylon in 539 B.C. he became the new ruler of the Middle East. Though Cyrus, a pagan, did not know it, God used him as an instrument to give freedom to his captive people. "I [God] called you by your name, giving you a title, though you knew me not."

The Hebrews paid tribute to the God of history who goes his own way to obtain his goals. "Say among the nations: The Lord is king, he governs the people with equity" (Responsorial Psalm).

Reading II
1 Thes 1, 1-5

Three Characteristics

This reading is from a Letter which is the oldest New Testament document, written by Paul from Corinth (Greece) in 50 A.D. Paul had founded a congregation at Thessalonica and sent Timothy to check how these new converts were coming along. Paul was pleased because they were doing fine and wrote them this letter of appreciation.

Notice the characteristics which marked Christian life in Thessalonica: "Proving your faith" —"laboring in love"— "showing constancy in hope in our Lord." God's word to your congregation and to you is that only if those three characteristics are present can your congregation (you) be like yeast in the dough and have an uplifting impact in your community.

Gospel
Mt 22, 15-21

Keep Balance

The Pharisees of Jesus' time were against paying taxes to the Romans, but the Herodians (supporters of Herod, puppet king of the Romans) collaborated and paid taxes. Jesus goes beyond the question they asked him: Legitimate government has its rights (see Introduction), but God has his rights too. "Give to God what is God's." In case of conflict, we should obey God rather than humans.

30th SUNDAY IN ORDINARY TIME
Love of God and Neighbor

UNTIL a few years ago, outsiders regarded Catholics as people who had to go to church on Sunday, did not eat meat on Friday, fasted during Lent and did not believe in divorce. With a grain of salt, that was the ordinary idea of a Catholic. And, indeed, a good Catholic was seen as a law-abiding citizen in the City of God. Judaism of our Lord's time suffered from legalism (i.e., strict adherence to a code of actions and observances as a means of justification). It was said that there were 613 precepts in the Law of Moses, and many interpretations on priority.

This danger of legalism ("lex" means law in Latin) exists also in our Church, though there is a shifting of opinions with some going to the extreme of doing away with laws entirely. Our Lord reacts against legalism by putting all laws in their proper framework: Love. Laws have reason to exist only insofar as they are explanations and adaptations of the great law of love of God and neighbor.

Christians should not see a law-abiding life as a tool for obtaining eternal salvation. It is love that makes the observance of laws compatible with human dignity.

Reading I Ex 22, 20-26
Love To Be Concrete

This passage introduces and concretizes Jesus' statement in the Gospel that it is love of God and neighbor on which the whole law is based. Love of God and neighbor should not be abstract, vague, and lacking in precision. Aestheticism and vague statements on love do not do much good for the poor, the stranger, the widow, the orphan. Christians who isolate themselves and their churches in comfortable exclusive neighborhoods must heed this.

The Responsorial Psalm (18, 2-4. 47. 51) is a beautiful song, but it needs to be applied to practical concern for the deprived of our society.

Reading II
A Model Church

1 Thes 1, 5-10

Paul has reasons to praise the congregation of Thessalonica: "You became a model for all . . . believers." "The word of the Lord has echoed forth from you resoundingly."

Can this be said of your congregation and you? Does your parish council have a committee on charity and social concern (Reading I and Gospel)? Is it active? If not a member, you are a constituent and should find out. Does God's word echo forth from your parish resoundingly to the inner city of your municipality?

Gospel
The Greatest Commandment

Mt 22, 34-40

This statement of Jesus is actually a combination of Deuteronomy 6, 5 (love of God) and Leviticus 19, 18 (love of neighbor). What is new is Jesus' interlocking of these two commandments, namely, that one cannot be thought of without the other.

Without love of neighbor the love of God remains a sterile figment of the mind, and without love of God love of neighbor may end up in a vague humanitarianism which usually does not last, especially when faced with disappointments. The vertical and horizontal must go together in sound Christian religion.

31st SUNDAY IN ORDINARY TIME
Our Priests

CHRISTIANS expect from their priests and bishops the service of the ministerial priesthood, which consists of both sacramental ministration and teaching of the Gospel. If citizens rightly expect from the politicians that they practice what they claim to stand for, all the more do Christians expect the same from their leaders, priests and bishops. Priests should not preach their own words, but the word of God. They should see their task as ministry, i.e., service to God's people.

Today's Bible readings have a few unkind words for the priests and leaders of the old dispensation. Priests of the new dispensation should heed them. Constructive critique on priests—their sermons, ministry, and leadership—is as wholesome in a parish as fraternal correction (23rd Sunday). The parish council meetings may be the opportunity to offer constructive remarks. An honest discussion, motivated by love and concern, may clear up a tense situation.

However, remember that only a few priests are endowed with genius. One man can seldom be "good" in all the aspects of Christ's ministry. Try to take your priest as he is, a limited human being like the rest of us. See in him the man with a message from God, and pray for him.

Reading I
Mal 1, 14—2, 2. 8-10
Good Leadership Needed

The author of this prophetic book is unknown. The book's title "Malachi" is taken from 3, 1 and means "my messenger." The work was written after the return of the exiles from Babylon (about 460 B.C.). During that time of reconstruction, public worship in the Jerusalem temple was in a bad state. Figuratively, the prophet lets God address the priests, who in particular neglected their duty of teaching the Torah (the Law of Moses): "You [priests] have caused many falter by your instruction; you do not keep my [God's] ways."

What could possibly be the message (God's word) to those who are not priests? Perhaps that we should pray for good leadership in our Church. We need it.

Reading II
1 Thes 2, 7-9. 13
The Message as Word of God

Today's first and third readings are critical of priests. This passage tells us how Christians should look at their priests with the eyes of faith. Not all priests are as gentle, great, saintly, and dedicated as Paul was. Whether a priest's sermon be good or bad, we should receive the message not as the word of humans, but as of the word of God.

Gospel   Mt 23, 1-12
Prayer for Priests

After the destruction of Jerusalem (70 A.D.), a bitter hostility had developed between Judaism and Palestinian Christianity. Indeed, Jesus had opposed the legalism of the Pharisees (30th Sunday), but Matthew, himself involved in the struggle between his Church and the Jewish rabbis, magnifies out of all proportions an element which was present in Jesus' teaching.

This shows the human factor already at work in the early Church. Priest should heed the lesson. They are rabbis (teachers) and fathers only in relation to God (Jesus does not dictate a vocabulary; he demands the right spirit!). And God's people could heed the message as explained in the Introduction.

———◆———

32nd SUNDAY IN ORDINARY TIME
Wisdom and Death

IT is wonderful if over the years persons acquire wisdom which results in a meaningful life. It is even greater if by the evening of their life persons have acquired the wisdom which helps them to die a meaningful death. Physicians, nurses, priests, and ministers take special courses which train them to accompany terminal patients in their last difficult days and hours. But one thing is certain: if counselors of terminal patients have to depend on human wisdom alone, they have a very difficult task in making the apparent absurdity of death meaningful.

We Christians possess a God-given wisdom which tells us not only that death is a sad and inevitable necessity, but that it has a positive meaning. Christians see death as the optimum opportunity for accepting God and full realization of one's self. Dying with Christ, Christians believe that they will arise with him. All Christians, not just nurses, physicians, and priests, should feel responsible for the suffering members of God's people. We should be able to share our wisdom of faith with a friend who knows that his/her sickness is terminal. Today's Bible readings deal with death and Christian insight which makes it meaningful.

Reading I Wis 6, 12-16
Wisdom Resplendent

The Book of Wisdom, the last of the Old Testament, was written in Greek by a believing Jew living in Alexandria, Egypt. In it, Wisdom is personified, a literary device used often in all literatures of the world. Wisdom, which incorporates that mysterious dimension called faith, is a gift of God. "She [Wisdom] makes her own rounds, seeking those worthy of her." This God-given wisdom is resplendent and unfading! We should be grateful for it (Responsorial Psalm).

Reading II 1 Thes 4, 13-18 or 4, 13-14
Being with the Lord Unceasingly

As already mentioned, Paul wrote this letter to his newly founded congregation in Thessalonica. Timothy had brought him a good report concerning the behavior of these new converts. However, they had a few questions, one about death and the return of Jesus. This passage gives the Christian's answer, which is inspired not by human wisdom alone, but by a human-divine wisdom which we call Faith. (See Introduction.)

Notice that the way the message is worded is conditioned by time and culture: (1) Paul is under the misconception that our Lord will return during his own lifetime. (2) He uses the traditional Biblical imagery of clouds, angels, blasting trumpets, etc., to describe God's splendor and our sharing in it. (3) He describes the event against the background of the world vision of his time: Heaven up—earth in the middle—nether world (hell) down. Only the message: "We shall be with the Lord unceasingly" is God's word to us. The way the message is worded is not part of it.

A — 33rd Sunday in Ordinary Time

Gospel
Mt 25, 1-13

Keep Your Eyes Open

Today's Gospel reading has the same message as found in the second reading, but now in the form of a parable. As we have this parable revised and edited by Matthew, it deals with two classes of people: the foolish ones who were not ready, and those who had wisdom and were ready when the groom (Jesus) arrived. Always be prepared to meet the Lord!

◆

33rd SUNDAY IN ORDINARY TIME
Creative Fidelity

FIDELITY to a commitment requires constancy, courage, dedication, perseverance and sometimes even heroism. "The fact is that when I commit myself, I grant in principle that the commitment will not again be put in question. . . . It at once bars a certain number of possibilities; it bids me invent a certain *modus vivendi* which I would otherwise be precluded from envisaging. Here there appears in a rudimentary form what I call *creative fidelity*. My behavior will be completely colored by this act embodying the decision that the commitment will not again be questioned. The possibility which has been barred or denied will thus be demoted to the rank of a temptation" (Gabriel Marcel, French Philosopher).

We may apply this to any commitment: baptismal, marital, religious, the promise to do a certain job. Today's Bible readings describe the fidelity of both woman (Reading 1) and man (Gospel) to a task to which they have committed themselves. We should check our fidelity to any commitment we have made.

Reading I
Prv 31, 10-13. 19-20. 30-31

Be Faithful

This passage describes a gracious wife and mother, faithfully dedicated to her marital commitment. She practiced creative fidelity in the marital setting of her time and culture. Women of our time and culture may have a few different occupations, but God's word of today is: Be faithful to your marital commitment!

"Creative fidelity" implies that my commitment will not again be put in question. "Give her a reward of her labors." The element of reward is there, but it should be kept in its proper perspective. (See 30th Sunday.)

Reading II — 1 Thes 5, 1-6
Awake and Sober

Paul continues his reply to the Thessalonians concerning the parousia (final coming of Christ), whose beginning we read about last Sunday. His answer to them is also God's word to us: Do not be too inquisitive about details concerning the hereafter. They have simply not been revealed to us. It is a reward (1st and 3rd readings). The message is: Stay awake and sober.

Gospel — Mt 25, 14-30 or 25, 14-15. 19-20
A Reliable Servant

The parable, as Matthew relates it, refers to Jesus Christ who will come back to judge the Church. All members have made their baptismal commitment and renew it every year at Easter or whenever they are godparents at a baptism. Today, God's question to us is: Do we practice "creative fidelity"? Or do we put our commitment in question by lack of faith or courage?

Notice that our baptismal commitment means acting within the framework of what is possible ("to each man's abilities!"). Passivity is culpable, as in the case of "the worthless, lazy lout." Is creative fidelity to an active Christian life possible? Yes, but there must be love for our Lord, which "the lazy lout" did not have. ("I knew you were a hard man.") Check yourself on "what I have failed to do?" (Penitential Rite of Mass).

◆

A — Christ the King

Last Ordinary Sunday
CHRIST THE KING
The Leadership of Our Lord

IN our democratic culture, we know about kings and emperors only from television and picture magazines. But we believe in leaders, "deriving (though) their just powers from the consent of the governed" (Declaration of Independence). Enlightened and reliable leadership is a great benefit to any society. We expect our leaders to be conscientious people, responsible to God, since we are "one nation under God." Our leaders must be equally concerned about all, since "all men are created equal."

If we had to describe what Jesus Christ means to Christians, we would most probably do so with this familiar terminology of the founding fathers. Hence, we should not be amazed that the Bible describes Jesus as a king, since leader and king were identical in Biblical culture. The Hebrews knew about the splendor of King Solomon, the heroic dedication and courage of their "founding father," King David, and the might and power of the kings of Egypt and Babylon; hence, they used these familiar images to describe Jesus' relationship to the people "he sanctified by his own blood" (Heb 13, 12).

Leadership is an alternative to a warped kind of freedom, which results in chaos and disaster. We experience it daily around us. Let us submit to Jesus' leadership: "Father all-powerful, bring all mankind together in Jesus Christ your Son, whose kingdom is with you and the Holy Spirit, one God, for ever and ever" (Alternative Opening Prayer).

Reading I   Ez 34, 11-12. 15-17
Tending the Sheep

Both the first and the third readings describe Jesus as king, using the imagery of shepherd and flock. There is a German saying: "He who wants to understand the poet, must go to the poet's country." Shepherds and sheep were part of daily life in the country of the Bible. Mentally, we should go there whenever we read Scripture and want to understand what God has to tell us through the author. God in his Messiah (Anointed King Jesus Christ) takes care of us.

The last verse with its note about judgment links this reading with the Gospel, where the king separates the sheep from the goats. "The Lord is my shepherd; there is nothing I shall want" (Responsorial Psalm).

Reading II
1 Cor 15, 20-26. 28
Handing Over the Kingdom

Paul teaches that Jesus' reign as king, inaugurated with his resurrection, will last until his second coming. Then he will hand over the kingdom to the Father.

The meaning is that God now acts toward the world "through Jesus Christ our Lord." At the end of time, God's relationship with redeemed mankind will be a direct one. Meanwhile notice that Jesus' kingdom is in constant warfare with evil. "Christ must reign until God has put all enemies [evil] under his feet." We should be part of that warfare against evil!

Gospel
Mt 25, 31-46
The Nations Assembled before Him

In this beautiful imaginative scene, which depicts the parousia, the second coming of Jesus, Matthew sees the core of Jesus' moral teaching. Notice that Jesus, introduced as king and judge, identifies himself with the deprived and the downtrodden of society, and that the supreme law of love will be the measure in judgment.

This Gospel about judgment marks the end of the liturgical year. We should judge ourselves. The last judgment does not mark an end, but a new beginning for those who have followed Jesus' leadership and heeded his great command of love.

———◆———

YEAR B

ADVENT

For a General Introduction, see p. 7.

1st SUNDAY OF ADVENT
Stay Awake!

WE can imagine the following embarrassing situation: A young baby sitter falling asleep or just stepping out for a short while, the children running all over the house, and the parents coming home from a party at midnight—a little bit earlier than anticipated! A soldier caught asleep on guard duty is court-martialed severely. And rightly so, for if the guards are sleeping, who can feel safe?

We Christians believe that "he [Jesus] will come again in glory to judge the living and the dead." According to the Bible, we are related to God in a sacred partnership (covenant). We are his co-workers in making this planet a better place to live for all. The moment you least expect it, the Lord may call you in. Make sure it is not going to be an embarrassing situation for you! "Be constantly on the watch" (Gospel).

Reading I   Is 63, 16-17. 19; 64, 2-7
We Are Sinful

This is a prayer in distress. God's people who have returned from exile in Babylon are experiencing frustration. The reconstruction has not worked as they had hoped. They attribute this to their own sins. May God interfere and help!

The Responsorial Psalm is a similar prayer. The "Shepherd of Israel" is God, leader of his chosen people, us. "The man of your right hand" is the king, representing the people, all of us. Our planet, our community, our family, and we ourselves—all need God to come and save us from the mess we have made of life so often!

Advent, the four weeks of preparation for Christmas, means "coming." May God come in his Messiah, Anointed One, Jesus Christ! But in order to receive him, we must open up. "Lord, make us turn to you, let us see your face and we shall be saved" (Responsorial Psalm).

Reading II 1 Cor 1, 3-9
As You Wait

Paul sees the community of Corinth as waiting for the revelation of our Lord Jesus Christ. He thanks God for the favors bestowed on them in Christ Jesus: the gift of speech and knowledge. Later in the Letter, he will tell them to use these gifts well! Waiting and persevering to the end requires the strength of God, but they will succeed. "God is faithful."

God's word to you could be: You are waiting for the final revelation of Christ. God has bestowed gifts on you. How are you using them? Persevering as a real Christian is not easy. Pray for it! God is faithful.

Gospel Mk 13, 33-37
Be on Guard!

The meaning of this parable is clear. Our Lord is "abroad." He ascended to heaven, but he will come back. Are we doing our job? Indeed, we are the "now" generation. The young want to enjoy everything they can right now. They are like high school drop-outs who lack the energy to work first so as to enjoy a more beautiful life later! Grown-ups may get drowsy, drift away from God, as can happen to partners in marriage.

God said to the Church of Ephesus: "I hold this against you: You have turned aside from your early love" (Rv 2, 4). "Be on guard! You do not know when the appointed time will come."

2nd SUNDAY OF ADVENT
All Mankind Shall See the Salvation of God

WAITING can be a tantalizing experience. Biding your time in a waiting room till the physician calls you in to hear the result of an x-ray of one of your beloved ones, you ask yourself questions: "Will it be a tumor? Is it malignant?" Waiting can take place with reference to the mail. A letter from a fiancée, for example, bearing good news or bad news! We had an unpleasant misunderstanding which culminated in an emotional outburst. On the way home we are waiting. How will it be straightened out?

In waiting, the question comes up as to how we will react to the outcome. Are we ready to accept all the consequences? We started our week with hope and expectations. What happened? What do we expect from life? Today's Bible readings shed some light on our often dim and hopeless situations. They constitute God's light shining upon us in the waiting room of life! Read and listen prayerfully with a great faith! "God of power and mercy, open our hearts in welcome. Remove the things that hinder us from receiving Christ with joy" (Opening Prayer).

Reading I Is 40, 1-5. 9-11
Have Hope!

In beautiful poetic language, the prophet tells the exiles in Babylon who were desperately waiting for freedom: "Have hope!" God will step in and lead you out of this hopeless situation back home! Notice God's tender love: "Like a shepherd he feeds his flock."

What do we learn as God's word from this ancient piece of poetry? It could be: God cares! "Your guilt is expiated. Here comes with power the Lord God." Whatever your problems in life may be, you can have a happy Christmas and celebrate "Emmanuel—God with us."

Make the Responsorial Psalm your prayer of today: "Lord, let us see your kindness and grant us your salvation."

Reading II   2 Pt 3, 8-14
While Waiting

The author uses the familiar imagery of the Bible (fire, a roar, flames, a blaze) to describe the awesome event of Christ's coming in judgment. Remember, God's timetable is not ours. God can call you at any moment, and this should be a motivation to preserve holiness.

While waiting, "make every effort to be found without stain or defilement, and at peace in his [God's] sight."

Gospel   Mk 1, 1-8
Repentance

Mark announces his Gospel as the good news of Jesus Christ, the Son of God. But before he actually tells us about Jesus Christ and his good news, he introduces John the Baptizer as our Lord's forerunner. Mark quotes Isaiah of the first reading. Just as in ancient times messengers went ahead of the king to announce his coming to town, so John announced the coming of the Messiah, God's Anointed vicegerent on earth, Jesus Christ. The mission of Jesus was prepared for by John. His mission was the same as that of Jesus, though he stressed a judgment whereas Jesus emphasized salvation.

Notice the two aspects of John's message: Repentance, baptism, forgiveness and the coming of One more powerful, who will baptize the people in the Holy Spirit (i.e., immerse them in . . . John thought of baptism by immersion!). If we are waiting for "salvation," a way out of a dim and unexciting existence, we should pay attention to these two aspects and apply them to ourselves.

3rd SUNDAY OF ADVENT
My Spirit Finds Joy in God My Savior

THE better the hostess has prepared for a party, scrutinizing all the details, checking the guest list and making sure that nobody has been overlooked, the more likely her party will be

B — 3rd Sunday of Advent

a success. The better we plan a vacation the more guarantee we have that it will be a great one. It is a joy to prepare well for the visit of friends and to know that they have enjoyed it.

Many people, though, want instant joy. They do not want to plan, to prepare, and to sacrifice. Moreover, they do not have the insight or the faith that service to others can be a source of joy!

One of the great contributions of Christianity is that it has brought "joy to the world." This is even a well-known Christmas hymn! The Scripture readings of today deal with this joy. It is a joy which cannot be obtained overnight. It is a joy which is found in service. Christianity does not have the answer for all questions. But if you are yearning for real joy, happiness and peace of mind, you should prayerfully go over these readings. "My being [that is,I] proclaims the greatness of the Lord, my spirit finds joy in God my Savior" (Responsorial Psalm).

Reading I   Is 61, 1-2. 10-11
Joy to the World

The prophet describes his mission as service to his people. He announces glad tidings to the captives back from exile in Babylon. The second part of this poem is the joyful reaction of Jerusalem (God's people). She is overwhelmed by the abundant goodness of the Lord, who has bedecked her with a robe of salvation and precious jewelry. This poem greatly influenced our Lord's understanding of his mission of service. In describing his mission, he refers twice to it (Lk 4, 16-22; Mk 11, 2-6).

God's word through this tradition could be that there is joy in service and that the riches which we possess through faith and baptism are a great source of joy as well. The Responsorial Psalm is the well-known song which Luke put into the mouth of Mary when she visited Elizabeth. We should pray it with her: "His servant . . ." is Israel, God's people, you and I. "My soul [that is, I] rejoices in my God": this is not instant joy. It is a kind of happiness which must be obtained and safeguarded time and again with faith and patience.

Reading II 1 Thes 5, 16-24
Rejoice always

Paul explains what kind of people we should be while waiting for the coming of our Lord Jesus Christ at Christmas, and in that perspective for his final coming to judge the living and the dead. Waiting with hope for final and complete happiness, Christians have reason for joy. "Lord, prepare our hearts and remove the sadness that hinders us from feeling the joy and hope which his [the Savior's] presence will bestow" (Alternative Opening Prayer).

Gospel Jn 1, 6-8. 19-28
Jesus the Answer

The question which no intelligent person can ignore is "Who is this Man, Jesus Christ, who started that worldwide movement, called Christianity?" It has existed for some 2,000 years. Apparently, it has satisfied the aspirations of millions. It has given a kind of joy and happiness for which martyrs have laid down their lives.

John the Baptizer explains it to us. Jesus is Light and Lord. Many do not recognize him yet but he is great. Notice the unselfishness of John. He himself is a preacher, but he bears witness to him, whose sandal he is not worthy to unfasten. John is the pattern of the Church's ministry today. There are many in every community who are searching. It should be our joy by word and example to point to the Lord Jesus as an answer.

———◆———

4th SUNDAY OF ADVENT
Jesus Christ Will Reign Forever

WHEN a mother is expecting a baby, in a way the whole family is expecting with her. There is joy in expecting a beautiful happening to come. There is excitement in expecting a vacation trip which is going to be an entirely new experience.

B — 4th Sunday of Advent

We ask friends who have been there. Expecting keeps us young. We look to the future instead of to the past. There are always new and exciting aspects in life, if only we have the eye to see them and the gift of wonderment, which children possess and grown-ups should never lose.

Christmas is such an event to come. It is God revealing "a mystery, hidden for many ages" (Reading II). He wants to be present to us. He wants to give us an image of himself in Jesus Christ, an image which we are able to perceive with our weak human senses. Christmas is great every year, but only for those who are expecting "Emmanuel—God with us" in faith and wonderment.

Reading I   2 Sm 7, 1-5. 8-11. 16
Fixing a Place for My People

David, full of goodwill, wants to build a temple for God. But instead of David buiding a temple (house) for God, God will build a "house," an everlasting dynasty, for David: "Your house shall endure forever." In today's Gospel, Luke sees this promise ultimately fulfilled in the universal kingship of Lord Jesus. With this in mind, we should make the Responsorial Psalm (89, 2-5. 27. 29) our prayer of praise and thanksgiving for what God gave us in Jesus Christ.

Reading II   Rom 16, 25-27
A Mystery Revealed

Only with the coming of Jesus Christ do we attain the right understanding of Israel's expectations. The mystery, hidden for many ages, is now revealed and made known to all the Gentiles. Salvation, coming to us through Jesus Christ, is for all. We should pray that all may see the real light of Christmas.

Gospel   Lk 1, 26-38
His Reign Without End

(See also commentary for the Immaculate Conception, December 8, p. 350.)

Here we concentrate on what Luke wants to teach us about this child about to be born. First, he wants our affirmation in faith that Jesus' origin is a transcendental one, that he is born from God. Secondly, Luke brings out what role this child is to play in salvation history. He finds the clue for understanding this in the Old Testament. God has promised David that his dynasty (throne) would stand firm forever (Reading I). Hence, the expectation that a descendant of David once again would rule the house of Jacob (Jacob, the Hebrew patriarch, stands for God's people), and that his reign would have no end.

Luke sees this political expectation, which was very much alive in his day, fulfilled on a higher level in Jesus Christ, who will reign over God's people forever. "The Lord God will give him the throne of David his father." Let us admire God's way every year again during Advent and Christmas time, and accept Jesus Christ as Luke wants us to do.

◆

CHRISTMAS SEASON

See p. 14.

CHRISTMAS

See p. 15.

Sunday in the Octave of Christmas
HOLY FAMILY
Family Life

WE are witnessing a breakdown of the traditional family and its values—filial respect for authority, exercised responsibly by parents—and a rising juvenile delinquency. Hence, our society can learn a few things from today's Bible readings. Of course, there is no easy available remedy for today's family crisis. Also, the Christian family is part of a culture in which humanity participates—neighborhood, school, television, friends and recreation patterns. But in stormy weather a ship may get at least some guidance from a beacon! And though authority from the earliest infancy on should be exercised perhaps

B — Holy Family

in a different way, it should not be done away with. Parents could discuss this with their children. A substitute for sound family life has not yet been offered by any of the behavioral sciences!

Today's readings on the family necessarily reflect the patriarchal family pattern, hence the subordinationist family ethic, of the Biblical culture. We should distinguish between the core of the Christian ethics and the cloth in which it is wrapped. This cloth is conditioned by time and culture and is not necessarily part of the divine message. But the message on family life as such is timeless.

Reading I   Sir 3, 2-6. 12-14
Filial Respect

By keeping in mind that the point of this passage (God's word to us) is conditioned by time and culture, a modern Christian can succeed in learning from it. Respect, reverence, and love are values that should be cherished. Take care of your parents when they are old. Show love and care, even if you soothe your conscience with the fact that he/she is well taken care of in an old people's home far away! "Happy are those who fear [show filial respect to] the Lord and walk in his ways" (Responsorial Psalm). Nature, hence God, wants the family!

Reading II   Col 3, 12-21
Family Bible Reading

The Holy Family, Jesus, Mary, Joseph, must have cherished the values brought out in this Bible passage. "Let the word of Christ dwell in you." Why not try regular family Bible reading, with a discussion afterward and an improvised prayer by one member of the family at the end? The idea of wives being "submissive to your husbands" may not appeal to "women's lib"; however, where there is genuine love, constantly fostered, a mutual pattern of "doing the loving thing" spontaneously originates. Love and bitterness are incompatible.

Gospel

Lk 2, 22-40 or 2, 22. 39-40

Parents Marveling

Luke describes the Jewish purification rite, observed by the Holy Family, as a manifestation of our Lord. He is introduced as "the Anointed of the Lord," the anointed king or Messiah, who meets two representatives of his people, Simeon and Anna. "He took him in his arms"; this was the customary ritual of blessing children. "You yourself [Mary] shall be pierced with a sword": indicates the pain experienced by Mary as the Mother of the Redeemer.

Are you willing to accept our Lord as controversial? His values, "do's and don'ts," are not always the same ones which your friends and associates go by! Take a stand!

OCTAVE OF CHRISTMAS

See p. 23.

2nd SUNDAY OF CHRISTMAS

See p. 24.

EPIPHANY

See p. 26.

B — Baptism of the Lord
Sunday after the Epiphany
BAPTISM OF THE LORD
The Servant of Yahweh

EVERY time we discover a new aspect in the person we love, we stop in wonderment. "I did not know him/her as such!" And this deeper insight and sharing in a person's self results in greater appreciation, intimacy, and love.

Today we celebrate the Lord's baptism by John in the Jordan. Matthew relates Jesus' baptism as another epiphany (manifestation), declaring that the Lord Jesus is the servant (Son) of Yahweh. His call in life is that of the Servant as depicted in today's first reading. This is an aspect of Jesus' personality, which gives us a deeper insight into who our Lord is. He is "the man for others." He is there for you and me. Experiencing this in prayer, we should appreciate and love our Lord more for it.

Everyone has his/her own calling in life. We must respond to it in the framework of our personal capacities and the circumstances of time and milieu. Serious and mature people understand that only a life of service is a meaningful life. What do you consider your main calling in life, and how do you fulfill it? "Almighty, eternal God, keep us, your children born of water and the Spirit, faithful to our calling" (Opening Prayer). Today's feast marks the end of the Christmas season.

Reading I
Is 42, 1-4. 6-7
A Call to Service

It is not clear what kind of person the inspired poet had in mind, when he depicted an ideal servant of God in the four "Servant Songs" as we have them in Isaiah. Is it the whole nation of Israel? Is it some prophet or king of the past? Is it a Messiah (Anointed King) to come?

Reapplied by the evangelists and the Church, the Servant is identified with Jesus, who is manifested as God's beloved Servant (Son) in his baptism. The song depicts what the Lord Jesus' mission is to all of us. Reapplied by the Church, the psalm refers to the voice of God "over the waters," when Jesus was baptized in the Jordan

B — 2nd Sunday in Ordinary Time

Reading II　　　　　　　　　　　　　　　　Acts 10, 34-38
Doing Good Works

Peter sees Jesus as in his baptism "anointed with the Holy Spirit and power" and so equipped for his calling: doing good words and healing all who were in the grip of the devil. A similar calling is ours as baptized Christians. Being a Christian does not mean just avoiding sin. We are anointed to do good and to be concerned about fellow human beings who are in the grip of evil. And God will be with you!

Gospel　　　　　　　　　　　　　　　　　　Mk 1, 7-11
Your Call?

When John the Baptizer speaks of baptizing, he thinks of baptizing by immersion. When, through the priest, the Lord Jesus baptized you, he immersed you in the Holy Spirit. We should always be aware of our Source of Inspiration! Accompanying Jesus' baptism is a theophany (manifestation of God).

"Like a dove": a dove was the symbol of Israel. Filled with God's Spirit, Jesus is the representative of the new Israel of God. Using the language of vision, the author describes Jesus' awareness of his mission. It was a tremendous task which he accepted obediently. How do you see your call as a baptized Christian?

―――――◆―――――

ORDINARY TIME

See p. 29.

2nd SUNDAY IN ORDINARY TIME
Call and Responses

MATURE people are aware that only a meaningful life can impart lasting happiness. What gives meaning to my life? It is a task, which I feel called to fulfill. Today's first and third Bible readings relate a call in life explicitly to God. But in daily life it is not always simple to find out what one's call is. God works implicitly through our inclinations, natural abilities, friends, parents, educators, and church affiliation. These will guide us in deciding how we are going to make a living and, as a rule, in choosing our partner for life.

It is a human call to make life together with a beloved one meaningful. However, there is a special call in life, which we are used to terming a "vocation." It is the invitation to follow Christ as a religious or priest. Christians who choose this kind of life, celibacy for the sake of God's reign, choose to relate their "openness to the other" not to one person but to the human community as a whole. They keep themselves free to dedicate themselves entirely to the establishment of universal human relations, and as such they are a living sign that the reign of God (a reign of love, justice, fidelity, and peace) has been initiated already in our history.

Young people should be open to God's call and challenge, and parents should generously cooperate if one of their children feels God's invitation to live a meaningful life of dedication in the ministerial priesthood or religious life. All of us should pray with the psalmist: "Here am I, Lord; I come to do your will" (Responsorial Psalm).

Reading I — Fidelity to Our Call
1 Sm 3, 3-10. 19

Samuel is one of the great prophets of the Hebrews. It is he who anointed David as king of Israel. By setting down this beautiful tradition, the author relates Samuel's work and life directly to a call of almighty God. God's word is clear: All of us must be faithful to our call in life, whether it is in married life or in celibacy for the sake of God's reign (see Introduction).

Reading II — Reasons To Be Faithful
1 Cor 6, 13-15. 17-20

Notice that in Paul's language "body" stands for the whole person. Paul gives two reasons for a morally responsible life. First, you are members of Christ; in other words, you belong to Christ by faith and baptism and should be faithful to your baptismal commitment. Secondly, you are a temple of the Holy Spirit. Through baptism, the Spirit of God dwells in you. Immoral behavior desecrates the temple of God. These are two important reasons to be faithful to our call as Christians.

Gospel

Jn 1, 35-42

Call and Response

Today's Gospel tells about our Lord's own call/task in life. John designates him as "the Lamb of God," a sacrificial lamb offered to God—in contemporary language, "the Man for Others," giving himself to God in his fellow humans. We also learn about the call of the first disciples. This call-vocation is a growing thing. It may be initially just curiosity, a disposition to inquire. "What are you looking for?" "Teacher, where do you stay?" "Come and see." The first day the disciples stayed with Jesus. Their final decision to leave everything and follow the Lord came later.

God's word to us asks us to question ourselves about our relationship with God. Is it a dynamic one of call and response? Is it an ongoing process? An ever more generous response should be the result of counsel and constant prayer.

———◆———

3rd SUNDAY IN ORDINARY TIME

Call, Reluctance and Repentance

WITH reference to our call/task in life, we may go through periods of reluctance when we just do not feel up to our previously made commitment. Such reluctance is part of human nature. However, our first reaction to do something about it should not be a visit to the lawyer. As mature people we should have an honest discussion, seek counseling, and pray to God. The first Bible reading has been taken from the Book of Jonah. Since this book is so beautiful and consists of only four chapters, you should take time today and read it entirely.

It is a didactic story used by the sacred writer to oppose the narrow nationalism of Judaism after the exile in Babylon. Salvation is not just for the Jews, but for all! The writer deals with two calls. First, he tells of the call of Jonah to go and preach repentance in the pagan city of Nineveh, and the prophet's reluctance to answer God's call. The story speaks for itself. Secondly, the writer describes a call to repentance addressed to sinful Nineveh, which responds and does penance.

The message, God's word, to us is: Our call in life may be a challenge and the future may not always be clear, but we must respond in faith, and in repentance, when we have failed.

Reading I Jon 3, 1-5. 10
A Call to Repentance

The theme of this passage is God's call and our response to be the kind of person the Maker has designed us to be. It is a call to repentance. The response: "They proclaimed a fast and all of them put on sackcloth" (Oriental sign of penance). This reading introduces Jesus' call for repentance in today's Gospel: "Reform your life!" It is a constant call to Christians of all times. We may pray: "Your ways, O Lord, make known to me; teach me your paths" (Responsorial Psalm).

Reading II 1 Cor 7, 29-31
Timeless Advice

We should first observe that Paul's statement of today is conditioned by his mistaken opinion that the parousia (Second Coming of Christ) would occur during his own lifetime. Does it make sense then to pay attention to this statement, since Paul's expectation was mistaken? Yes, it does because it is still true that "the world as we know it is passing away."

We should heed Paul's timeless advice that all human values, possessions, and even marriage are relative to the ultimate values of the hereafter: "They neither marry nor are given in marriage" (Mt 22, 30). Married people are necessarily involved in the cares of this world, but they should be careful not to attach their hearts to it. Their call involves both this life and the hereafter.

Gospel Mk 1, 14-20
Two Calls

Like the author of Jonah (see Introduction) Mark also deals with two calls. He first sets forth the call for repentance to all of us: "Reform your lives and believe in the good news."

Conversion, time and again averting yourself from evil in all its forms and converting yourself in even more perfect love to God, is a lifetime job which requires perseverance! Secondly, Mark relates another call of the disciples. Last week, we referred to "call-vocation," in particular to total dedication to Christ, including one's sexuality, as an ongoing process. The disciples have just spent the day with our Lord. In today's reading we see a definitive decision. "They abandoned their nets [their father] and became his followers."

The first call to repentance is addressed to all Christians, the second one to those whom God calls to a life of service in the ministerial priesthood and/or religious life. It requires generosity to respond. Pray that it always may be found among God's people!

4th SUNDAY IN ORDINARY TIME
He Speaks with Authority

MEETING people for the first time, hearing them in a public address, may prompt various reactions. We might state: "He/she did not impress me too much," that is, as a person, he/she does not have much to offer. Our reaction could also be: "I was very much impressed," that is, we see a person who stands for something, who is a real "somebody." This first impression, though perhaps mainly intuitive, is often decisive for our final opinion about a person. Only for very good reasons do we revise it.

The Lord Jesus must have impressed people as a real "Somebody." He was so impressive that he has prompted people to agree with him, to give up everything and follow him, not just in his own time and country, but all over the globe and already for some 2,000 years. What is that mysterious authority which people felt during his lifetime and which they still feel when they read the faith experience of his early followers in Scripture? Today's Gospel reading describes such an initial reaction and it should provide much food for thought for us.

B — 4th Sunday in Ordinary Time

Reading I
Dt 18, 15-20
To Him Shall You Listen

Meditating on the great prophet Moses, the writer of Deuteronomy assures his readers that the prophetic office will be an ongoing process in Israel. "I [God] will raise up for them a prophet like you [Moses], and will put my words into his mouth." God will always guide his people through his "mouthpieces," the prophets.

Later, this text came to be regarded as teaching that God would send a final (end-time) prophet. These are the terms in which Jesus saw himself, and more explicitly in which the early Church understood him. Just as Moses spoke with authority, so did the Lord Jesus. "If today you hear his voice, harden not your hearts" (Responsorial Psalm).

Reading II
1 Cor 7, 32-35
Celibacy—Marriage

Notice that Paul does not condemn marriage or sex as something inferior. He recommends celibacy as a way of life for those who are called to it, and offers just one reason for it (freedom to be concerned with things of the Lord). There are many more. You should read this passage in its total context of chapter 7, and remember that the background from which Paul reasons is the partriarchal marriage pattern of his time and culture, which as such is not part of divine revelation.

Gospel
Mk 1, 21-28
Spellbound

"The people were spellbound by his teaching—a new teaching in a spirit of authority." The prophets, including the great Moses, used to say: "Thus says the Lord." Jesus says: "I tell you. . . ." The exorcism accompanying Jesus' teaching in Mark's account underlines this authority. Where God's word breaks through in human history, announcing the coming of his kingdom of justice, love, and peace, there evil must cease!

Listen often and with faith to the Lord Jesus and his teaching with authority, as we have it in Scripture. "Spellbound" by his words, you will keep balance in a society where so much other "wisdom" is for sale.

5th SUNDAY IN ORDINARY TIME
He Heals the Brokenhearted

OUR community hospitals and mental clinics are hopeful havens for suffering mankind. But they also constitute the signs that pain and misery form an integral part of the human condition. We would hail the genius who could make it possible for our species to have no more need of physicians and hospitals. It would be wonderful, but it will never be realized. Pain and suffering, both physical and mental, and ultimately death, are going to remain with us. Hence, how do we handle this facet of our human existence?

The Bible discusses the problem of pain and suffering quite often. It does not offer a final solution, but under God's guidance the sacred writers attain some very consoling insights which help us Christians to cope with pain when it strikes us. Scripture should be the constant companion of each suffering person. The Gideons put Bibles in motel rooms. They should be found in all hospital rooms and be available for patients whose health permits them to read.

Reading I   Jb 7, 1-4. 6-7
Life a Drudgery

In the framework of a folktale, a Hebrew sage tries to approach the mystery of suffering. If possible, take time today to read the prologue: Job 1, 1-22; 2, 1-13, and the epilogue: Job 42, 7-17, which constitute the original folktale. Between those sections the author composed the poetical dialogues on the problem of suffering, but no clear solution is offered. Today's passage is very pessimistic about the human condition. Notice that the author of Job did not have a clear idea of a life hereafter, which formed part of the fuller revelation brought us by Christ.

We should connect this passage with the healing ministry of Jesus in the Gospel and the Responsorial Psalm: "Praise the Lord who heals the brokenhearted and binds up their wounds."

B — 6th Sunday in Ordinary Time

Reading II — 1 Cor 9, 16-19. 22-23
"For the Sake of the Gospel"

Paul considered it his call in life, his duty, to preach the Gospel. And he asked for no reward, though he could rightly expect it. Jesus had told his disciples: "The laborer is worth his wage" (Lk 10, 7). Paul did not want to make full use of the authority which the Gospel gave him. He earned his living by tentmaking. This was only one of the features that made him a great man.

Gospel — Mk 1, 29-39
"He Helped Her Up"

In reading about the healing ministry of the Lord Jesus, we should keep in mind that the ancient Hebrews did not see a scientific relation between medication and healing, as we do. Their understanding of medication was mainly a magical one. Sickness was caused by evil spirits. Hence, a sick person turned first of all to the priest or a holy man for help. Healing was identical with expelling demons. Hence, the ministry of healing is one of the signs of the messianic era, the time of salvation from the power of Satan and of God's reign on earth. Proclaiming the good news and healing went hand in hand. According to Mark, these healings foreshadowed the ultimate healing of all the brokenhearted by Jesus' death on the Cross.

When we are depressed and suffering, and perhaps tempted to think as Job did (Reading I), we should meditate on our Lord's death and resurrection, and see pain as our passage to eternal life with him.

6th SUNDAY IN ORDINARY TIME
Spiritually Unclean

FOR one reason or another society expels members from its midst. Reasons may be crime, disease, inability to live up to community standards or simply discrimination based on prejudice. Society confines outcasts to prison, isolates them in quarantine, or just ignores them. In any case, outcasts are unhappy persons. They feel unwanted and often turn to bitterness and hatred.

Over the centuries, leprosy, for which no cure existed until recently, was a reason to ostracize one's fellow humans. Mostly in the developing countries, there are still thousands of lepers considered as unclean, contagious, and dangerous, who live in leper colonies, often in utter misery and filth.

The first and third Bible readings deal with leprosy and uncleanness, but transferred to another plane, the uncleanness of heart through sin. Sinners are unhappy outcasts and the Lord Jesus came to show care. Sinners, all of us who fail, should turn to the Lord for help: "I turn to you, Lord, in time of trouble, and you fill me with the joy of salvation" (Responsorial Psalm).

Reading I   Lv 13, 1-2. 44-46
"Unclean!"

In ancient times, there was no scientific diagnosis of leprosy, and many other curable skin diseases were included in this designation. These diseases were considered dangerous and detestable not only because they were contagious, but also because they made a person religiously unclean and unworthy to take part in community worship. Notice that disease, and certainly this kind of disease, was thought to be caused by sin! These sick people had to present themselves to the priest who decided how long they had to stay in quarantine.

Avoided by fellow citizens, these outcasts lived in miserable, poor, and squalid quarters. Scientific health care is a luxury of recent times in affluent societies! When the sick thought that they were cleansed of their disease, they had to go and see the priest again (Gospel) and could return to normal life in the community. Sinners are spiritually unclean. They should confess their faults to the Lord! (Responsorial Psalm).

B — 6th Sunday in Ordinary Time

Reading II   1 Cor 10, 31—11, 1

Be Considerate!

Paul encourages us to imitate the Lord Jesus who was considerate and thoughtful. The problem in the congregation of Corinth was that of eating meat sacrificed to the pagan gods which was available at the market. Informed Christians knew that such gods did not exist and thus could eat this meat without thinking anything more about it. Paul himself sees no harm in eating sacrificed meat, but he knows that such an action might well scandalize less instructed fellow Christians (perhaps those of Jewish background). Hence, Paul's advice, "Give no offense to Jew or Greek"; in other words, do not eat sacrificed meat for that reason.

God's message is: Be considerate! Do not hurt others' feelings! Both "progressives" and "conservatives" in the manner of Church renewal should heed this message.

Gospel   Mk 1, 40-45

"Moved with Pity"

The healing of a leper and sending him to the priest (see comment on Reading I) should not be seen as just a proof of Jesus' power. St. John calls Jesus' miracles "signs." They are signs that indicate the breakthrough of God's reign of love, justice, concern, peace and happiness into human history. Jesus shows why he has come, namely, to share our helpless and miserable human condition and to redeem us from evil.

The Responsorial Psalm invites us to pray: "I turn to you, Lord!" Do you take part in any of your parish penitential services? Confession of guilt is part of Christian life!

———◆———

7th SUNDAY IN ORDINARY TIME

Penance and Forgiveness of Sin

THE beautiful song "Miracle of Miracles" in the Broadway musical *Fiddler on the Roof*, of some years ago, brings out how Jewish tradition regards miracles. It refers to the traditional Biblical miracles of Daniel in the lion's den, the parting of the waters of the Red Sea, and the manna in the wilderness. But it is a miracle too that God made people and "has given you [my wife] to me." The Biblical miracles are not just unexplainable interferences of God with his laws of nature. In the Bible, any event, whether natural or supernatural, in which one sees an act or a revelation of God, is considered a miracle.

Mark, whose gospel we are reading this year, does not want Jesus to be seen as merely a wonderworker, a kind of magician. He wants to see Jesus' miracles as signs or prefigurations of the great miracle of God's reign to come with Christ's death and resurrection. The healing of the paralytic in today's Gospel is a good example.

We are familiar with contemporary symbolism: the burning of a man's effigy, hunger strike, peace signs, *et al*. We should develop a feeling for symbols and signs. They often speak a language which is more suggestive than words alone.

Reading I   Is 43, 18-19. 21-22. 24-25
Something New

The prophet tells the Jews who are about to return from exile in Babylon that in their worship services they should not only remember/celebrate the events of the past (the traditional exodus from bondage in Egypt), but also the new exodus—from bondage in Babylon. "I [God] am doing something new! In the desert I made a way for you," so that you can go back to your homeland. This new exodus is a generous gift of God, even offered to a people who have burdened him with sins.

The reading refers to the healing of the paralytic in today's Gospel, which is seen as a sign that "God in Christ" offers free-

B — 7th Sunday in Ordinary Time

dom/exodus from the bondage of evil. "O Lord, have pity on me: heal me, though I have sinned against you" (Responsorial Psalm).

Reading II — 2 Cor 1, 18-22
God Keeps His Word

Paul has been accused of being unstable. Going back to the basics of the Christian message, he refers to God's promises which are stable and to which all of us attach our "Amen" ("So be it") when we worship together. Have trust in God!

Today's message of penance and forgiveness of sin shows clearly that God has promised mercy! Once persons have committed a crime, their police record will follow them wherever they go. But this is not the case before God—once forgiven of our sins, we have no more record!

Gospel — Mk 2, 1-12
Your Sins Are Forgiven

Mark tells the healing story of the paralytic, as tradition had couched it, to bring out a point. He wants to stress not just that Jesus is a wonderworker, but that his miraculous healings are signs of a mysterious reality—in this case the authority of the Church to forgive sin in God's name. (See Introduction.)

Over the centuries the Church, God's people, has been aware that this authority has been entrusted to her. It has been exercised in various ways and even in our time we see some changes. But the authority is there and we should call upon it. (See comment of last week.) Do you make the penitential rite before the Eucharistic Celebration meaningful, as far as you are concerned? "I confess to Almighty God and to you, my brothers and sisters."

◆

8th SUNDAY IN ORDINARY TIME
The Covenant of Love

A PERSON'S "dos and don'ts" are greatly determined by how he/she is related to others. A young lady at home may not be very happy when mother asks her to do the ironing of the week's family clothes. But ironing her boyfriend's shirt on Friday night is different! Love casts a very particular kind of light on our habits and way of life. This becomes even more evident when, by contrast, love has gone. Things people in love did so happily for one another become a burden once love is absent.

Apply this to your "dos and don'ts" as far as God is concerned. Are they boring and burdensome where once they were pleasant events? Love of God can get stale if it is not kept alive. When married love loses its tang, usually both partners are to be blamed. In our love relationship with God, it is only we ourselves who drifted away. God is faithful. If we have failed by indifference, we should return to him who "is slow to anger and abounding in kindness" (Responsorial Psalm).

Reading I   Hos 2, 16-17. 21-22
Espoused in Love

As mentioned often, the Bible sees human beings as related to God in a sacred partnership, called a covenant. Hosea is the first prophet to attribute marital characteristics to this sacred partnership. God wedded Israel in the desert. However, once she attained the promised land, enjoying the promised milk and honey, she became unfaithful to God by seeking out Baal, the god of the Canaanites.

Hosea takes his own unhappy marriage as an example. His wife has betrayed him, but he is willing to take her back. God is willing to do the same with his unfaithful people.

Reading II   2 Cor 3, 1-6
A Covenant of Spirit

As easily as the people of Corinth accepted Paul's message, they often followed other preachers. Paul states that he does not need credentials. He goes by one credential, namely the one written in the hearts of his converts. As the first and third readings do, Paul also views the covenant between God and humans as a partnership of intimate love, "a covenant not of a written law but of spirit. The written law kills, but the spirit [of love] gives life."

Gospel
At a Wedding — Mk 2, 18-22

The early Church was in constant conflict with Judaism. The Jews often fasted twice a week, though a wedding was a legal reason to make an exception. The Christians did not follow that rule. Mark uses a tradition on Jesus in conflict with the Pharisees to explain why Christians do not follow the Jewish laws on fasting. He states: "One doesn't fast at weddings."

The first reading shows that when Mark compares a Christian's covenant with God to the partnership of husband and wife, he is on solid Biblical ground. Do you see yourself as related to God in a partnership of love? Then love should be guiding your Christian "dos and don'ts' " for example, your decision to serve the parish when you are asked to.

———————◆———————

9th SUNDAY IN ORDINARY TIME
Freedom for Love

ON the weekends we "take off." We take off from the work we do to make a living. All agree on that, but not all will agree on the question, "What do you take off for?" Freedom from and freedom for are two sides of one coin, but they are not the same. On weekends we should be glad to be free for more time with those we love, not excluding God. However, this entails a love which is very much alive and makes togetherness a happy event.

If love is stale, we will escape togetherness by means of the various excuses available: an extra job, meeting a business friend, just walking out "for a while" (how long?) or endless hours before the television. Furthermore, excuses for not being together with God [Sunday worship] are very simple since God does not ask questions. (Read the Introduction of last Sunday again). It is love which determines our "do's and don'ts," including those of our weekends. What do you take off *for* this weekend?

Reading I   Dt 5, 12-15
The Sabbath of the Lord

Notice that the author of Deuteronomy mentions two elements concerning the Sabbath (meaning roughly, "to leave off"): abstinence from work and "remembrance." Abstinence from work should give ample opportunity for "remembrance." The Sabbath was seen as a grateful response to the exodus from bondage in Egypt. Initially, Christians from Jewish background continued to observe the Sabbath and celebrated the Eucharist on the Lord's Day (Day of his resurrection). Later, when even more Gentiles joined the Church, the Lord's Day (Sunday) became the Christian day of worship.

Freedom from work should give opportunity for "remembrance," for the memorial of our exodus from evil through Christ's death and resurrection, celebrated in the signs of bread and wine. Partaking of this "memorial of our redemption" (Mass) is an integral part of a Christian's Sunday.

Reading II   2 Cor 4, 6-11
Revealing the Life of Jesus

Paul is really disappointed that his converts blame him for failing to be spectacular. They have been listening to other preachers who claim that their miracles, eloquence, and even visions are manifestations of God's power in them. Paul states that God's revelation was indeed given to him—but as a treasure in an earthen vessel.

Paul is a human being, crushed, struck down. The Corinthians should look to the treasure, God's light, as shining on the face of Christ, and understand that the real Gospel is not the spectacular, but Christ crucified. Paul opposes any triumphalism in the Church.

B — 1st Sunday of Lent

Gospel
Mk 2, 23—3, 6 or 2, 23-28
The Sabbath Made for People

Initially, the gradual substitution of Sunday (the Lord's Day) for the Sabbath caused hard feelings especially in mixed congregations with Christians from both Jewish and Gentile backgrounds. By relating these two traditions about the Jews, Mark puts few things in their right perspective: (1) "The Sabbath was made for people, not people for the Sabbath." The observance of the Sabbath was essentially a law to enable people to be free. But the Pharisees had made it an unbearable yoke by adding many details concerning what could not be done. Jesus opposes such legalism (making the law an end in itself). (2) "Jesus is Lord even of the Sabbath." Hence, Christians of Gentile origin observe the Lord's Day but will not be forced to observe the Sabbath.

Regardless of our changing observance of the Sunday, we should not let any activity interfere with our time for worship, unless it is really necessary. (See Introduction.)

LENTEN SEASON

For General Introduction, see p. 43.

1st SUNDAY OF LENT
Overcoming the Powers of Evil

SEEING New York from the Empire State Building gives a view which the person in the street cannot have. The astronauts saw the earth and life on it from a distance. This has changed them. Many of them have admitted that they experienced a new sense of God. We can only surmise their experience by looking at their pictures of that bluish ball silently circling around in an unfriendly universe. The POWs in Vietnam had a similar experience. That time of isolation has done something to them.

In the Catholic tradition, we have our retreat houses, parish missions, and annual Lenten observance. It is the idea of getting off "the merry-go-round" for a while and standing away from life in order to take a realistic look at ourselves. Through the mass media modern life is constantly imposing its neon-light values on all of us. These values are glittering and tempting. Francis of Assisi was fed up with this kind of life and "dropped out." In the sixties many quit society to live in communes away from the cities. The Lenten season should help us to focus our attention on the real thing and prepare for the feast of our redemption, Easter.

Put aside some extra time for meditative Bible reading and take part in the Lenten exercises of your congregation. Doing things together makes it easier!

Reading I — My Bow in the Clouds — Gn 9, 8-15

In order to understand the common theme of today's Bible readings, we must keep in mind the belief of the ancients that disasters of nature, such as a flood, were caused by evil spirits, wicked angels, the power of evil and sin. But if people were faithful to God's covenant, they could overcome the power of evil with God's help.

The flood story with its rainbow is a beautiful allegory containing a very meaningful and universal lesson. God will preserve the universe if human beings want to cooperate. Ecology is a Christian concern! Responsibly using the resources of the planet and not wasting them is overcoming the evil of destruction.

Reading II — Saved by Baptism — 1 Pt 3, 18-22

By his death Christ overcame the power of evil: "He went to preach to the spirits in prison," announcing their defeat to the cosmic powers of evil, including the disobedient spirits at the time of Noah (Reading I). The author sees an analogy between the waters of the flood and the baptismal bath. A few persons escaped in the ark through the water and were saved. A baptismal candidate goes through the water (immersion), is saved, and is able to overcome the powers of evil.

The author warns, however, that the baptismal water as such does no good, unless it is accompanied by the pledge to God which proceeds from a good conscience.

B — 2nd Sunday of Lent

Gospel
Mk 1, 12-15
Angels—God—Protection

In this passage, we read about the test (temptations), Satan (the devil), the wild beasts (every kind of threat and evil), and angels (God's protection). Nothing has changed. All of this is still in and around us! The temptation to fall for warped values is perhaps even more powerful than it has ever been.

Jesus gives the example of going into solitude. Making a retreat occasionally is very beneficial. Observing Lent can be done by all. Jesus is victorious over the powers of evil. Angels will wait on us, if only we ask God for help. Have a realistic look at yourself and reform your life.

2nd SUNDAY OF LENT
"If God Is for Us, Who Can Be Against Us?"

A TIME of obscurity in our lives can constitute a more severe mental pain than any physical suffering. It may be a time of doubt about values which we have cherished as sacred in the past, fidelity in a stale marriage situation, commitment to religion in parish setting which does not excite us, or dedication to a job under changed circumstances and with all other avenues closed. In each case, we do not know where to turn.

Young people have problems with their faith. In their process of maturation they question all values, religion included, till they find themselves. More serious is the obscure situation grown-ups may go through.

We think of the professionals who work daily with test tubes, statistics, and computer results. They must know exactly what is going on. But this kind of one-sided pragmatism does not work in the field of interpersonal relations. How can we keep values like love and faith alive even when they are tempted by obscurity, confusion, and doubt? Today's Liturgy deals with this problem. Prayerful reading and listening may shed some light on it!

Reading I

Gn 22, 1-2. 9. 10-13. 15-18

"Yes, Lord!"

In Hebrew tradition, Abraham represents the classic example of faith. This tradition describes an honest man, how he goes through a tormenting experience of uncertainty, and how he finally resolves it. Guided by God, the author brings out a timeless message to all who wrestle with the problem of fidelity, faith, and trust in a future. He teaches that there is a way out if we dare to persevere, hoping against all hope, and in faith get on our knees to pray. "I believed, even when I said, 'I am greatly afflicted' " (Responsorial Psalm). This could well have been said by Abraham!

How do we stand fast when shadows of uncertainty and doubt are tormenting us? We could pray: "Father of light, free us from the darkness that shadows our vision. Restore our light that we may look upon your Son who calls us to repentance and a change of heart" (Alternative Opening Prayer).

Reading II

Rom 8, 31-34

God Is for Us

"If God is for us, who can be against us?" This one line states in a nutshell what the other two readings teach in story form. Abraham experienced it when he was faithful in the darkest moment of his life (Reading I). The three apostles felt it when, in their doubt and embarrassment about the necessity of suffering in life, they enjoyed a moment of light and glory on the mountain (Gospel).

We, God's chosen ones, should find consolation and courage in these words when we pass through the valley of darkness, doubt, and mental suffering.

Gospel

Mk 9, 2-10

We Will Overcome

What does Mark try to bring out by relating this tradition about Jesus' transfiguration? He knew the Abraham story of the first reading: Abraham's faith, his suffering and mental pain, and finally God speaking! Mark follows the same pattern:

He has Peter's profession of faith: "You are the Messiah" (Mk 8, 27-30), Jesus foretelling his suffering (8, 31-33) and our partaking in it (8, 34-38), and finally God speaking (in today's Gospel). We must suffer physical and mental pain, but like Christ we will overcome. Notice that there is a mountain as in the first tradition, as well as the traditional cloud as sign of God's presence.

Our prayer could be: "God, grant me the serenity to accept the things I cannot change, courage to change the things I can, and the wisdom to know the difference."

◆

3rd SUNDAY OF LENT
Laws and Worship

WE are proud to be a nation ruled by laws and not by whims of individuals. There is much wisdom invested in our Constitution and in most of our other laws as well. But when we permit things to get out of control and do not let the laws work as was intended by the founding fathers, the country is in trouble. However, when the insight that we are a nation under the laws prevails once again, and we let the system work, we recover from setbacks.

Today's Scripture deals with laws (Reading I), derivation from them (Gospel), and the reaction by a man who was concerned. We must be careful, though, not to regard God's commandments as mere civil laws. In our relation to God, we Christians see ourselves in a family setting. The wish of a father who cares for his children is not a law in the same sense as a law found in our civil code of Laws. We are related to God as children to a loving father.

There is one absolute rule we go by and that is love for God and neighbor. Other commandments derive their reason for existence only from the law of love (Mt 22, 40), and we should understand them in the light of Jesus' Sermon on the Mount (Mt 5). Obedience of the commandments should always be motivated by love!

B — 3rd Sunday of Lent

Reading I   Ex 20, 1-17 or 20, 1-3. 7-8. 12-17
"All These Commandments"

Since civil and religious laws were so intimately intertwined in Hebrew culture, we must read the laws of the Old Testament with this in mind. Civil laws and laws clearly conditioned by time and culture (e.g., dietary laws) do not bind us any longer. The Ten Commandments, however, are timeless. Millions of Christians and Jews alike live by these laws. There is not only human but also divine wisdom imbedded in them.

But remember, in observing laws, we Christians should be motivated by love: "You did not receive a spirit of slavery leading you back into fear, but a spirit of adoption through which we cry out, 'Abba!' (that is, 'Father')."

Reading II   1 Cor 1, 22-25
God's Folly

Jews demand "signs" (Gospel). They want the spectacular. Greeks want "wisdom." Everything must be clearly understandable. There is no room for intuition, vision, mystery. It may be that Paul's Jews and Greeks characterize two kinds of Christians.

The first comprises those who hanker for the spectacular in worship. It must be exciting, or else they will not come. They are people who ask, "What does a worship service offer me?" and not, "What can I do to make it meaningful?" The second comprises the rationalists who crave wisdom, analysis, insight, but do not realize that values like mystery, intuition, love, or faith cannot be analyzed without being destroyed. Paul offers his vision to both groups, namely, the cross, Christ crucified. What is your stand? There is a law of worship (Reading I; Gospel).

Gospel   Jn 2, 13-25
Zeal for God's House

In chapter two, John relates the wedding at Cana as the first of Jesus' "signs." Then he relates the cleansing of the temple. Again "signs" are in the picture. "What sign can you show us?" "Many believed . . . , for they could see the signs he was performing." John wants to teach that Jesus put an end to the old way of worship (in the temple), and inaugurated a new worship "in spirit and truth" (Jn 4, 23). This transition was accomplished by Jesus' death and resurrection.

Organized worship and laws for participating in it make sense only if worship is motivated by Spirit and truth! God is not interested in hypocritical display. Make your worship meaningful today!

◆

4th SUNDAY OF LENT
The Son of Man Lifted Up, That All May Have Eternal Life in Him

TIME and again we see them pass by on our television screens, the refugees, driven away from their homes by floods, famine, wars. They live in miserable shacks or refugee camps. Clothed in rags, with starving babies on the hip, they stand in line with a plate, waiting for some meager food. What human misery! These people are homesick. They want desperately to go back to their homes and farms, but often machine guns and barbed wire prevent their return.

The Jews carried away into exile in Babylon were exactly like the dislocated persons of our day. And since the Hebrew writers saw exile and suffering as a divine punishment for sin, the miserable situation, famine, want, and longing for home of these exiles point to the sinful human condition of all.

The Lenten season invites us to be aware of how alienated sinful humankind is. Return is possible through Christ our Lord, who was lifted up on the cross, died, and rose again, "that all who believe may have eternal life in him" (Gospel)

Reading I   2 Chr 36, 14-17. 19-23
Alienated by Sin

The Jews in Babylonian exile stand for all who are alienated from God by sin. Only those who are aware of their alienation and are longing for home, salvation, lasting happiness, and peace can be saved. The Responsorial Psalm (137, 1-6) is a prayer of displaced Jews. "Zion" is the holy mountain in Jerusalem on which the temple was built. Both "Zion" and "Jerusalem" stand for "home."

Every sinner is a displaced person. Make this psalm your Lenten prayer!

Reading II   Eph 2, 4-10
Saved by God's Favor

Paul states that the salvation which the repentant sinner is hoping for is not our own doing. It is God's gift which we should accept in faith. Good works as such do not justify us but should be the consequence of our purification. Grateful for God's abundant love, the justified sinner spontaneously desires to do something in return.

Gospel   Jn 3, 14-21
Looking to Christ

The Book of Numbers (21, 4-9) relates a beautiful tradition. In the desert on their way to the promised land, some of the chosen people were bitten by serpents and many of them died. At God's command, Moses made a bronze serpent and mounted it on a pole. Whenever those who had been bitten by a serpent looked at the bronze serpent, they recovered. The serpent stands for the evil one (Jn 3, 6). All who have been bitten must die, but looking to the Son of Man, lifted up on the cross, will save them.

Looking to Christ means, of course, looking with faith and repentance! Those who love darkness rather than light cannot be saved. Do you have a crucifix in your home and do you ever look at it with faith and repentance?

———◆———

5th SUNDAY OF LENT
Death as a Metamorphosis into a Better life

OBSERVING nature carefully makes us wonder about the mysterious cycle of life, death and through death new life again. It is the mystery of the grain of wheat, which falls to the earth and dies in order to produce an abundance of new life, which transcends itself in both quality and quantity. From biology in high school, we remember "metamorphosis," the post-embryonic change in form of an animal, as when the larva of an insect becomes a pupa, or a tadpole changes into a frog. Metamorphosis is a mysterious development of life.

In dealing with the mystery of human life and death, the Bible refers to these phenomena in nature in order to indicate that, for the Christians, death is a metamorphosis (transfiguration: Mk 9, 2) into a better life. Mark (9, 2) says that on the mountain Jesus was "metamorphosed"—transformed. For a brief moment the disciples saw Jesus as he would be in the resurrection. And in today's Gospel, the Lord Jesus uses the mystery of the dying grain of wheat to refer to his impending death and resurrection to a new life.

All of us will have to face death. But our lives are patterned after that of Jesus. As he did, we must go through the mystery of death, but in faith we know that death is a metamorphosis, and it will result in a glorious life with Christ.

Reading I — The New Covenant — Jer 31, 31-34

Jeremiah addresses the exiles in Babylon. They are being punished for their infidelity to the Mosaic covenant (partnership of God with human beings), but there will be a new start. Christians see Jeremiah's vision fulfilled in the new covenant (partnership), established by the blood of Christ. Unlike the Mosaic covenant which was written on stone tablets, the new covenant is written on our hearts. In a sacred partnership. "I will be their God, and they shall be my people."

Lent is the time to check where we have failed to be faithful to our partnership (covenant) with God. Make the Responsorial Psalm (51, 3-4. 12-15) your prayer of repentance!

B — Passion Sunday [Palm Sunday]

Reading II Heb 5, 7-9
Our Source of Salvation

We are saved, and can see death as a transfiguration into eternal life, because of Jesus' prayer and obedience to the will of God. "When perfected" refers to the time after he reached his final goal in the resurrection. In our human condition, still waiting for our final transfiguration into eternal life (see Introduction), we are happy to have " a source of eternal salvation," namely, our Lord, who prays for us in heaven.

Gospel Jn 12, 20-33
Life and Death

Jesus speaks about his impending death. It will be a shock for the disciples and the final test of their faith in him. By referring to the mystery of the grain of wheat, which dies in order to produce new life, he tries to prepare them for that final decisive moment. "Hates his life" is a Semitic idiom for "willing to give up his life." "Once I am lifted up from earth" refers to the cross. From his cross (by his death of atonement), Jesus will draw all to a glorious life with him.

With the disciples we must try to see death as a mysterious metamorphosis (transformation) which Jesus went through and we must go through with him in order to live forever. "Father in heaven, help us to embrace the world you have given us, that we may transform the darkness of its pain into the life and joy of Easter" (Alternative Opening Prayer).

PASSION SUNDAY

[PALM SUNDAY]
Death and Life

GREAT people were often controversial figures during their lifetime. It is history, which can look on from a distance and see things in proper perpective, that rectifies the often limited judgment of contemporaries. Something like this has happened to the Lord Jesus. His contemporaries, even his closest

B — Passion Sunday [Palm Sunday]

coworkers did not understand him, especially not his strange ideas on suffering and death as a necessary passage to a better life. Only later did all of this become clear to them.

Today Christians celebrate Passion, or Palm Sunday. "Christ entered in triumph into his own city to complete his work as our Messiah: to suffer, to die, and to rise again" (Procession Rite). The triumphal entry celebrated at the beginning of the passion-week emphasizes that the three elements: suffering, death and resurrection belong together. Jesus' death was not a defeat. It was a victory. It is the genuine insight of Christianity that the events of Jesus' earthly life were the execution of God's saving purpose. This genuine insight should be ours also concerning our own lives, when suffering strikes us.

How do you deal with suffering in your life and when you encounter fellow humans who die in suffering and distress? Paul states: "If we believe that Jesus died and rose, God will bring forth with him from the dead those also who have fallen asleep believing in him" (1 Thes 4, 14). "Lord, the death of your Son gives us hope and strengthens our faith. May his resurrection give us perseverance and lead us to salvation" (Prayer after Communion).

Gospel Mk 11, 1-10
Who Is This

Like King David and all kings in his culture, Jesus enters the capital riding on the traditional animal. In the midst of the people, he is the Son of David, a Messiah sent by God to give freedom and self-determination to his country. But Jesus is a humble and peaceful king, not in favor of worldly display. He enters Jerusalem, "meek and riding on an ass" (Zec 9, 9). All four of the evangelists relate this tradition as an introduction to Jesus' passion and cruel death. Why? To teach us that Jesus is indeed the Messiah, though on a higher level than the people thought.

Jesus is sent by God to establish his reign (kingdom) on earth. His impending suffering and death will not thwart this divine plan but must be seen as the means to fulfill it, as will be clearly understood after the resurrection. "Did not the Messiah have to undergo all this so as to enter into his glory?" (Lk 24, 26). Participating in the Liturgy of Holy Week, we should keep in mind that suffering, pain, and death are also mysteriously part of our passage to a glorious life with our Lord.

Reading I   Is 50, 4-7
"The Lord Is My Help"

This reading is taken from the third song of the Servant of Yahweh. As mentioned at the feast of the Baptism of our Lord, it is not clear whom the inspired writer had in mind when he composed these four songs, describing the ideal Servant (Son) of God. Is he a collective person: Israel, God's people? Is he a king of the past or the Messiah (anointed king) to come?

In any case, the Christian community applied these hymns very early to Jesus and they are used throughout Holy Week as a beautiful commentary on the passion narratives. Indeed, "the Son of Man [Jesus] came not to be served but to serve, and to give his life for the ransom of many" (Mt 20, 28). Read the Responsorial Psalm (22) meditatively applying it to the Lord Jesus dying on the cross.

Reading II   Phil 2, 6-11
Your Attitude

This text is actually a Christ hymn, sung in church. It beautifully describes our Lord's utmost humiliation which he suffered on the cross. By being obedient, he made up for our sinful disobedience. But this hymn sings also of Christ's exaltation by the Father.

Meditating on the Lord's suffering and death, as Christians do during Holy Week, we should keep both sides of the Christ event in mind. It is suffering-and-death, which actually constitutes a passage to exaltation. Good Friday and Easter belong together even in our lives!

Gospel   Mk 14, 1—15, 47 or 15, 1-39
No Greater Love

Paul states: "For our sakes God made him [Jesus] who did not know sin, to be sin so that in him we might become the very holiness of God" (2 Cor 5, 21). Jesus identified himself entirely with sinful humankind, whom he freed from sin and death. Each of the evangelists relates the narrative with only a few different memories of the tragedy. In Matthew and Mark, Jesus' last words are: "My God, my God, why have you forsaken me?" Luke remembers that on the cross Jesus said: "Father, into your hands I commend my Spirit." All three relate the Lord's Supper, which Jesus gave us to celebrate as a memorial of his passion, death, and resurrection.

Prayerful meditation on Jesus' passion should make us grateful for what Jesus did. He has said: "There is no greater love than this: to lay down one's life for one's friend. You are my friends" (Jn 15, 13-14).

EASTER SEASON
See p. 55.

EASTER VIGIL MIDNIGHT MASS
See p. 56.

EASTER SUNDAY
See p. 57.

2nd SUNDAY OF EASTER
Faith and Fellowship

"BIRDS of a feather flock together." With respect to certain instincts, we humans are no different from cows in a pasture flocking together when a thunderstorm is threatening. We need one another's company and inspiration to keep going. Marital love can survive only if the partners daily foster togetherness with all the means nature and religion suggest. The survival of faith is subject to the same conditions. A Christianity lived "alone," all by oneself, does not last.

The first reading describes the communal life of the early congregation in Jerusalem. "Koinonia" (fellowship, brotherhood, communion) should be an important element in the life of Christians of all ages. Faith, like love, is constantly exposed to the temptation of doubt and indifference. We need one another's support. You are blessed, if you have/belong to a family where Christian fellowship is part of family life; where the members pray/worship together, read the Bible together, practice the Christian values of love, justice, mutual respect, decency, and concern together. In such a case, the members of the family carry one another and that fellowship keeps faith alive.

Fellowship should also be part of every congregation though this poses a problem in a large parish. We need belonging! Parish Councils should discuss available options. Participate in some activity of your parish. Do not be a loner! Without being exclusive, have friends who feel the same as you do in matters of faith. And at meetings, contribute to the value of "belonging" for all. Listen, be open to others, exchange ideas and experiences, share time and talents. "The brethen devoted themselves to the apostles' instruction and the communal life." The above may suggest how to realize this in our time and culture.

Reading I   Acts 4, 32-35
"One Heart and Mind"

This passage depicts the early Church of Jerusalem. The emphasis is on being of "one heart and mind." Responsibility

B — 2nd Sunday of Easter

for one another was so deeply felt that they shared everything in common. It is a beautiful ideal which is still practiced in the Church's religious societies. It is a way of life which cannot be imposed on all. It must be freely chosen with the firm belief that "my strength and my courage is the Lord, and he has been my savior" (Responsorial Psalm).

Reading II
Is Your Faith a Power?
1 Jn 5, 1-6

"The power that has conquered the world is this faith of ours." In reading about the enthusiasm of the early Church (Reading I) and recalling the sophisticated way of life and moral decay in the Roman Empire which Christianity gradually overcame, one finds the clue for this accomplishment in John's statement. It is faith.

In our day, we see the power of sophistication and moral decay all around us. Seemingly, the Church is losing ground. Why? What about your faith? Is it still a power? Is it still very much alive?

Gospel
Faith from Hearing
Jn 20, 19-31

The second reading has made the point that "without seeing you [Christians] believe in him [Jesus]." By relating the well-known tradition of the unbelieving Thomas, the writer of John wants to shed further light on this point. He indicates that even seeing, as Thomas did, is no guarantee of faith. Faith comes by hearing the word of the risen Lord who addresses Thomas personally.

Christianity knows the golden rule: Faith comes from hearing. It is God, personally addressing you in an "I-Thou" situation! This intangible situation can never be fully explained just as we cannot explain exactly what happens when someone falls in love! Respond when the Lord says: "Shalom—peace" to you in any situation of your life and keep that faith alive!

◆

3rd SUNDAY OF EASTER
May the Lord Open Our Minds for Understanding of the Scriptures

IN our confused and limited human condition, we are daily confronted with ignorance, knowledge, and understanding. Every human being starts out as a "tabula rasa" (a smoothed tablet, without impressions on it.) Only by hard work can a youngster overcome ignorance, gather knowledge, and attain insight and understanding. We need knowledge in order to achieve insight. When a teenager states: "But I think . . .," and it turns out that he made his statement without first gathering information, most people will take this youthful blunder in stride. They know that a teacher will tell the youngster what one is supposed to do before a statement is made. But when a grown-up does the same time and again, that person comes through as a big talker!

Today's Bible readings deal with ignorance (Reading I), knowledge (Reading II), and understanding of the Scriptures (Gospel). Living in an isolated and closed society, Catholics could perhaps afford to leave knowledge and understanding up to the priest. But such a closed society of Catholics is a thing of the past. Through the mass media everybody enters our home today. We owe it to ourselves and others to be informed Christians. If not, the flood of information which overwhelms us daily will confuse us.

However, even the grown-ups can come to insight and understanding only by exerting themselves. Adult Christians should read the Bible, the diocesan newspaper, and good books, and watch television programs that deal with their religion. Ignorance can be culpable and lead to disaster as the first Scripture reading clearly implies.

Reading I   Acts 3, 13-15. 17-19
Ignorance

The sacred author has Peter say harsh words to the Jewish people. He blames them for killing the Holy and Just One, the Author of life, our Lord Jesus Christ. But he adds quickly: "I know you acted out of ignorance." Judging others should be left up to God. But it is clear that ignorance on the part of those who should know is blameworthy and causes harm and disaster.

Poorly informed Christians, though they may hold a doctorate in science, are a danger to themselves and others. One cannot possibly cope with other visions on life, glittering and seemingly so much more appealing, if one knows one's own only poorly. Do you keep up-to-date on your religion? Is there an adult education group in your parish?

Reading II   1 Jn 2, 1-5
Knowledge

There is a difference between knowing about your marriage partner and knowing him/her. Knowing a great deal about God and religion does not make one necessarily a good Christian. The greatest theologians were not always the greatest saints!

The author of John states that knowing God is a religious experience in which you are involved. Love has very much to do with it! "The way we can be sure of our knowledge of him [Christ—God] is to keep his commandments," in other words, to do what he wants us to do. This kind of knowledge is acquired not only by study but also and much more by prayer!

Gospel   Lk 24, 35-48
The Understanding of Scripture

Luke states that our Lord opened the minds of the disciples to the understanding of the Scriptures. Experiencing God/Jesus Christ in meditative and prayerful Bible reading is the clue to Christian renewal. Understanding the human writers' word in the Bible is a necessary condition for understanding God's word in Scripture.

Hence, partaking in a study group is important. Doing things together under capable leadership makes study easier. But the real understanding of the Scriptures requires prayer and meditation, because the Lord must open your mind and give you insight.

4th SUNDAY OF EASTER
There Is Salvation in the Name of Jesus Christ

THE collective representatives of the people of the United States are responsible for our safety. We have a National Safety Council and such agencies as the Federal Bureau of Investigation (FBI) and the Central Intelligence Agency (CIA)—all concerned with safety. The sooner a threat to our safety is detected, the better it is. Yet many are not aware that a dangerous threat to our personal safety is posed by a meaningless existence. Psychiatrists and mental institutions are reminders of it. Once a person has to be referred to them, harm to that person's safety has already been done.

Christianity, the movement started by Jesus of Nazareth, wants to save people from precisely such a meaningless existence which the Bible calls darkness. The word "salvation" is mentioned on almost every page of Scripture. A mental breakdown is a tragedy, resulting from the fact that a person cannot cope with life. Counseling and medication may help. Christianity, however, offers something which prevents it. Christians who faithfully live their faith will not break down easily. They have reserves unknown of elsewhere.

Today's Liturgy deals with your safety. Let us hope that you will discover a few untapped reserves that could keep you going on your way to a great future.

Reading I   Acts 4, 8-12
Cripple—Perfectly Sound

In this reading, pay attention to the affinity between the sign (the crippled man restored to health—"saved" in the Greek original) and what is signified (all human beings "saved" in the name of Jesus). In other words, the saved man is a sign of all of us saved in the name of Jesus. Israel has rejected him. But there is no salvation in anyone else!

The Responsorial Psalm states the same: "It is better to take refuge in the Lord than to trust in man." Where do you turn in times of depression or when you are "crippled" because things do not go your way?

Reading II
Children of God
1 Jn 3, 1-2

In faith, following Jesus of Nazareth, we see the ultimate reality as a person, and are privileged to call him "Father." The author of John uses similar language. If God can be called "Father," then we are his children and feel safe, because we are taken care of.

A living relationship of child-Father may save us from ourselves when all around us seems absurdity. The key to such a living relationship with God our Father is to keep in touch with him by prayerful Bible reading.

Gospel
Turn to the Lord!
Jn 10, 11-18

This reading brings out the idea of salvation with another sign or image, namely, that of the shepherd tending his flock. As suggested in the first reading, do not turn somewhere else, to a hired hand, who lets you down when you need help most.

The Lord Jesus knows you and is concerned. He laid down his life for you. Turn to him in prayer and meditative encounter in your Bible and you will find peace of mind.

5th SUNDAY OF EASTER
Our Union with the Lord in the Community of the Church

WHEREVER physically strong animals like water buffaloes are together in herds, they are said to be harmless. But whenever you meet one alone, an outcast from the herd, you are well-advised to be careful. He might be vicious and attack. Human beings follow a similar rule. A loner, an outcast, easily turns criminal. In order to develop harmoniously as human beings, we need the feeling of "belonging." Alone, a human being is insufficient.

Today's Scripture readings deal with this theme of "belonging." But a Christian who fails to develop relationships on the everyday level usually fails also to develop a sound relationship with God. Children must learn that relating to one another means both listening and talking, both giving and taking. Grown-ups should practice this. Only when they are able to do this in the family, with friends, and on the parish level, can they have a beautiful relationship with God and Christ. It is time-tested wisdom that the supernatural builds on the natural!

Reading I   Acts 9, 26-31
Staying with Them!

If one is acquainted with what Saul, later called Paul, had done to the Church of Jerusalem (see Acts 8, 1-3) one can understand that at his return this Church did not trust him. Only after Barnabas consented to sponsor him was Paul accepted as a disciple. This reading brings out to us that a living relationship with God and Christ alone is not enough. Our relationship with God should be carried by a living relationship with a congregation. Back in Jerusalem, Saul tried to join the disciples. Once accepted, Saul stayed on with them.

Do not try to "go it alone" as a Christian. You need a congregation and the congregation needs you. Without being exclusive, have some Catholic friends who feel about religion as you do. There are very few things we do alone successfully. "I will praise you, Lord, in the assembly of your people" (Responsorial Psalm).

Reading II   1 Jn 3, 18-24
Love Implies Deeds

The sacred author teaches that we should accept all the consequences of being a Christian. Love implies deeds! Only talking about it is not truthful. Faith implies keeping the commandments. Check your conscience!

Gospel

Jn 15, 1-8

"Live On in Me"

Since the Bible originated in a country where vines and grapes were part of the daily scenery, it is understandable that the vine-image is used so often to explain religious values. In this passage it is used to tell us that Christians must live in Christ and let Christ live in them. There should be an "I-Thou," a person-to-person relationship between you and the living Lord Jesus.

As already mentioned (see Introduction) this is possible only if we have first learned to relate to one another. A human openness to others is a condition for openness to the transcendent, God and Jesus Christ. Develop both! Encounter the Lord Jesus in prayerful Bible reading, listening and responding, but also in your fellow human beings.

6th SUNDAY OF EASTER

God Is Love

DID you ever meet a person who told you bluntly that he/she did not believe in love? Social workers, prison chaplains, teachers in both ghetto and middle-class high schools meet such persons all the time. People who do not believe in love often have a sad history behind them. It may be a broken home, parents neglecting them, friends cheating and lovers double-crossing them. Where love was expected, rejection was received! The result is that entirely negative outlook of the lonesome and unhappy outcast.

Today's Liturgy deals with love of God and fellow humans. God loves you but it does not make sense even to mention this if the addressee does not believe in love at all. Love is something that must be learned and experienced from early infancy. It must be developed and fostered first on the human level; only then can it be given its religious dimension of God and (because of God) the neighbor. It is so important that all of us who must be witnesses of Christianity make outsiders first believe in our love on the human level. Only then can they believe in God's love.

Reading I Acts 10, 25-26. 34-35. 44-48
God Shows No Partiality

We learn that God's Spirit of love came down on a Gentile, non-Jew, even before he was baptized. Why does Luke narrate this tradition? He wants to teach first that, authorized by Peter, Christianity should be preached to all without imposing the laws of the Jewish faith upon them, and secondly, that the Spirit can take an initiative wherever he wishes.

Faith in Jesus Christ sealed by baptism is the way to salvation for all who are called. It does not mean that God is unable to bestow salvation outside the framework of organized Christianity. God's salvific will is universal. God's will that all be saved follows the definition of God given by the author of John in the second reading, where he states: "God is love."

Reading II 1 Jn 4, 7-10
Where Does Love Fit In

We want a meaningful life. In today's Gospel our Lord says: "Bear fruit. Your fruit must endure." But in trying to attain your goals in life, where does God fit in? This Scripture states: "God is love." Hence, we could just as well ask: In trying to attain your goals in life, where does "love" fit in? "The man without love knows nothing of God." Only love makes your life meaningful and worth living. Pray for selfless love because it is from God. "Ever-living God, help us to celebrate our joy in the resurrection of the Lord and express in our lives the love we celebrate" (Opening Prayer).

Gospel Jn 15, 9-17
"Live On in My Love"

John teaches us about love of God and neighbor, friendship and complete joy which result in a meaningful life, "bearing fruit." But why do so many fail in love even after starting out so beautifully? Over the years, did they try to listen to one another? Was there an emphasis on mutual understanding, forgiveness after failures, and fidelity to an initial "yes" when it was difficult? Love, like a plant, must be cared for daily; otherwise it withers.

Check your own life, have an honest discussion if necessary, pray and pattern your love after Jesus' example: "Love one another as I have loved you."

◆

ASCENSION

Heaven and Earth

NOT all members of our species have the same outlook on life. There are people for whom this life means everything and "heaven" nothing. Naturally good people, they may cherish love as a great value, but when one breathes his last, that is the end. There are others for whom "heaven" is all-important and this life almost completely unimportant. Save your soul! Many Christians have cherished this outlook, especially concerning others and as long as the self was not involved. Finally, we have those for whom "heaven" is realized already on earth in love.

If we understand Jesus' philosophy of life well, and try to understand the exaltation of his humanity as we celebrate it today, we could give it a try. We may live life, including marital sex and love, as an earthly reality. We may develop our potential as earthlings to its fullest. We may make use of the results of science (sociology, etc.) to achieve a better life on this planet. We may consult marriage counselors and psychiatrists and seek the best medical care available. Yet in our best moments ("disclosure situations"), we know that there must be something more than all of this, a transcending reality.

In faith, following Jesus of Nazareth, we see this "transcending reality" as a loving Father who is waiting for us. He (Jesus) is the beginning: "Where he, our head, has gone, we, his members, hope to follow him" (Preface). "God, our Father, may we follow him [Jesus] into the new creation, for his ascension is our glory and our hope" (Opening Prayer).

B — Ascension

Reading I
Acts 1, 1-11

Lifted Up

The wording of this tradition on the ascension of our Lord is clearly conditioned by the limited understanding of the universe during the writer's lifetime. This wording is not part of divine revelation. There is no absolute up or down. Heaven is not a place somewhere up in outer space. Heaven is a situation outside our concepts of time and space. What the evangelists have tried to do is describe the final appearance of Jesus and/or the fact that the Lord Jesus is "sitting at God's right hand," which is a Hebrew idiom for "sharing power with God." (For both this reading and today's Gospel see the general introduction to the Easter Season, p. 55.)

Luke's message is: Christ has died ("in the time after his suffering"), Christ has risen ("he showed them that he was alive"), Christ will come again ("this Jesus . . . will return"). That is the way we word it in our second Memorial Acclamation at Mass.

Reading II
Eph 1, 17-23

In Heaven

Paul, a learned Jewish rabbi, relates the same message as Luke and the evangelist do in the first and third readings, only he does it in difficult theological language. Paul relates the risen and ascended Christ to all that exists. Christ is supreme, above all creatures, seated at God's right hand (a Hebraism for "sharing power with God").

Paul prays for the Ephesians and for all of us: "May God grant you a spirit of wisdom and insight to know him [the Lord Jesus] clearly."

Gospel
Mk 16, 15-20

Preaching Everywhere

In this tradition, we are told what the mission of the Church is: In continuing the Lord's visible presence on earth, the Church, you and I, must do what the Lord himself has done and wants us to do in his name. By word and example we should preach the Good News.

The signs that accompany the Church's mission over the centuries indicate that the kingdom is established. "The Lord continued to work with them" indicates that Jesus Christ is with his Church until the end of time.

◆

7th SUNDAY OF EASTER
That All May Be One

WHEREVER people are "one," in other words, establish a group, be it a garden club, a sorority, a fraternity, or the family, we may ask: "What motivates such people to come together and stay together?" Bypassing business concerns, we can pinpoint mutual interests and various levels of friendship and love. There is loyalty to the group and a body charged with the administrative and executive work.

The group charged by our Lord to establish God's reign on earth, and though marred by human deficiencies still together after 2,000 years, evokes the same question: "What motivates Christians to come together and stay together?" Today's Liturgy dwells upon this question. As a Christian dedicated to establishing God's reign of love and justice in and around you, you may have doubts about the way groups are organized. A prayerful reading of today's Scripture may help you.

Reading I   Acts 1, 15-17. 20-26
Creative Loyalty

In this reading we find one answer to the question: "What keeps the Christian community together?"—though not the essential one, which is given in the second and third readings. We read that the apostles were concerned to keep the executive branch of the group going. Jesus had appointed the "Twelve" as a sign of "the Israel of God" (Gal 6, 16), the community of followers, and so Matthias would replace Judas, the deserter.

The Church at large, your diocese, and your parish need executive bodies to keep the group together and make its mission of establishing God's reign possible. Believing in organized religion means believing in authority, and, since those in charge are human, accepting the fact that this authority is not perfect. Creative loyalty should guide us when we deal with authority in the church!

Reading II 1 Jn 4, 11-16
Love for One Another

Here we find the essential answer to the question: "What keeps the Christian community together?" It is love of God and neighbor. God abides in us and we in God, if we abide in love.

The sacred author refers to the Holy Spirit, whose outpouring we will celebrate next Sunday. It is that mysterious Spirit of love which keeps us together, especially when we are together to celebrate the Eucharist. "May all of us who share in the body and blood of Christ be brought together in unity by the Holy Spirit" (Eucharistic Prayer II).

Gospel Jn 17, 11-19
Being With Your Church

It is love that keeps the Christian community together and makes its mission in the world possible. Persevering in love, however, is not easy. As long as our Lord was with his little flock visibly, he could guard it more tangibly. But after his ascension into heaven, he is still with us through his prayers. The Lord prays that we we may remain one. He prays that God may protect us and guard us from the evil one: "Consecrate them," or make them holy as priests are consecrated; "I consecrate myself" (I offer myself as a sacrifice to you) . . . , "that they may be consecrated in truth," holy and dedicated to you, God.

Are you loyal to your Church as an institution? Do you contribute constructive criticism if things are not going your way? What about discussing issues with your elected parish board members? Defecting or undermining the group by bitter and destructive criticism has never done any good in history! Be with your Church by your creative fidelity!

PENTECOST SUNDAY

See p. 73.

ORDINARY TIME (cont'd)

See p. 79.

Sunday After Pentecost
TRINITY SUNDAY
The Ineffable Mystery of God

THE first thing our parents taught us about our religion was most probably the sign of the cross. The last thing a priest will do at our graveside is make the sign of the cross over our body. A Christian's life is marked "in the name of the Father, and of the Son, and of the Holy Spirit." The Sunday Bible readings often speak to us about the Father (as originator of all life related to creation), sending his Son or Word (for our salvation) and communicating the Spirit (related to our rebirth from water and the Spirit).

The revelation of God as Father, Son, and Holy Spirit tells us first of all what God is for us. But as to the mysterious unity of Father, Son and Holy Spirit, we can only stammer with inadequate human concepts, which are not able to express the ineffable mystery of God in himself. We want to know. But we must realize that more important than knowing about God the way two beloved know one another! An intimate person-to-person relationship gives a knowledge which cannot possibly be expressed in human terminology. It is that kind of knowledge of God which ultimately satisfies a human being. "How deep are the riches and the wisdom and the knowledge of God! How inscrutable his judgments, how unsearchable his ways!" (Rom 11, 33).

B — Trinity Sunday

Reading I
Dt 4, 32-34. 39-40
Experiencing God

We learn from this reading how the Hebrews experienced God. It is their great contribution that, inspired by God, they experienced him as one. In the beginning, they believed that other nations could have their gods, as is still reflected in this passage ("or did any God venture?"), but gradually the Hebrews became aware that their God was the greatest and finally the only one, the creator of heaven and earth.

The Old Testament did not know about Father, Son, and Holy Spirit. This is a New Testament revelation. However, there is a triple aspect in the experience of this passage: (1) "God in himself, immanent ("on earth below") and transcendent ("in the heavens above"), (2) revealing himself ("speaking from the midst of fire": Ex 3, 2-3), and (3) creating a response in the hearts of the faithful ("keep his statutes").

How do you experience God in your life? It should be an experience in which you are involved like that of the author of the Responsorial Psalm (33, 4-22).

Reading II
Rom 8, 14-17
Led by the Spirit

Paul stresses the difference between a slave and a son, as related to the master of the household. We are related to God as his adopted children. Notice how, in a few lines, Paul expresses an experience of total involvement in the triune God. It should be our approach as well. Our knowledge of God should be an experience in which we are totally involved.

Gospel
Mt 28, 16-20
I Am with You Always

In Biblical thought, discipleship does not mean merely following and learning from a teacher; rather it is seen as establishing a strong person-to-person relationship. It involves faith in the teacher. And, as we learn from this passage, this faith is sealed by baptism. By immersion into the water, the candidate is initiated into the family of believers, intimately related to Jesus, to his Father, with whom he is one, and to the Spirit, who proceeds from both.

B — Corpus Christi

Sunday After Trinity Sunday

CORPUS CHRISTI

Sharing Life with Christ

IN an affluent society basic food such as bread and water is no problem. However, for many people in the world it still is. Thus, they can understand better than we do that it is a real sign of love and care when God intervenes to feed his people. For them, water and bread are a question of life and death. But we are often hungry and thirsty for other values than sustenance of physical life. In a depersonalized society we suffer from absence where there should be presence. We hunger and thirst for companionship, love, concern, mercy, respect which are no problems in the great family of primitive people. Whose need is greater?

Where we suffer from absence, the Lord Jesus wants to be present to us with all the concern and love of a friend for a friend. In the signs of plain daily food for Orientals, water, bread, wine, Jesus indicates what he intends by being present to us. He wants to share life. He wants to strengthen. He wants to mean something to you and me. When we celebrate the Eucharist, we celebrate this mysterious presence of the Lord Jesus with the community. Open up to make "Communion" possible. "Whoever eats my flesh and drinks my blood will live in me and I in him, says the Lord" (Communion Antiphon).

Reading I Ex 24, 3-8
The Blood of the Covenant

This reading points out how the early Christians understood Christ's death on the cross (Reading II) and the memorial of Christ's death and resurrection, the Eucharist (Gospel). The covenant (partnership of God and human beings) is ratified by a sacrifice, in this case young bulls which stand for human beings offered to God. According to the ancients, blood is the seat of life. Moses splashes half of the blood on the altar, symbol of God, and sprinkles the other half on the people, who promise to be faithful to the covenant. "This is the blood of the covenant."

B — Corpus Christi

The New Testament sees God's people as a "New Israel," related to God in a new covenant, new partnership. Be aware that you are God's partner! "God and Sons." And your task is to establish God's reign of justice, love, and peace on this planet, in yourself, and in those for whom you are responsible. We Christians celebrate our partnership-relation with God whenever we partake in the memorial of Christ's sacrifice on the cross at which he shed his blood and ratified the new covenant between God and humankind.

Reading II   Heb 9, 11-15
The Blood of Christ

The sacred author sees our Lord shedding his blood on the cross as a high priest offering God a sacrifice of atonement similar to that of the first reading. Christians of Jewish background were familiar with the activities of the Jewish high priest in the temple of Jerusalem, who entered the sanctuary to sprinkle blood, as Moses did, to ratify the covenant (Reading I).

Jesus on the cross is a high priest. He sheds, however, not the blood of goats and bulls, but his own blood to ratify a new covenant (partnership) of God with "a New Israel," God's people, the Church. Be aware of your beautiful relationship with God, made possible by our Lord shedding his blood in atonement for our sins.

GOSPEL   Mk 14, 12-16. 22-26
My Body— My Blood

The Lord's Supper is a Christian Passover Sacrifice and Sacrificial Repast. It is an anticipated memorial of the Lord's sacrificial death on the cross (Reading II), and we repeat it time and again "in memory." Our Lord's blood was shed in atonement, to ratify a new covenant between God and humankind. "This is my blood, the blood of the new covenant." When you partake in the memorial of Christ's death, make his body and blood present in the signs of bread and wine a token of your self-surrender to God.

As you partake of the Sacrificial Repast, Holy Communion, let it be a real encounter, a growing oneness of mind with our Lord. "In memory of his [Christ's] death and resurrection, we offer you, Father, this life-giving bread, this saving cup. Grant that we, who are nourished by his body and blood, may be filled with us Holy Spirit, and become one body, one spirit in Christ" (Eucharistic Prayer II and III).

10th SUNDAY IN ORDINARY TIME
Evil To Be Conquered

IN any contest it is of the utmost importance that those involved have the firm determination to win. Those who are not sure of themselves lose out. Coaches know this, hence their pep talk to the team with the assurance that they are going to win. Civil rights demonstrators in the sixties often started their marches in church, where they listened to a talk and prayed for strength and determination.

Evil exists and has tremendous power. We feel its strength in us and experience its sinister threat around us. We encounter corruption and pursuit of self-interests where we would expect dedication and fidelity to an oath of office. There is the evil of social injustice, juvenile delinquency, and an ever-rising crime rate. Values such as right to life and fidelity to the marital commitment are openly questioned. And we see rich nations abusing the poor ones shamelessly.

The first and third readings of today call this total phenomenon of evil: Satan—Beelzebul—the serpent. Can we overcome it? Christians should never give up. The reign of God, a reign of justice, love, fidelity, and peace, was initiated in this world, when its Redeemer died on a cross but rose from the dead. Determination is the key to overcoming evil. In improving the world, start with yourself, your family, your direct environment. Your word and example do oppose evil! Then, collectively, see what your parish can do to oppose evil in your community. "We shall overcome, one day," completely, though only in the world to come.

B — 11th Sunday in Ordinary Time

Reading I   Gn 3, 9-15
Overcoming Evils

(For comment, see the Solemnity of the Immaculate Conception, December 8, p. 350.) Notice the promise of a Redeemer, who will overcome evil by striking at its head. The sacred writer is convinced that God will intervene. He knows this from his national history. God has helped his people to defeat enemies and threats of evil so often that he will do it again. Hence, we too can pray: "With the Lord there is mercy and fullness of redemption [from evil]" (Responsorial Psalm).

Reading II   Cor 4, 13—5, 1
"Do Not Lose Heart"

Paul makes a few beautiful statements which may encourage those of us who are getting on in years. He says: "We do not lose heart, because our inner being is renewed each day, even though our body is being destroyed at the same time." Although we are aging, we can continue to grow into even more beautiful persons, in spite of the fact that the agility and physical functions of our body decay. "You," the person you make of yourself now, will live forever. "We have a dwelling provided for us by God—a dwelling to last forever."

Gospel   Mk 3, 20-35
Expelling Demons

The gist of today's Gospel is the ongoing battle between good and evil. Jesus expels demons and indicates that the final defeat of evil, promised for the world to come, has been initiated in our history. But we are part of this battle. "On then Christian soldier" is a hymn we still hear in our churches. Be determined that we shall overcome, since God is with us.

11th SUNDAY IN ORDINARY TIME
Hope

ALL of us have our expectations in life and, related to our hope for fulfillment, our disappointments. Hope implies

B — 11th Sunday in Ordinary Time 185

an element of uncertainty. A student works hard and hopes for a beautiful future. Young people fall in love, discuss their future, and hope to do better than most grown-ups have ever done. Parents rear children and hope to be proud of them. A dedicated social worker hopes to improve society drastically. Christians also have expectations as far as their Church is concerned.

It is important for our hope to be realistic. Hoping too much leads necessarily to disappointment and even despair. Today, we apply this to the reign of God and the Church. We should realize that these two are not the same. The reign of God, a reign of justice, love and peace, is found in the Church. The Church itself, a community of human beings, is not necessarily God's reign on earth. Keeping this in mind, our expectations (hope) for the Church will be realistic.

Hoping for the spectacular, impressive statistics, and dazzling buildings is unrealistic. Hoping for a perfect Church society is a utopia. It leads to disappointment and even defection. The reign of God is a hidden reality. Today's Bible readings deal with the Church and our expectations.

Reading I — The Lowly Tree Lifted High — Ez 17, 22-24

Ezekiel consoles his troubled and despairing fellow citizens with the promise of God's kingdom to come. It will be a kingdom of prosperity and peace, with a Messiah, an anointed king, as God's vicegerent to rule them. Have hope! It is still a tender shoot but it will grow. God can do whatever seems impossible: "I, the Lord . . . lift high the lowly tree, and make the withered tree bloom."

This reading prepares for the Gospel wherein God's kingdom awaited by the Hebrews becomes the Christian reign of God with Jesus as the Christ (Messiah-Anointed King) and God's vicegerent.

Reading II — Walking by Faith — 2 Cor 5, 6-10

Paul also preaches a message of hope: "We continue to be confident." But we must have patience both with ourselves and with our fellow Christians. "We walk by faith, not by sight." Not all members of our congregation do things our way. Do not blame them! Perhaps there will be a few surprises when "the lives of all of us are . . . revealed before the tribunal of Christ."

Gospel
Have Hope and Patience!
Mk 4, 26-34

Christian hope implies uncertainty and requires patience. Ezekiel told his people this when he referred to a Hebrew kingdom of God to come (Reading I). Mark teaches the same lesson. God's word is like a seed in us. Through Jesus Christ he scattered it on the ground. We want this seed (God's word) to bear bountiful fruit in the Church right now.

There are members who leave the Church if things do not go their way. They have in mind an ideal Church with the reign of God already realized in it. But it does not work that way. The reign of God—justice, love, fidelity, peace—is submitted to the slow process of growing (a mustard seed!). Its fully realized splendor will appear only in the world to come. Meanwhile, have hope and patience. If you want to improve the Church, start with yourself.

———◆———

12th SUNDAY IN ORDINARY TIME
Prayer in Faith

MANY of us have experienced the awesome power of a hurricane or tornado. All of us have seen on television what their devastating force can do. Small wonder that in prescientific times people saw God's anger and threat in storms and bad weather. "They cried to the Lord in their distress; he hushed the storm to a gentle breeze, and the billows of the sea were stilled" (Responsorial Psalm). Today, there are still Christians who light a blessed candle and pray to God when thunder and lightning threaten. Nor is this such a bad thing! Prayer in faith is meaningful in any anxiety because it gives strength. God is with us!.

B — 12th Sunday in Ordinary Time

In Biblical times the threatening forces of nature were so automatically related to God that they became the customary imagery used to describe a theophany (manifestation of God). See the great theophany of Mount Sinai (Ex 19, 16-19) and today's first reading where God speaks out of the storm. This same imagery is still applicable. Life can be like a storm. We can lose hope and be on the brink of giving up. The sight of the Church, the bark of Peter, being so frighteningly rocked nowadays may confuse us. But, while we are doing whatever is humanly possible to solve our own problems, we should never forget to pray with faith. "When I called, you [God] answered me; you built up strength within me" (Ps 138).

Reading I   Jb 38, 1. 8-11
Out of the Storm

(For comment, see 5th Sunday in Ordinary Time.) In lengthy dialogues Job and his friends have discussed the mystery of suffering, but no one of them has come up with an adequate answer to the question: "Why must a just man suffer?" Finally, God speaks out of the storm (see Introduction) and asks Job: "Who created the sea?

God is the Lord of creation. He has power to do things which humans cannot explain: "Thus far shall you come but no farther." Job in his suffering should be mindful of this. The reading introduces the theme of the Gospel, where Jesus shows a similar power by stilling the storm.

Reading II   2 Cor 5, 14-17
A New Creation

Paul defends himself against "the false preachers" who have captivated the minds of many in the congregation of Corinth. These preachers regard Jesus as just another miracle-worker. Paul condemns this viewpoint as one made solely "in terms of mere human judgment," though at one time (before his conversion) he subscribed to it himself.

We should look at Christ as the one who "died for all and was raised up," and as such inaugurated the new age. "Anyone in Christ is a new creation." We should regard Christ the way Paul wants us to do and be grateful that we are "a new creation" in Christ.

Gospel   Mk 4, 35-41
"Quiet! Be Still!"

"Who can this be that the wind and the sea obey him?" Jesus has a power similar to the one God claimed for himself in the first Bible reading: "And here shall your proud waves be stilled" (Reading I). "Quiet! Be still!" The wind fell off and everything grew calm (Gospel).

This clearly indicates Mark's answer to the question: "Who can this be?" Jesus is "God with us," and we should turn to him in faithful prayer whenever difficulties overwhelm us.

13th SUNDAY IN ORDINARY TIME
That We May Have Life

ALL of us treasure life as the highest good. We cherish our physical lives. We try to keep ourselves in good shape. Many make regular trips to the doctor and the beautician. We care for the health of our children. We also care for the quality of the life we are living. Mental health clinics are filled to capacity. We do not want to destroy life, yet we do not want a miserable life. Many, though, are not so interested when the lives of others, who are not close relatives, are involved, when they have to go out of their way to improve other people's quality of life.

The quality of human life is measured by the quality of its relations with others. Improving life means actually improving relations, first our relations on the human level (with our marriage-partner, children, parents, friends, co-workers) and then our relationship with God, which is called grace. Being in "the state of grace" means being in good standing with God.

This good standing, close relationship of love with God, is also called "life." Life is a free gift of God to human beings.

Hence, he is the absolute Lord of life. People are merely life's stewards. Today's first and third readings deal with life. "I will praise you, Lord, for you have rescued me" from death, which is alienation from you (Responsorial Psalm).

Reading I Wis 1, 13-15; 2, 23-24
Formed To Be Imperishable

"By the envy of the devil, death entered the world." If we understand this word of Scripture as referring only to physical death, we run into the problem that the righteous also dies. The sacred writer has in mind a spiritual death, which consists in alienation from God and of which biological death is a sign.

It is death by alienation from God, a broken relationship of love, which Jesus Christ overcame by his death and resurrection. Through him human beings who had drifted away can relate to God again in love and have life. This reading introduces the theme of the Gospel on life.

Reading II 2 Cor 8, 7. 9. 13-15
"The Relief of Others"

Paul has promised the Church of Jerusalem that he will take up a collection in the churches he has founded abroad to help the poor of Jerusalem. He urges the congregation of Corinth to be generous and offers motivations for giving. These reasons may also motivate us to be generous in Church support and contribute to help those who are poor.

Gospel Mk 5, 21-43 or 5, 21-24. 35-43
"Little Girl Up"

Mark inserts the healing of the woman with the hemorrhage into the tradition concerning the raising of a little girl. Although both miracles prefigure our salvation, we are here limiting ourselves only to the account of Jairus' daughter. Physical death is a sign of that spiritual death which is conscious aversion from God (Reading I). By overcoming death in this little girl, Jesus prefigures his victory over the death of alienation from God. Mark brings out that Jesus is the prophet of the end-time, who has come to bring life, in other words, to restore our relationship of love with God.

14th SUNDAY IN ORDINARY TIME
The Priest's Ministry

"WHO does that person think he (or she) is?" This remark is often made when a person of well-known humble stock has become a success and issued a statement of some kind. Is it reasonable to act in this way? We know that children do not learn well with a teacher they dislike. Children go by their instinctive likes and dislikes and let these influence their behavior. Adults, on the contrary, should have outgrown them and be able to distinguish between *what* is said, *how* it is said, and *who* says it. However, it is not an easy thing to do.

Listening time and again to the sermons of a priest whom we do not like humanly speaking can be a problem, but one that can and should be overcome. No bishop can guarantee to have pastors available who are liked by all the members of every congregation in a diocese. The priest represents Christ and his ministerial priesthood in our midst. However, no priest is such a saint or genius that he can reflect all the beautiful characteristics of our Lord and be "good" in all the facets of his ministry.

Today's first and third Bible readings deal with this problem. We hope your priest will not have to pray these words with his congregation in mind: "Have pity on us, O Lord. Our souls are more than sated with the mockery of the arrogant, with the contempt of the proud" (Responsorial Psalm). Pray for your priests!

Reading I   Ez 2, 2-5
I (God) Am Sending You

The prophet is God's spokesman, sent specifically by him. Ezekiel is sent as a prophet to his own compatriots, a people "hard of face and obstinate of heart." He is told to preach the message whether they "heed or resist." Not an easy task!

Many prophets have had to suffer. Think of Jeremiah, Isaiah, Amos, John the Baptizer, and modern prophet-like personages. And our Lord himself was no exception, as we will see in the Gospel reading.

B — 15th Sunday in Ordinary Time

Reading II
2 Cor 12, 7-10
In Weakness

Paul encounters problems similar to those of Ezekiel (Reading I) and Jesus himself (Gospel). "False preachers" have confused the congregation of Corinth. They have bragged about supposedly having received extraordinary revelations from God. Paul, on the contrary, will boast of nothing except his physical situation which is miserable: "And so I willingly boast of my weaknesses instead, that the power of Christ may rest upon me." He thus invites his converts to see in him Christ whom he represents.

God's word to us is: We should do the same wherever people preach the word of God.

Gospel
Mk 6, 1-6
Their Lack of Faith

Jesus is shown as being unable to accomplish much in his hometown because of the people's lack of faith. Why does Mark recount this tradition? He has no intention of entertaining us. Guided by God, he wants to teach his word. It may be as follows: Without faith it is impossible to be aware of the truth and the sacred in our midst.

A child, a hobo, a neighbor, a coworker, any person even without formal education can teach us the truth. Do we accept it? Faith is of the utmost importance when we are listening to our priest. (See Introduction.)

15th SUNDAY IN ORDINARY TIME
Acceptance and Rejection

WHAT do you expect from the Church, which is not only the hierarchy (the leaders) but all of God's people, you and I included? What is its mission? There are conflicting ideas. Many are in favor of a kind of civil religion ("ole time religion"?) which stands for the status quo and stern patriotism.

We think of political prayer breakfasts, worship services in the White House, and of how civil religion would approach the draft evasion versus how it should be done in the light of the Gospel.

After the Second Vatican Council, there is a clear change, of course. The Church is stripping itself of the many human-made burdensome matters that had accumulated over the centuries and designedly going back to a more original evangelical pattern. Change causes friction. This is necessary and even good. Both "progressives" and "conservatives" in the Church need one another's corrective attitude. The bond of love and mutual respect should keep us together.

Reading I   "Off with You!"   Am 7, 12-15

In this passage we see two opposing conceptions of religion. Amaziah, the priest of the sanctuary in Bethel (the Northern Kingdom of Israel), favors a religion that stands for the status quo, is loyal to patriotism, and is loath to "rock the boat," which might upset the constituency. Amos, an "outside agitator" (from Judah, the Southern Kingdom), preaches the word of God and does not follow the line of smooth talkers. He blames the congregation for its social injustice, and consequently is expelled from the sanctuary.

Read also Amos 2, 6-8; 4, 1-5. His fate points to the Gospel, where the Twelve are told that something similar could happen to them.

Reading II   Eph 1, 3-14 or 1, 3-10
"To Be Full of Love"

Paul outlines a beautiful picture of who we are as Christians. We should be grateful for our election as God's adopted children and have understanding when preachers of the Gospel constantly refer to it. They are not allowed to water down the message in order to avoid hurting feelings!

Gospel   Mk 6, 7-13
If Not Being Received

The mission of the Twelve consists in preaching the need for repentance, which necessarily implies confrontation with evil. In addition to preaching, mention is made of exorcism (expelling demons), and healing, including anointing. The possibility of not being accepted (as was true of Amos) should be considered.

What is the mission of the Church? It is similar to that of the Twelve and Amos of the first reading, and we should consider whether or not a "civil religion" fits this mold.

◆

16th SUNDAY IN ORDINARY TIME
As a Shepherd Tends His Flock

A HIGH school teacher, discussing the importance of mutual care in the family, mentioned the nightly television flash: "Do you know where your children are?" and a senior snapped: "They'd better ask: 'Do you know where your parents are?'" So many youngsters drop out of our impersonal and anonymous society to join communes! Broken families and homes where parents have no time for their children are not without guilt concerning this phenomenon.

Nobody can live in the vacuum of loneliness. We need care. Parents should provide it. Wherever possible, we should try to personalize situations in which we are together as human beings: schools, offices, jobs, church.

Using the familiar image of shepherd and flock, the Bible readings emphasize the necessity of a real person-to-person care, which all of us need.

Reading I   Jer 23, 1-6
"You Have Not Cared"

Jeremiah attributes the woes that beset Israel (defeat and deportation) to lack of leadership. The kings of Judah, shepherds in the name of God, have failed in tending the flock. Remember that in Biblical thought the king was the Supreme Shepherd's vicegerent on earth (Responsorial Psalm). Where he fails, disaster follows.

But Jeremiah foresees an ideal king to come. He will be a righteous shoot of David (of the dynasty of the great King David). He shall govern wisely and do what is just and right in the land. The early Church saw this vision ultimately fulfilled in God's ideal vicegerent, the Lord Jesus, a shepherd who really cares (Gospel).

Reading II   All Welcome?   Eph 2, 13-18

Paul teaches that Jews and Gentiles ("you who once were far off") were brought together by Christ. It is he "who made the two of us [Jews and Gentiles] one by breaking down the barrier of hostility that kept us apart." He abolished the law (all the rules of the rabbis) to create *one* new man from us, who follows the great universal law of love for God and neighbor, on which "the whole law is based" (Mt 22, 40).

Why do we read this passage which deals with an issue (Jews and Gentiles) of 2,000 years ago? Perhaps the Bible with God as author wants to question us about a current similar issue. Can people of a different race feel welcome in your congregation, or do they go home with the feeling that they were just politely tolerated?

Gospel   Mk 6, 30-34
Sheep Without a Shepherd

The image of shepherd entails first of all the idea of ruling, but it also implies the notion of feeding and providing. In the Sunday liturgy, the Lord Jesus shepherds by teaching his word during the Liturgy of the Word, and by "spreading the table before us" (Responsorial Psalm), during the Liturgy of the Eucharist. Jesus still has compassion for any vast crowd which is like sheep without a shepherd, but he has only us to show this.

Do we make everyone, especially visiting strangers, feel at home in our congregation? Does your congregation have a committee of members to welcome strangers? What about your handshake of peace? What is done to give young members a feeling of belonging? Your parish council could look into this.

17th SUNDAY IN ORDINARY TIME
The Hand of the Lord Feeds Us

EATING together not only signifies togetherness but also sustains and promotes it. It constitutes a beautiful means of communication. One must have been exposed to a warm and animating table fellowship time and again to savor it as an inspiring symbolism of person-to-person relationship. Happy the family that still insists on at least one meal together every day! It should be a meal begun with a blessing and, if possible, concluded with a short Bible reading and spontaneous meditative prayer. The family that prays (eats) together stays together!

A well-understood table fellowship at the family level is a prerequisite for appreciating the table fellowship of the Eucharist and the Biblical banquet symbolism which describes the end-time (Mt 22, 1-10). Today's first and third readings utilize the symbolism of eating to bring out a message. "The eyes of all look hopefully to you [O Lord] and you give them their food in due season; you open your hand and satisfy the desire of every living thing" (Responsorial Psalm).

Reading I 2 Kgs 4, 42-44
"They Shall Eat"

This beautiful little tradition prefigures the miraculous feeding of the Gospel. Notice that the bread is multiplied to feed the poor!

Reading II Eph 4, 1-6
Preserve Unity!

From prison Paul exhorts the congregation of Ephesus to preserve unity. We symbolize our oneness as congregation when we celebrate the Eucharist. "Make every effort to preserve that unity." All should heed this plea: grown-ups and young people, progressives and conservatives, charismatics and those who favor a less emotional way of living the message! "May all of us who share in the body and blood of Christ be brought together in unity by the Holy Spirit" (Eucharistic Prayer III).

Gospel
Jn 6, 1-15

"Fed with Five Barley Loaves"

Just as Moses fed the people in the desert by giving them the miraculous manna, our Lord, the new Moses, re-creates that ancient desert wonder and feeds the crowds in the wilderness. Like Elisha (Reading I), Jesus does not have enough, but he organizes the meal anyway. He presides, as he does at our Eucharistic Celebration, when we break Bread together.

Does our participation in the Eucharistic Banquet really promote togetherness with fellow Christians? Where two-thirds of our fellow humans are hungry, we should never go home without thinking of them. We break Bread with our Lord, but should also do it with our brother or sister in need. "God, our Father, help us to cherish the gifts that surround us, to share your blessings with our brothers and sisters and to experience the joy of life in your presence" (Alternative Opening Prayer).

18th SUNDAY IN ORDINARY TIME
The Lord Gave Them Bread from Heaven

WE can look at flowers in various ways. For example, I can see them from the viewpoint of a florist, a painter, or an artist who loves to arrange them. When I see flowers in church, I take them as symbols of life. When I glimpse flowers around a casket, I regard them as symbols of sympathy and signs of the resurrection. If flowers are sent to me as a present, they become for me a symbol of attention, love, and friendship; accordingly, I will love these flowers and think of the person who did me this honor.

We should develop a feeling for symbolism since it plays such an important role in religion. Water, bread, wine, salt, yeast, fire, light, rain, dew, thunder, lightning—time and again these are used to impart a message and when properly understood they do so more efficiently than theoretical concepts can do. Symbolism contains an intuitive (suggestive) power which appeals not only to the intellect but to the total person, heart and mind.

B — 18th Sunday in Ordinary Time

Today's readings utilize the symbolism of bread to bring out the message that God wants to feed us, to take care of us on all levels of human existence. "The Lord gave them bread from heaven" (Responsorial Psalm).

Reading I
Ex 16, 2-4. 12-15

You Shall Have Your Fill

Wandering through the desert, living the life of nomads, God's people had to rely on God. The author is a keen observer of the human condition. Human beings can be like ungrateful children who take love and care for granted and complain when things fail to go their way. Prudent parents understand. They know that maturation is a slow process and they help the child on its way to adulthood.

God's word in this tradition brings out to us that growing toward maturity in Christ is a lifetime process. As long as we are a pilgrim Church, wandering through the desert of life, we must work hard to attain such maturity. But God is with us, providing bread and quail, in other words, giving whatever in his infinite wisdom and love he knows we need.

READING II
Eph 4, 17. 20-24

Learning Christ

"That is not what you learned when you learned Christ." Note that Paul does not say: "when you learned *about* Christ." No, you learned Christ, whom you accepted as a person in faith, with all the values he stands for.

Christianity is not primarily a doctrine to go by; it is a person-to-person relationship with our Lord. Partaking in the Eucharist, the bread of life, should help us to "learn Christ" ever more intimately.

Gospel
Jn 6, 24-35

Food for Life Eternal

Jesus states that he is the manna, that bread from heaven which human beings need on their way through life. Feeding the crowd was a sign which those who had eaten did not understand. Patiently, our Lord explains: "You should not be working for perishable food but for food that remains unto life eternal. . . . I myself am the bread of life."

We should be aware of this whenever we encounter our Lord in the signs of bread and wine. "Lord, you give us the strength of new life by the gift of the eucharist. Protect us with your love and prepare us for eternal redemption" (Prayer after Communion).

◆

19th SUNDAY IN ORDINARY TIME
Christ Our Viaticum, Food for Our Journey

LOOKING back to our past, we remember people we have met. Some of them hold a prominent place in our memory. They are people who have meant something to us: our parents, a parish priest, a schoolteacher, an aunt or uncle, a close friend, or someone who helped us make a difficult decision, one perhaps that determined the course in life we have chosen. The latter may have been a friend who stood by us in dark moments of life or a teacher who with patience and understanding convinced us to finish our education. We are grateful to these people, and we realize that we would be different persons if we would not have met them.

Suppose you would not have met Christ? What would be your outlook on life? It is difficult to visualize this since we are part of a culture that is so deeply rooted in the Judaeo-Christian tradition. Even without knowing it, many live by Christian values. But without Christ in our lives we would be entirely different.

Again using the symbolism of bread, the Bible readings bring out what Christ means to us. "Taste and see how good the Lord is; happy the man who takes refuge in him" (Responsorial Psalm).

Reading I 1 Kgs 19, 4-8
"Strengthened by That Food"

The prophet Elijah is depressed. Queen Jezebel has forced him to get out of the kingdom. In fear, he is fleeing for his life. On his journey through the desert to the mountain of God,

B — 19th Sunday in Ordinary Time

Horeb, he is strengthen by a hearth cake and a jug of water provided by the Lord. "Then strengthened by that food, he walked forty days and forty nights."

God's word in and through this tradition could be: On our lifetime journey to the mountain where we hope to meet God, we need the food, which today's Gospel indicates as Christ, the bread of life.

Reading II   Eph 4, 30—5, 2
"Don't Sadden the Holy Spirit"

"Follow the way of love, even as Christ loved you." Serious Christians are concerned with the great value of love as the value without which there can be no lasting happiness. It is the quintessence of Christ's message. What kind of person would I be if I would not have met Christ? (See Introduction.)

Let us not be like children, who take wealth for granted. God chose you and me, but he did so freely, not out of necessity. Let us show our appreciation by being guided by the precious insight that there is no greater value than love.

Gospel   Jn 6, 41-51
Christ the Bread of Life

Using the symbolism of bread, Jesus indicates that we need him on our journey through life. "I [Jesus] am the bread of life. . . . If anyone eats this bread he shall live forever." In other words, a person closely related to Jesus Christ will not die the death of alienation from God. (See comment on Wisdom at 13th Sunday in Ordinary Time—B.) The essential condition for this is faith (trust) in the Lord Jesus: "He who believes has eternal life."

Christians see the Eucharistic bread and wine, signs of Christ's mysterious presence to us, as a viaticum, "food for our journey" to the mountain where we hope to meet God (Reading I). Gratefully, we should "take and eat it" as the Lord has told us to do.

20th SUNDAY IN ORDINARY TIME
The Eucharistic Celebration

ABSENCE, alienation, loneliness, communication gaps are the ailments of modern life. We yearn for presence and the loving care of a person who is close by. The great consolation which Christianity offers to mankind, haunted by the threat of alienation, is that God is close by, Emmanuel, in Jesus Christ.

The Lord Jesus is always present in his Church, especially in the liturgical celebrations. He is present in the sacrifice of the Mass, not only in the person of the minister, but especially under the Eucharistic species. By his power he is present in the Sacraments, so that when a person baptizes it is really Christ himself who baptizes. He is present in the word, since it is he himself who speaks when the holy Scriptures are read in the Church. He is present, finally, when the Church prays and sings, for he promised: "Where two or three are gathered for my sake, there am I in the midst of them' " (Mt 18, 20) (Vatican II, *Constitution on the Sacred Liturgy*, 7).

Whenever you feel the need of presence, and perhaps have been disappointed on the human level, know that Jesus Christ is present to you. Turn to him in faith!

Reading I   Prv 9, 1-6
"Come, Eat of My Food!"

Personalizing Wisdom and Folly as two women (a figure of speech used in many literatures of the world), the author has both of them invite guests to a banquet. This passage concerns the invitation of Wisdom; verses 13-18 of the same chapter deal with the invitation of Folly to her banquet.

Human beings are free in their choice of where to go. Eating the food of Wisdom and drinking her wine makes human beings live. Sharing the table of Folly, know "that in the depths of the nether world are her guests" (v. 18). This reading relates to the Lord's banquet in which he himself is the living bread (Gospel).

B — 20th Sunday in Ordinary Time

Reading II — Eph 5, 15-20
Togetherness

In order not to act like fools and not to continue in ignorance, we should be filled with God's Spirit and sing praise to the Lord with all our hearts. Our communal worship services should inspire us. We need one another's inspiration. That is why we should not skip Mass without serious reasons.

Each of us is responsible for an inspiring worship service. We are there *together*, listen to God's word *together*, pray and sing *together*, partake in the Eucharist celebration *together*, not only to get inspiration, but also to give it to others by the mere seriousness of our presence. A Christian alone is unthinkable. Only through togetherness and a sense of belonging do Christians live up to their name.

Gospel — Jn 6, 51-58
Real Food—Real Drink

This is the third consecutive Sunday that we are reading from the "Discourse on the Bread of Life" as we have it in the sixth chapter of John's Gospel. The previous two portions of this discourse were primarily figurative references to our Lord's teaching and referred secondarily to the Holy Eucharist. In this reading we have reference to how the early Church and the Lord Jesus himself saw the Eucharistic Banquet. "The man who feeds on my flesh and drinks my blood remains in me, and I in him." By his mysterious presence our Lord heals the wounds caused by absence and alienation. (See Introduction.)

By your participation in the Eucharistic Banquet time again, Jesus' presence to you should become ever more intimate, a closer sharing of life together. "God of mercy, by this sacrament [Eucharist] you make us one with Christ. By becoming more like him on earth, may we come to share his glory in heaven" (Prayer after Communion).

◆

21st SUNDAY IN ORDINARY TIME
The Risk of Faith

ENGAGEMENT, bethrothal, and marriage imply the faith which two young people have in one another. Though there are and should be reasons for this mutual faith, it cannot possibly be thought out logically. Attempting to do so would destroy the intuitive element of love in it. Dissecting a rose results in insight but kills the beautiful flower in the process. Applying this remark to our faith-relationship with God, we observe that faith is not understanding but taking the risk of the engagement. We have reasons for faith. In our best moments intuitively we feel there must be a transcendent element in reality—an ultimate reality. But the ultimate reason for faith escapes analytical thinking.

Like love, faith also knows its dark moments in which we think that God is absent, maybe even "dead." Great mystics have gone through this and in their writings refer to it as "the night of faith." It is not God who causes doubts and uncertainty, but our own frail human condition which blurs our vision so often.

Today's Bible readings deal with the faith-love commitment. Keep it exciting and alive as long as you live. "Taste and see the goodness of the Lord" (Responsorial Psalm).

Reading I   **Jos 24, 1-2. 15-17. 18**
Faith—Experience

After Moses' death, Joshua took over as army commander and led the Hebrews into the Promised Land. Those who had been wandering nomads settled down as farmers. This reading describes the covenant at Shechem, a renewal of the Sinai Covenant. The people pledge their faith-commitment not to the local gods of the country they have invaded, but to Yahweh, the God of their fathers. Notice that the "why" of this faith-commitment is not calculation but the concrete experience of God's goodness.

As always, we ask: Why do we Christians read this tradition in the Bible? The answer is that, guided by God, the Bible

B — 21st Sunday in Ordinary Time

wants to teach us through this narrative about our own faith-commitment which cannot be founded on deliberate prudence, but ultimately only on a mysterious interference of God in our lives.

Reading II — Eph 5, 21-32
Love and Faith Interrelated

Many a bride, choosing the readings for her Nuptial Mass, may object to this traditional reading. The idea that "wives should be subject to their husbands" seems contrary to the ideals of most contemporary women. However, we should not forget that God's word is necessarily conditioned by time and culture. Paul reasons from the patriarchal marriage setting of his time, which as such is not part of God's revelation. We should pay attention to the core of the message, which focuses on love as most essential in marriage and as giving a different color to everything married people do.

Referring to Genesis 2, 24 ("the two of them became one body"), Paul states that this text has a higher level of meaning and portrays the unity of Christ and the Church, from which we should understand the earthly reality of marriage. Keep in mind that love (mentioned in this reading) and faith (Reading I and Gospel) are interrelated. There is no love without faith and no faith without love. Both should be dealt with in the same way. (See Introduction.)

Gospel — Jn 6, 60-69
"We Have Come To Believe"

This is the conclusion to the "Discourse on the Bread of Life" which we have been reading for several Sundays. Note that "flesh" does not refer to the Eucharistic "flesh" of the passage of last Sunday. It is simply "nature" in us which cannot give eternal life. Jesus speaks here about faith in him, the bread of life.

God's word to us could be an invitation to spontaneous faith: "Lord, to whom shall we go? . . . We have come to believe."

22nd SUNDAY IN ORDINARY TIME
The Human and the Divine Element in Religion

ON leaving the safe family setting and going to college, many young intellectuals begin to have doubts about their religion. An agnostic professor may make a sneering remark about "The Good Book"; fellow students, though ostensibly Catholics, may show by their behavior that they could not care less about religion. Although there are many reasons for such confusion in young minds, one may be that many do not make a distinction between what is God-made and what is human in religion, especially as we used to live it in the Catholic tradition

Basic Christianity is a beautiful way of life, but many object against the way it has been institutionalized over the centuries. Many human-made details were added and some of them are/were undoubtedly outdated. The renewal movement begun by the Second Vatican Council aims at divesting the Church of human baggage picked up along its path through history. Naturally, this requires sound and informed leadership in order not to "dump the child with the bathwater," in other words, in the process of cleaning not to do away with divine elements.

As the saying goes: "Pope John wanted to open the windows to let in fresh air, not to throw out the furniture!" Young and old should update themselves. If programs are available, take part in them, or ask your parish council to take constructive initiatives.

Reading I   Dt 4, 1-2. 6-8
Observing the Law Intelligently

Meditating on the Law of Moses, the author of Deuteronomy saw the danger of human traditions, usually created by pious and well-intentioned churchmen, which could obscure the original will of God for his people. In your observance of the commandments of the Lord, "You shall not add to what I command you nor subtract from it."

From the Gospel we learn that the Pharisees and experts of the law in Jesus' time had not heeded this advice of Deuteronomy too well. The Responsorial Psalm (15, 2-5) mentions a few things which cannot be done away with.

B — 23rd Sunday in Ordinary Time

Reading II Jas 1, 17-18. 21-22. 27
Worship without Stain!

The sacred author stresses that the word of God is a genuine benefit from above, freely given by God. If this word is humbly welcomed in faith, it will save us. But we should do more than just listen to God's word. We should also live it.

Gospel Mk 7, 1-8. 14-15. 21-23
Ongoing Church Renewal?

This passage, as we have it now in Mark, consists of two pronouncements. In the first one Jesus castigates the experts of the law for the countless human-made traditions they want the faithful to follow. "You disregard God's commandment [love for God and neighbor?] and cling to what is human tradition." In the second pronouncement, Jesus refers to the human-made dietary laws of the Jewish Religion, the *prohibition* of certain foods (e.g., pork) that would make people impure and not fit to partake in cultic worship.

In the early Church, Christians of Jewish origin tried to impose these laws on Christians of Gentile background! Mark does not agree and refers to Jesus' statement that only what comes out of people (evil words and actions) makes them unclean. In both cases, Jesus stresses the relativity of human tradition versus the divine elements in religion. What is your attitude toward Church renewal? (See Introduction.)

23rd SUNDAY IN ORDINARY TIME
The Healing Activity of Our Lord

A HEALTHY person, who seldom or never needs a physician, finds difficulty in understanding the anguish, frustration, and never-to-be fulfilled desires of the physically handicapped. In primitive societies and prescientific times, the condition of the handicapped was even worse than it is today. There were no rehabilitation programs for them, no wheelchairs or any equipment that gave them at least some relief. Since religious beliefs

B — 23rd Sunday in Ordinary Time

regarded their misery as related to sin and moral guilt, they were often outcasts for whom nobody cared.

We find it altogether natural, therefore, that the writers of the Bible used the wretched situation of the lame, the blind, the deaf, the epileptics, and the lepers (all of whom they believed to be in the power of demons) as a figure to describe humankind's alienation from God, and the healing of these people as the sign of God's powerful and caring presence. Ethically speaking, we could be like some of those handicapped. Pray that the Lord may open your ears to listen to his message.

Reading I
"He Comes To Save You"
Is 35, 4-7

This passage is attributed to Second Isaiah and addressed to the exiles in Babylon, who are about to go home. The return from exile was seen as God's redemptive act, hence one accompanied by miraculous healings as sign of God's redemptive presence. "Here is your God, he comes to save you."

Later the early Church applied this poem to the saving ministry of Jesus, and we have an example of this in today's Gospel. Human beings, handicapped in various ways, turn to God and pray with the words of the Responsorial Psalm (146, 7-10).

Reading II
Discrimination?
Jas 2, 1-5

James has some advice for the hospitality committee of your parish and for all of us. Can strangers, people of other races, young and old feel welcome or are they just tolerated in your church? What can you do?

Gospel
Deaf to God's Word?
Mk 7, 31-37

We must be careful to note that Mark wants us to see the miracles of Jesus as signs of a hidden reality to come. Jesus is not like the traditional miracle-workers circulating in his day; his miracles are not ends in themselves. Mark brings this out by having Jesus order silence time and again after each miracle. Hence, we must meditate on what Mark wants to teach by relating this tradition.

We offer a few suggestions. We may know some people who are deaf to God's word. As the friends of the deaf man did, we could make them acquainted with our Lord. The reading shows that Jesus is concerned; he takes the handicapped man aside and heals him utilizing some of the gestures which healers of the time also use and are thus likely to be understood by the poor man before him who is undoubtedly a pagan (symbolism of our Sacraments!).

Are you concerned about those who are deaf to God's word? You could talk with them and introduce them to your priest.

24th SUNDAY IN ORDINARY TIME
Taking Up Our Cross

OUR affluent society does all it can to do away with the reality of suffering. In the eyes of those who are blind to the transcendent, suffering and pain are incompatible with happiness. Funeral homes make it their profession to blur suffering. Medical science alleviates pain, the drug commercials on television advertise their painkillers and sleeping pills, and dope peddlers make it possible to escape a harsh reality. Not all of this is bad. It is service to alleviate pain, to arrange a worthy funeral, and to pray to God for help when we suffer.

However, we should regard as un-Christian an attitude which desires at any cost or with dubious means (dope abuse) to do away with both mental and physical suffering that is unavoidable! Since our lives are patterned after the life, death, and resurrection of our Lord, we should in faith be willing to die with him (die to our egotistic selves, which is a painful process, and accept unavoidable suffering) in order to live with him forever. Today's Bible readings deal with the theme of taking up our cross and following in our Lord's footsteps.

B — 24th Sunday in Ordinary Time

Reading I
Is 50, 5-9
"I Have Not Rebelled"

This reading is taken from the third song of the Servant of Yahweh. As mentioned at the feast of the Baptism of Our Lord, it is not clear whom the inspired writer had in mind when he composed these four songs describing the ideal Servant (Son) of God. Is he a collective person: Israel, God's people? Is he a king of the past or the Messiah (anointed king) to come? In any case, the Christian community applied these hymns very early to Jesus.

The song used today introduces the Gospel theme on the necessity of taking up our cross and following the Lord Jesus who suffered and died for us. "I fell into distress and sorrow, and I called upon the name of the Lord, 'O Lord, save my life' " (Responsorial Psalm).

Reading II
Jas 2, 14-18
Faith Without Works Is Useless

James teaches that faith without good works is no good. Real Christian charity, going out of your way to help the other, may require sacrifice which we should not shun, as the other Bible readings tell us.

Gospel
Mk 8, 27-35
Taking Up Our Cross

Mark, writing 40 years after our Lord's resurrection, time and again has Jesus imposing silence on others, sometimes about his miracles and other times (as here) about the fact that he is the Messiah. This represents a literary device which Mark uses to teach that Jesus' real Messiahship was fully revealed only by his death and resurrection.

In this tradition as Mark relates it, Peter cannot combine the idea of suffering with that of Messiahship. Jesus corrects him in clear language and teaches all Christians about taking up our cross and following in his steps. We should think of this when things do not go our way and pray for strength.

25th SUNDAY IN ORDINARY TIME
Church Management Is Service

WHEREVER people establish a group, the necessity of management arises. No enterprise can do without it and the executives of any group are human beings, hence subject to human failings, such as jealousy and strife. Furthermore, they will "manage" according to a pattern which they are used to in their own time and culture. The Christian movement came into being in the Roman empire, hence institutionalized itself according to the pattern of which it was a part—Roman law and order. In the feudalistic Middle Ages with its pompous and splendiferous kings, Church management shaped itself automatically after that system. And the Church in the United States is today inclined to manage dioceses and parishes as General Motors manages its enterprise.

From the very beginning, the Founder of the Church, the Lord Jesus, had to remind his human coworkers that his movement to establish the reign of God on earth should not be managed by human standards alone. Today's Gospel tells us that the twelve apostles had been arguing about who was the most important! Jesus' words to them on this occasion give us an idea of how he envisioned the management of the Church—from the parish council level to the diocesan and as far as the top or Vatican level!

The key characteristic of his type of Church management is *service*. All of us are the Church. All of us should be active in parish activities, but always guided by the desire to serve!

Reading I Wis 2, 12. 17-20
Let Us Try His Patience

The setting is the city of Alexandria in Egypt, a port town with a sophisticated Greek culture; the time about 50 B.C. There was a Jewish congregation there, a minority, which because of its own way of life had its opponents. Some Jews tried to find a middle way, compromising between pagan culture and the rules of their Jewish faith; others remained strict and very faithful Jews. This led to friction and even violence.

The early Church applied this passage to Jesus Christ, the Son of God, in a very special way. As such, it introduces us to the theme of the Gospel: service and suffering as part of Christian life, if one takes it seriously. If in serving the congregation, we incur disappointments caused by human strife and jealousy, we should pray with the psalmist: "For haughty men have risen up against me. Behold, God is my helper" (Responsorial Psalm).

Reading II   Jas 3, 16—4, 3
Jealousy and Strife?

James refers to what can happen in any parish organization. Jealousy and strife may be part of it. "You envy and you cannot acquire, so you quarrel and fight." Church workers should go by the rules Jesus lays down in today's Gospel.

Gospel   Mk 9, 30-37
"The Servant of All"

Mark has fashioned this tradition of Jesus and the earliest disciples to teach his Church (about 70 A.D.) that Jesus was not just a divine miracle-worker and that certain spectacular preachers should not be seen as his genuine successors. The task of the Church is ministry (i.e., service) which must imply humility, more or less the simplicity of a child, and even readiness to suffer!

The Church as institution the committee on finances included, is not General Motors! In Church enterprises we must go by rules the Lord Jesus has given us. Whenever we take part in Church activities, we should keep this service idea well in mind.

26th SUNDAY IN ORDINARY TIME
Open-Minded Respect and Love for All

IT seems to be an inborn instinct to mistreat and disqualify people who are different from us. Let a bearded and long-haired youngster or a lady whose dress code is not ours appear and immediately eyebrows are raised! The more isolated life is, be it geographically in rural areas or socially by self-imposed isolation (the railroad dividing black and white sections of little towns in the South or the inner city versus the suburbs of the North), the more narrow-minded and biased people are, even to the extent of expelling the "outside agitator" violently ostracizing him socially.

This very thing happened to our Lord, who came to his own "yet his own did not accept him" (Jn 1, 12). He was *different*. In his hometown of Nazareth the people even became hostile. "They found him too much for them" (Mk 6, 3). Being a Jew, our Lord would be refused membership today in many a country club! Over the centuries, Christian denominations have isolated themselves socially. Small wonder then that they mistrust one another. An imprudent proselytism may have contributed to religious bias as it still exists in our country, though the ecumenical movement has done much good by trying to eliminate a "ghetto mentality" which has been with the Churches for a long time.

Today's Bible readings deal with this topic. Since bias (whether social, racial, or religious) is so subtle, we should check ourselves honestly and pray: "Cleanse me from my unknown faults" (Responsorial Psalm).

Reading I
Nm 11, 25-29
"Are You Jealous?"

The "spirit" in this passage is not the Holy Spirit. It is a "charism to prophesy," which is somehow related to God. Moses enjoyed this charism and shared it with the seventy elders. But this spirit was directly given to some others also. Joshua did not take it, which made Moses ask: "Are you jealous?"

As God's word to us, this tradition teaches that God's gifts are not limited to certain people only. It introduces the theme of the Gospel, which deals with the same issue.

B — 27th Sunday in Ordinary Time

Reading II   Jas 5, 1-6
"Your Wealth Has Rotted"

In this reading James has severe words of warning for the rich who exploit the poor. A generous Church contributor who sins against social justice in any form is a hypocrite. Underpaying domestics and soothing our consciences by giving them the leftovers of our food and some old clothes is a crime against justice.

Since this sin too can be "hidden," pray with the psalmist of today: "Cleanse me from my unknown faults" (Responsorial Psalm).

Gospel   Mk 9, 38-43. 45. 47-48
No Ghetto Mentality

The spirit (charism) to expel demons was given to Jesus and his disciples first, but also to others. John did not like it and tried to stop one who had it from using it. Jesus said in reply: "Do not try to stop him." We should learn to see God's Spirit at work wherever we meet good people. "For or against Jesus" does not necessarily follow Church-denomination lines, but acting honestly according to one's conscience. "Anyone who is not against us is with us," be it often anonymously!

This does not blur the truth as we see it in the Catholic tradition; it simply recognizes that a ray of truth and much goodness are found everywhere. We should respect and love every conscientious person no matter how different he or she may be!

27th SUNDAY IN ORDINARY TIME
Unshakable Fidelity

IN a rapidly changing world, many values are questioned. One of them is the lasting marriage commitment. There is no doubt that the outlook on marriage has changed with a changing culture. The patriarchal marriage pattern of the Bible is no longer our own. The point is: What can be changed in marriage and what constitutes its core which cannot be called

B — 27th Sunday in Ordinary Time

into question? Our Lord's statement in today's Gospel: "Let no man separate what God has joined," is the rule Christians follow.

The New Testament gives the Church the authority to make a few concessions that are pastorally necessary. Rather than going into the matter of complicated exceptions (ask any priest for literature!), let us meditate on the beauty of commitment, in other words, the reason why the law was made. Much depends on how one looks at the cherished value of freedom. For some, freedom claims unshakable fidelity; for others, freedom is incompatible with a definitive commitment.

We should check which opinion is most in line with the dignity of the human person and assures the happiness of all involved, wife, husband, and children. Even more depends on what role love plays in one's life and on the art of keeping it exciting!

Reading I — A Suitable Partner — Gn 2, 18-24

In this beautiful allegory that teaches the oneness of husband and wife, it is the man as God's coworker who gives a name (meaning) to all of creation, in particular to sex. "Rib" suggests that both male and female belong to the one human race. "Flesh" and "body" in the Bible stand for the whole person. Hence, "become one body" refers to more than the physical union. It indicates also the total oneness of two persons.

Notice that the author of this passage, who lived after the Babylonian exile, had a more advanced view on the dignity of the woman than many writers after him. He sees the woman as a suitable partner for the man, which clearly suggests equality. In today's Gospel our Lord refers to this passage.

The Responsorial Psalm (128, 1-6) pictures an ideal marriage, one as it should be. Married people should never give up pursuing ideals!

Reading II — Called Brothers! — Heb 2, 9-11

The next seven Sundays we will read from the Letter to the Hebrews. Its author writes for Christians of Jewish background. He wants to strengthen their faith and to encourage them to grow with the Christians of Gentile origin into Christian maturity. The author refers to many details of Jewish worship (e.g., the Jewish high priest officiating in the Jerusalem temple), which his readers were familiar with and we can understand only if we read our Bible.

This passage describes what Jesus has done for us Christians. "God made our leader [Jesus Christ] in the work of salvation perfect" (that is, he made him achieve his goal to save us) through his suffering on the cross.

Gospel Mk 10, 2-16 or 10, 2-12
Becoming as One

In this reading we have a section on marriage followed by a section on the family. As far as marriage is concerned, we should constantly search for the values which underlie the law of lasting fidelity. We should utilize all the means which nature, sound sexology, and religion indicate. They should be used to keep marriage an exciting event. By living the earthly reality of their marriage as it should be done, Christians should be a beacon for so many who waver in their commitments.

As far as family life is concerned, children are part of marital fidelity and happiness. Accepting "the kingdom of God" on marriage presupposes some of the spontaneousness of love which children possess and grown-ups have so often lost.

28th SUNDAY IN ORDINARY TIME
Renunciation and Stewardship

A SONG from the musical *Godspell* has these lines concerning Jesus of Nazareth: "See [know] him more clearly, love him more dearly, follow him more nearly." Millions have done so over the centuries and countless others are still doing so today; and all have found the key to a meaningful life. In the Catholic tradition we know of two life-styles in which Christians search for meaning and happiness.

B — 28th Sunday in Ordinary Time

One of them is marriage, which is the life-style of most people. Facing life together, they try to see the Lord Jesus more clearly, love him more dearly, and follow him more nearly through the good stewardship of all the beauty and goodness of life that God has bestowed upon them. The other life-style, for those who are called to it, is "celibacy for the sake of the kingdom." It is a life of renunciation not as an end in itself but for a life of discipleship.

If they are well understood, both life-styles should witness to the same Christian mystery, namely, God's reign of justice, love, and peace as already initiated in human history. Today's Scripture readings deal with the issue of life-style.

Reading I   Wis 7, 7-11
A Good Philosophy of Life

Figuratively, the author puts these words into the mouth of King Solomon. The king had asked for wisdom, which in Biblical language is not only learning but practical skill and insight as well. Actually, it stands for a good philosophy of life, which is worth more than wealth or comeliness, if one does not know how to manage it prudently. The rich young man of the Gospel narrative did not understand this.

Wisdom is a gift of God for which we should pray: "Teach us to number our days aright, that we may gain wisdom of heart" (Responsorial Psalm).

Reading II   Heb 4, 12-13
We Must Render an Account

God's word to us insists on a decision. By their life-styles Christians should witness to real values that lead to happiness—in Biblical terms, values that witness to the reign of God as initiated already here on earth.

Whether married or celibate for the sake of God's reign, our way of life should be marked by that all-penetrating word of God. Someday we must render an account!

B — 29th Sunday in Ordinary Time

Gospel   Mk 10, 17-30 or 10, 17-27

A Challenge

Apparently, the rich young man of this reading was searching for something. Jesus challenges him to a life of total renunciation, which he cannot accept. Peter and the Apostles have accepted it and Jesus gives his vision of this kind of life.

And what about those who are wealthy and do not feel able to live a life of renunciation? Can they be saved? It is difficult, because of the innumerable pitfalls. But "with God all things are possible." They should keep the commandments, in other words, exercise good stewardship.

29th SUNDAY IN ORDINARY TIME

Being of Service

"OUR business is to serve you"—we see this advertised in enterprises of various kinds. From the local gas station up to the congress, service is offered. Those who serve us in government are called "public servants." The Prime Minister of Great Britain is the "First Servant" (minstry means service) of the nation. Professional service is offered by physicians and psychiatrists with a few days later a substantial bill in the mail.

The business of the Church is also to serve. Time and again our Lord emphasizes this aspect. What is the difference between service as mentioned above and the ministry (service) of the Church? It should be the quality of service and the personal touch in it, though many public servants, doctors, nurses, salespeople, waitresses, and bank tellers "serve" as true Christians should—with dedication and a personal touch. If so, they are the "Church of Christ" and carry out what our Lord says in today's Gospel: "You must serve the needs of all."

Our service is more clearly Christian when no bill follows. We do such a free service to a poor or suffering person whenever possible; children should do it to parents. Church workers, religious, and priests offer free service wherever service is needed.

B — 29th Sunday in Ordinary Time

Reading I
Is 53, 10-11

My Servant

This passage is taken from the fourth of the Servant Songs of Second Isaiah, which have already been encountered on Palm (Passion) Sunday. (Consult the commentary there.) This part brings out the idea of Jesus in today's Gospel that the Church (you and I) is there to serve.

Christian service implies self-denial and sacrifice, giving of self, sharing not only money but also time and concern, to an extent even that it may hurt. Jesus has done so and that is why the Church applies this song to him and all of us, his followers is service of "the brethren."

Reading II
'Heb 4, 14-16

Finding Help in Time of Need

As already mentioned (see 27th Sunday), the author is writing to Hebrews, meaning Christians of Jewish (Hebrew) origin. He refers to the Jewish high priest, who entered the sanctuary of the Jerusalem temple time and again to offer a sacrifice to God, and says that now Jesus is our high priest, who entered the sanctuary of heaven to pray for us.

To be sure, he (Jesus) is man and knows what it means to be a weak human being. Hence, turn to him confidently in time of need!

Gospel
Mk 10, 35-45 or 10, 42-45

Aspiring to Greatness

What makes a person really great? Society lays down rules for greatness: success in business, a charming personality, physical beauty, exellence in the performing arts. One must have done something spectacular! Our Lord has a few ideas of his own: "Anyone among you who aspires to greatness must *serve the rest.*"

We may admire those who are great in unselfish service to others. But do we realize that Jesus' statement is also directed to us, and that service which makes us great in eyes of God does not have to be spectacular?

30th SUNDAY IN ORDINARY TIME
Rabboni (Teacher), I Want To See

"I HAVE never seen it that way," we might exclaim when a friend opens our eyes. "I did not know him/her that well," we might murmur when circumstances have shown us some beautiful facets of his/her personality which we had overlooked during years of social contact. Meeting good persons may change our lives. Such persons may open our eyes to values we have overlooked. They may broaden our way of looking at things and encourage us when we are "down in the dumps." They may show us danger where we do not see it.

The miracle narratives of the Gospel tell us about deprived and unhappy people who started a new life once they had met our Lord. Have you "met" our Lord to such an extent that he fascinates you, that you are convinced that doing things his way will brighten your life? Pray that your eyes may be opened to see it! Blindness of mind may deserve blame, if it is caused by indifference and lack of care.

Reading I "A Father to Israel" 'Jer 31, 7-9

The setting is the long-awaited homecoming of the Israelites from their exile in Babylon. "Shout with joy for Jacob [Israel, God's people]." The author never lost trust in God that sometime or somehow he would heal the wounds of his people. The weak, lame, and blind (see Gospel!) are with the returning exiles. God cares!

The fact that "God cares" is also God's word to us now. "The Lord has done great things for us; we are filled with joy" (Responsorial Psalm).

Reading II Heb 5, 1-6
Christ Representing Human Beings to God

(See two previous Sundays.) The author refers again to the Jewish high priest officiating in the temple of Jerusalem. He represents human beings to God by offering gifts and sacrifices. It is stated that Jesus is the high priest of the community and as such appointed by God.

B — 31st Sunday in Ordinary Time 219

Jesus exercises his priesthood in heaven. Constantly referring to his sacrificial death on the cross, he pleads for mercy for all of us.

Gospel   Mk 10, 46-52
Healing Christological Blindness

Mark wrote his Gospel to heal a certain "Christological blindness" in the Church of his day. Spectacular preachers, themselves a kind of miracle-workers and faith healers, had come along. They preached Jesus as a divine miracle-man and themselves as his successors. Mark did not find this picture of Jesus compatible with Jesus as he really was: the one who redeemed us by his suffering, death, and resurrection. Hence, Mark describes Jesus' miracles as signs that indicate a spiritual reality.

In the healing of the blind man the reality is the healing of a "Christological blindness," a blindness of mind which kept Mark's congregation from seeing Jesus as he really is.

———◆———

31st SUNDAY IN ORDINARY TIME
Two Loves Not To Be Separated

NO value in human life has been sung about so much as love. Poems, songs, and novels of all literatures of the globe deal with it endlesslsy. Almost no motion picture leaves it unmentioned. Jokes caricature it, wise sayings try to define what love really is, and suicide/murder quite often follows upon the failure of love. Hebrew literature, that is, the Bible, is no exception. It deals often with love, but relates it constantly to its deepest root, love of God.

Especially in the awareness of the New Testament writers, love of God and neighbor cannot be separated. "Whoever loves God must also love his brother" (1 Jn 4, 21). Any attempt to separate these two loves is bound to fail in Christian experience. "If anyone says, 'My love is fixed on God,' yet hates his brother, he is a liar" (1 Jn 4, 20). And the other way around, loving the brother, but not paying enough attention to God in prayer and worship, results in failure as well. Many a social worker has tried to love God mainly or only "horizontally" (i.e., in the brother or sister). Usually this does not last long. When frustrations undo our best efforts to love others, love of God is needed to keep going.

Today's first and third Bible readings deal with this issue. Do you balance your love for God and neighbor in such a way that it is lasting?

Reading I "Love the Lord!" Dt 6, 2-6

The Hebrews saw themselves as related to God in a sacred partnership, called covenant. God had chosen them to be his partners. In this passage, Moses emphasizes their part of the deal: Fear the Lord (meaning: pay filial respect to . . .) and keep his commandments. In the second part of this passage, we have the so-called "Shema, Israel—Hear, O Israel." It is the daily Jewish prayer.

This passage mentions only love of God. One may miss reference to love of the neighbor. It is found in Leviticus 19, 18. In today's Gospel Jesus refers to both. Clear awareness that both loves are closely interrelated is a New Testament awareness. "I love you, Lord, my strength" (Responsorial Psalm).

Reading II Heb 7, 23-28
Forever Making Intercession

The attempt to explain what Jesus means to us with reference to the functions of the Jewish high priests in the Jerusalem temple is a very fecund one. Christians of Jewish origin to whom this letter was addressed understood clearly what the author was talking about. The condition for us to savor this comparison is that we be acquainted with our Bible by regularly reading it.

On the altar of the cross our Lord offered himself once and for all as a sacrificial lamb to God. Hence, there is no need to offer new sacrifices day after day as formerly was done in the temple of Jerusalem. In the Eucharistic celebration, Jesus' sacrificial intercession in heaven is made present. Make it a symbol of *your* love for God and neighbor (Reading I and Gospel).

Gospel

Mk 12, 28-34

Love for God and Neighbor

The scribe states: "[Love for God and neighbor] is worth more than any burnt offering or sacrifice." This is a Jewish hyperbolic (exaggerated) saying for: "Sacrifices which are routine and void forms have no value." Isaiah makes the same kind of strong statement (Is 1, 13). The meaning is that formalism and void symbols in religion are worthless.

The conclusion, however, is not: "Stop praying and worshiping!" Rather the clear lesson is: "Love God in your neighbor and show him/her your love directly in meaningful prayer and worship!" Do both and your love will be lasting.

◆

32nd SUNDAY IN ORDINARY TIME
Self-Giving to God

A PRIEST was asked: "Father, how much should I spend on my wife's Christmas present?" In plain language the answer was: "If you love her, you know. And if you do not love her, give nothing!" Around Christmas, Mother's Day, and Father's Day millions are made on our desire to express our affections for loved ones by giving presents. ("Say it with flowers!") Giving is a beautiful symbolical way of saying: "I love you—I am grateful—I'm sorry, forget what has happened!" expressing meanwhile a whole gamut of feelings in between.

Mainly in primitive cultures, we see that people use a similar symbolism of giving to placate and favor their gods. They offer the gods sacrifices of food, lambs, bulls as a sign of submission, and atonement for sins, as a preliminary to asking them for favors. The Jews offered daily sacrifice in the temple of Jerusalem to Yahweh the God of Israel. Small wonder, then, that the Jewish writers of the New Testament have used this well-known symbolism to explain the redemptive act of Jesus' suffering and death on the cross.

They saw Jesus' act of freely accepting his death as similar to the function of the Jewish high priest who offered lambs to

God. Hence, Jesus was seen as our high priest and simultaneously as the lamb of God who takes away the sins of the world. Understanding this ancient symbolism is a condition for intelligent Bible reading.

Reading I 1 Kgs 17, 10-16
The Symbolism of Giving

Both tradition and the Gospel for today deal with the symbolism of giving. Most important is not what you give, but why you give. All giving should symbolize self-giving. In both stories "poor widows" are giving a little, but it is precious in God's eyes, because it stands for a generous giving of self.

We learn from this tradition as God's word to us: "Make your giving to God always a meaningful symbol of genuine self-giving." Then God will reward it, as we read in the Responsorial Psalm (146, 7-10).

Reading II Heb 9, 24-28
An Everlasting Gift to You

(See also the previous five Sundays!) The author elaborates on the Jewish high priest and his function in the temple in Jerusalem: offering lambs to God and carrying the blood of those lambs (seat of life for the ancients!) into the sanctuary. (See also Introduction.) The author compares our Lord with the Jewish high priest and his activities. The sanctuary, however, is heaven, where Jesus prays for us and refers to his sacrifice, which he offered once and for all on the cross.

Our Lord and his sacrificial prayer are present to us in the Eucharistic celebration. (See 20th Sunday.) In partaking we pray: "[God] we offer you in thanksgiving this holy and living sacrifice. May he [Christ] make us an everlasting gift to you" (Eucharistic Prayer III). Make every Eucharistic celebration an act of genuine self-giving to God through our Lord Jesus Christ.

Gospel Mk 12, 38-44 or 12, 41-44
Jesus' Idea on Giving

This tradition deals with two kinds of people as they were found in the Jewish synagogues and perhaps still are found in our churches: the scribes, desiring front seats in the synagogues, and the poor widow, "contributing more than all the others who donated to the treasury." Jesus offers his idea on giving! See comments on the first and second readings. This lesson is the same.

33rd SUNDAY IN ORDINARY TIME
Hope for a Brighter Future

THE fall of the year prepares us for the great death of nature about to come. It is the time of "The Last Rose of Summer left blooming alone. All of their lovely companions are faded and gone." During this nostalgic season, the Church invites us for several Sundays to meditate on the great themes of the end. Death will come for all of us. There will be a final judgment.

Is this a message which shocks us? Is reminding us of the end also Gospel, good tidings? Yes, since we Christians know that whatever happens, no destruction is final. New roses will bloom on the same apparently dead bush. The seed dies in the soil in order to bear new life.

The Bible readings chosen for this season are often so-called "apocalyptic (revelation) literature." This sort of "underground" literature which the author uses to console and encourage his fellow faithful suffering persecution because of their religious convictions. He speaks in symbols, utilizes allusions and indirect references which are known to the insiders but not understandable to the persecutors. We must try to hear "God's word" also in this kind of "human word," though it requires some effort. In it, God wants to give hope for a brighter future to believers of all ages.

READING I   Dn 12, 1-3
"The Wise Shining Brightly"

The setting of this book is Israel occupied by the Syrians, who tried to impose Greek language, culture, and religion on the Jews. Many of the faithful Jews chose death rather than accept the pagan gods or violate the Mosaic Law. By using a mythological language of speech, a language with double and veiled meanings (see Introduction), the writer offers a message of hope. God will help—if not in this life (many chose death!), then in the hereafter. "Some shall live forever, others shall be an everlastinsg horror and disgrace."

The message to us, when we are depressed: Have faith in God. "Keep me safe, O God; you are my hope" (Responsorial Psalm).

Reading II   Christ Praying For Us   Heb 10, 11-14 18

(For comment, see previous six Sundays.) ["Jesus] took his seat at the right hand of God" is a Hebraism, which means "Jesus shares power with God in heaven" where he prays for us. Knowing this gives us hope in our often confused human condition.

Gospel   A Message of Hope   Mk 13, 24-32

Both the theme and the language are the same as in the first reading: A message of hope, offered in apocalyptic language (see Introduction). "The sun will be darkened . . . ," etc., are familiar Biblical images to describe God's awe-inspiring greatness. (See 11th Sunday —A, Reading I.) The setting is the early Church, harassed by persecutors. Though mistakenly, Christians are still expecting Christ's second coming in their own lifetime. Mark consoles his congregations with a message of hope: Christ will come.

What is God's word to us? We are not an occupied country; there is no Church persecution in our land; neither do we expect Christ to return during our own lifetime! We might suggest: The tribulation and distress, which besets the Church today is not the same as in Daniel's and Mark's time, but could be similar. We think of defections, criticism, unbelief, flight into Eastern religions, and escape into drugs. Do not despair. Have hope! The final achievement of God's saving purpose cannot be thwarted by human beings: "The heavens and the earth will pass away, but my words will not."

———◆———

B — Christ the King

Last Ordinary Sunday
CHRIST THE KING
God's Reign in the Process of Being Established

ARE you satisfied with the achievement of your Church? First, we should make a distinction between Jesus' movement to establish God's reign of justice, love, and peace on earth, and the Church as institutionalized over the centuries. Let us confine our question to the Christian movement as such and ask again: Has it achieved its goal of establishing God's reign on earth during the 2,000 years of its existence? The answer is obviously: We may speak only of a partial success! Seeing so much evil around us, we cannot state that God's reign of love, justice, and peace has been fully realized on planet earth. But was the Christian movement designed to be a one-hundred percent success?

In today's Gospel, Christ, stating that he is king, says also: "The reason why I came into the world is to *testify* to the truth." Earlier our Lord had said that the Church would be like yeast in dough (Mt 13, 33). The dough is the world. Jesus never promised that the whole world would become yeast! The Church (God's people), as yeast in the dough, should have a constant uplifting impact in the community in which it is situated, and testify to the truth! If you have an uplifting impact, wherever you are, and testify to the truth by word and example, you are establishing God's reign of which Jesus Christ is the Messiah, the anointed king.

Reading I   Dn 7, 13-14
"His Dominion Everlasting"

The setting is the same as in Daniel's reading of last week. Using apocalyptic language, the author wants to encourage people in trouble. (See Introduction of last week.) "Son of man" is God's people, standing before the throne of the ancient one (God). We shall overcome! One day, the Syrian empire will be destroyed, and Israel will "receive dominion, glory, and kingship." In later literature the concept "Son of man" becomes a heavenly agent of judgment and salvation, and finally it is applied to Jesus Christ. The author of Revelation (Reading II) applies this passage to the final, end-time victory of Christ and God's people.

The Responsorial Psalm (93) refers to God's kingship. The Church applies it to God's kingship as invested in Christ the King. As such we pray it today.

Reading II   "Ruler of Kings"   Rv 1, 5-8

Again we deal with apocalyptic language. (See Introduction of last week!) The imagery is clearly borrowed from Daniel. The author wants to encourage his fellow faithful, as Daniel does, but he does so by referring to Jesus Christ. "Alpha and Omega" are the "A" and "Z" of the Greek alphabet, hence mean: "I am the first and the last."

Note that final victory over all the peoples of the earth will only be achieved at the end, when Christ will present to his Father "an eternal and universal kingdom: a kingdom of truth and life, a kingdom of holiness and grace, a kingdom of justice, love and peace" (Preface of Christ the King). Be part of it!

Gospel   "You Are a King?"   Jn 18, 33-37

Jesus was crucified on the charge that he claimed to be a Messiah, freedom-fighter. Pilate's inscription: "Jesus the Nazorean the king of the Jews," placed on the cross, was a sarcastic warning to all Messiah-pretenders to be careful, if they planned to revolt against the mighty Roman empire. Jesus reinterprets what kingship means to him. It is not political in character!

Note Jesus' statement that he came to testify to the truth. His kingdom (the reign of God) will never be fully realized on earth. There will always be evil and enemies of the good. Jesus is king, though, and shares power with God (in Hebrew idiom "sits at God's right hand"). In heaven he constantly intercedes for us "and waits until his enemies are placed beneath his feet" (Heb 10, 13), which will happen at the end of time. God's word, conveyed in this passage, may be as suggested in today's Introduction.

YEAR C

ADVENT SEASON

See p. 7.

1st SUNDAY OF ADVENT

"By Patient Endurance You Will Save Your Lives" (Lk 21, 19)

THE virtue of patience is not as a rule one of the strong points of people today. They want things to be done quickly and efficiently. Promises and appointments should be kept as accurately as they were made; otherwise an outburst of impatience may follow. We have all experienced the impatient and compulsive driver behind us who takes unreasonable chances and causes disaster quite often. Patients in a hospital or nursery obviously must practice the virtue of patience. They have to wait for recovery patiently and when they are old or sick for a long time they often have to wait for company or friends with even more patience.

A classic example of impatience is that of the Jews at Mount Sinai. In waiting for Moses' return from the mountain, they lost patience and constructed the golden calf. They said to Aaron: "Come, make us a god who will be our leader" (Gn 32, 1).

Advent is a time of waiting for the coming of Christ. Promises have been made to us about a way out of our distress. Salvation will come, but when? We pray, but does God listen? The Advent Bible readings deal with this problem. Waiting for somebody to come, i.e., Jesus Christ, supposes patience. We must accept the human condition of "not yet" with the patient hope for better things to come.

Reading I — "We Shall Be Safe" — Jer 33, 14-16

"I will raise up for David a just shoot." King David's dynasty came to a fall with the destruction of Jerusalem by the

Babylonians in 586 B.C. It was like a stump. But from that stump God will let grow a shoot. A new Davidic king will be on the throne of Israel. Meanwhile, the Hebrews were in exile in Babylon. They knew God's promises, but were tempted to lose patience when time dragged on. Christians see this promise fulfilled with the coming of Jesus Christ. Then Judah, Jerusalem, God's people, received lasting salvation.

But this salvation is only initiated in all of us. Full salvation from all evil and perfect bliss with God will be ours with Christ's final coming for you and me. When, depressed by life's tribulations, you are tempted to lose patience, make the Responsorial Psalm your prayer! "God, for you I wait all the day."

Reading II 1 Thes 3, 12—4, 2
"At the Coming of Our Lord"

The Christians of Thessalonica were waiting for Christ's return during their lifetime. Many lost patience and did not live blamelessly. Paul prays that God may strengthen their hearts, so that they may be holy at the coming of our Lord Jesus.

Advent is a time of repentance, a change of attitude, if necessary. We wait for Christ's renewed coming at Christmas and in one perspective his final coming which will be final for you or me at the moment God calls! "All-powerful God, increase our strength of will for doing good, that Christ may find an eager welcome at his coming" (Opening Prayer).

Gospel Lk 21, 25-28. 34-36
"Be on Guard!"

The core of this tradition comes from Jesus, but it has been embellished extensively by oral tradition and the editing by Luke, who adapted it to the needs of his congregations. As mentioned before, signs in the sun, moon, and stars, gathering clouds, and the shaking of powers in the heavens constitute the familiar imagery utilized by Biblical writers to describe the awe-inspiring event of manifestation of the divine. The early Christians expected the return of Christ to take place in their own lifetime. They were waiting, ran out of patience, and gave in to laxity (characterized by Luke as indulgence, drunkenness, and worldly cares).

What is God's word to us in this passage? It is true that we do not expect Christ's second coming right now. However, it is equally true that God can call you and me the moment we least expect it. That moment represents "the great day" for each of us. "Be on guard."

◆

2nd SUNDAY OF ADVENT
All Mankind Shall See the Salvation of God

IN our computerized society each necessity for change is carefully calculated. One wants to avoid mere chance. Every step in a new direction should be pondered on its pros and cons first. Hence, one is suspicious of any prophetic enthusiasm. Prophets see the necessity for change in a society, but, according to the calculators, they are motivated too much by intuition and great visions of a better future. Nevertheless, in order to have things done, we need the prophetic element.

We need men like St. Francis of Assisi, who did not calculate but by a life of poverty effected a change in the Church back to evangelical simplicity. We need women like St. Catherine of Siena, who counselled the Pope on evangelical values and was listened to.

The society of Jesus' time was waiting for a change. John the Baptizer initiated Jesus' mission (Gospel). Both were assassinated! But we need the prophets' intuition, their enthusiasm and dedication to a better future. Share it! The moment you start thinking: "It will last for my time," you are old and stale!

Reading I   Bar 5, 1-9
"Up, Jerusalem!"

The writer of the Book of Baruch actually lived during the 2nd or 3rd century B.C. However, he made use of a fictitious setting: the Babylonian exile from which the people were delivered, in order to get his message across to the Jews who were in Egypt at this time. Life in the big cities was not easy for the Jewish minority groups. In enthusiastic and poetic language, the sacred author encourages his fellow faithful: "God will show all the earth your splendor."

He sets forth a prophetic vision which we can easily apply to ourselves. "Jerusalem," the capital of Israel, stands for God's people, you and me. We should "look to the east," toward the rising sun, which in the Christian tradition signifies Christ, the light of the world. The message of Advent is faith in a better future. Christ will come. With this in mind, let us make the Responsorial Psalm (126, 1-6) our Advent prayer of hope.

Reading II   Phil 1, 4-6. 8-11
Your Priority of Values

Paul writes about "the day of Christ Jesus." It is the day of Christ's coming. In waiting for his coming, Christians must "learn to value the things that really matter." What is the priority of your values?

During Advent we prepare for the Lord's coming at Christmas and his final coming to each of us. Could you explain your priorities if the Lord were to call you right now? (See the example of John the Baptizer in today's Gospel!)

Gospel   Lk 3, 1-6
Making Ready the Way of the Lord

Luke relates John the Baptizer's call to be a prophet, i.e., God's mouthpiece or spokesman. In God's name, he is to deliver a message of repentance. Change in attitude is necessary to make ready the way of the Lord. Later, Jesus himself will inaugurate his mission with a call for repentance (Mk 1, 15).

John was committed to his task. He did not preach only what people wanted to hear. He openly rebuked King Herod for wrongfully living with his brother's wife and this zeal for God's law cost him his life (Mk 6, 14ff). Calculators would say: "He should have been more careful!" But men like John with their great visions and enthusiastic commitment have changed the world!

Do you consider "commitment" as a value? It does not mean that you should give up planning. We need both the calculations of the computer and the commitment of the prophets!

While waiting for Christ and his ideals to spread throughout the world, we should seek creative participation in his mission. John prepared for Christ's mission. We should continue it, so that all mankind will "see the salvation of God."

3rd SUNDAY OF ADVENT
"God Is Indeed My Savior; I Am Confident and Unafraid (Is 12, 3)

LIFE could be compared with a doctor's waiting room where people tell one another about their ailments. It could be the emergency room of a hospital where a mother waits with a sick child. She shares her anxiety with others whom perhaps she does not even know. This is the instinctive need for concern. Everyone hopes that the doctor can help and take away fear and anxiety.

Life is a waiting room, and Christians make themselves more aware of this during the time of Advent. All of us have our ailments and anxieties, like the rich people (having "two coats"), the tax collectors, and the soldiers of today's Gospel. We wait for Christ's coming into our lives. Hope for salvation is an integral part of the Christian life-style. And this hope is founded on our firm faith that somebody is concerned!

"Cry out with joy and gladness, for among you is the great and Holy One of Israel" (Responsorial Psalm). In Jesus Christ, God shows us his real face, namely, that of a concerned father and friend.

Reading I Zep 3, 14-18
God Will Save Us

This reading invites "daughter Zion" (Zion is the holy temple mountain in Jerusalem, hence stands for God's people) to rejoice because salvation from all enemies and evil is at hand. We should read this passage to inspire our Advent awareness that God will save us.

Life has meaning. It can be beautiful. "God indeed is my savior; I am confident and unafraid" (Responsorial Psalm).

Reading II
"God's Own Peace"
Phil 4, 4-7

"The Lord himself is near." Whatever our ailments and anxieties are (see Introduction), we can turn to him. "Dismiss all anxiety from your minds." Rejoice, because we Christians know to whom we should turn for peace and happiness. This reading offers a "crash program" for your preparation for Christmas.

Gospel
Full of Anticipation
Lk 3, 10-18

We see by this reading that there were people who reacted to John the Baptizer's sermons. "What ought we to do?" In searching for meaning in life, we ask this question too. It all depends whether or not we are "full of anticipation." Do we look at a future? Do we believe in Jesus to come, who will baptize us (immerse us) in the Holy Spirit and fire?

There are wheat and chaff also in our lives. With our doubts, problems, and anxieties, we should turn to the Lord Jesus. He is concerned. Immersed in the Holy Spirit, we should come to new life! Christmas could be a new start for us.

4th SUNDAY OF ADVENT
Faith and Obedience of Mary To Be Followed

WHEN candidates for public office are campaigning, they often bring their wives and children into the picture. They expect that their family setting will tell the voters something about them as persons. And when they have been elected to office, they make their first public appearance with their wives. What we are as persons is greatly influenced by the human beings to whom we are related. Many great men admit that they forged their career through the inspiration of their wives.

The New Testament writers describe Jesus of Nazareth as a celibate. There was no wife who inspired him to greatness.

But a woman is mentioned, namely, his mother Mary. Luke states: "[Jesus] was obedient to them [his parents]. . . . [He] progressed steadily in wisdom and grace before God and men" (Lk 2, 51-52). It was Mary who reared the man Jesus.

In preparing for the Lord's coming, we do not leave Mary out of the picture. It was her faith and obedience which made the incarnation of God's Son possible. Mary's faith and obedience should also inspire us to greatness as Christians.

Reading I　　　　　　　　　　　　　　　　Mi 5, 1-4
Coming Forth From . . .

Because of the great traditions of the Golden Age of Israel with David as its fabulous and astounding king, expectations for freedom and new self-determination in Jewish thought were always connected with a restoration of David's dynasty-house-throne. The Messiah, God's vicegerent, who will bring salvation to Israel, must be a descendant of David. "You, Bethlehem-Ephrathah. . . ." King David came from Bethlehem.

Israel is waiting for the birth of the Messiah. Hence, she is likened to a woman in labor. But "until the time when she who is to give birth has borne," Israel will be ruled by other nations: "The Lord will give them up." Christians see this oracle fulfilled in the birth of Jesus who brought final salvation. Waiting for the coming of the Messiah, we make the Responsorial Psalm (80, 2-3. 15-16. 18-19) our own prayer.

Reading II　　　　　　　　　　　　　　　Heb 10, 5-10
Coming To Do Your Will

(See commentary on Reading II for the 29th to 32nd Sundays in Ordinary Time—B.)

Christ took a body in order to be able to sacrifice himself in total obedience to God. This reminds us of the reason for the incarnation, which is closely related to our Lord's sacrifice of atonement on Golgatha. Bethlehem and Calvary cannot be separated. We learn what is most characteristic about Jesus: "I have come to do your will."

Gospel

Lk 1, 39-45

"The Mother of My Lord"

Filled with the Holy Spirit, Elizabeth calls Mary "blessed," because of her faith and the obedience with which she bore her child. The Second Vatican Council's *Constitution on the Church* states: "Mary devoted herself totally as a handmaid of the Lord to the person and work of her Son." By her faith and obedience to God's design, Mary was the great woman behind Jesus.

On the 2nd Sunday of Advent, we learned about the commitment of John the Baptizer. Today we learn the same virtue from Mary. Preparing for the Lord's coming and accepting him implies a total commitment to what he stands for.

CHRISTMAS SEASON

See p. 14.

CHRISTMAS

See p. 15.

Sunday in Octave of Christmas

HOLY FAMILY

Family Life

WE are witnessing a breakdown of the traditional family and its values—filial respect for authority, exercised responsibly by parents—and a rising juvenile delinquency. Hence, our society can learn a few things from today's Bible readings. Of course, there is no easy available remedy for today's family crisis. Also, the Christian family is part of a culture in which human beings participate—neighborhood, school, television, friends and recreation patterns. But in stormy weather a ship may get at least some guidance from a beacon. And though authority from the earliest infancy on should be exercised perhaps in a different way, it should not be completely eliminated. Parents could discuss this with their children. A substitute for sound family life has not yet been offered by any of the behavioral sciences.

Today's readings on the family necessarily reflect the patriarchal family pattern, hence the subordinationist family ethic, of the Biblical culture. We should distinguish between the core of the Christian ethic and the cloth in which it is wrapped. This cloth is conditioned by time and culture and is not necessarily part of the divine message. But the message on family life as such is timeless.

Reading I   Sir 3, 2-6. 12-14
Filial Respect

By keeping in mind that the point of this passage (God's word to us) is conditioned by time and culture, a modern Christian can succeed in learning from it. Respect, reverence, and love are values that should be cherished. Take care of your parents when they are old. Show love and care, even if you soothe your conscience with the fact that they are well taken care of in an old people's home far away! "Happy are those who fear [show filial respect to] the Lord and walk in his ways" (Responsorial Psalm). Nature, hence God, wants the family!

Reading II   Col 3, 12-21
Family Bible Reading

The holy family, Jesus, Mary, Joseph, must have cherished the values brought out in this Bible passage. "Let the word of Christ dwell in you." Why not try regular family Bible reading, with a discussion afterward and an improvised prayer by one member of the family at the end.

The idea of wives being "submissive to your husbands" may not appeal to "woman lib"; however, where there is genuine love, constantly fostered, a mutual pattern of "doing the loving thing" spontaneously originates. Love and bitterness are incompatible.

Gospel
Lk 2, 41-52

Accepting in Faith

Entire villages joined the annual Passover pilgrimage to Jerusalem. It is quite normal that Jesus' parents did not worry about their son till the first night on their way home. Jesus listened and asked questions. At twelve, a year before his "bar mitzvah," he had learned the Torah, the Law of Moses, and its interpretations by the rabbis. "In my Father's house" indicates the close personal relationship between Jesus and the Father. Mary had to realize that Jesus was not simply her son, but the Father's Son, who had a special mission which would mean separation and pain for her.

"They did not understand" indicates that Mary did not understand Jesus as God's Son from the very beginning. In faith she had to accept a mystery, which became clear only in the light of the Easter event. Christmas, God sharing our human condition, is a mystery which we must accept in faith, as Mary did.

―――――――◆―――――――

January 1 to the Epiphany

See pp. 23-27.

Sunday after the Epiphany

BAPTISM OF THE LORD

The Servant of Yahweh

EVERY time we discover a new aspect in one we love, we stop in wonderment. "I did not know him/her as such!" And this deeper insight and sharing in a person's self results in greater appreciation, intimacy, and love. Today we celebrate the Lord's baptism by John in the Jordan. Matthew relates Jesus' baptism as another epiphany (manifestation), declaring

C — Baptism of the Lord 237

that the Lord Jesus is the servant (Son) of Yahweh. His call in life is that of the Servant as depicted in today's first reading.

This is an aspect of Jesus' personality which gives us a deeper insight into who our Lord is. He is "the man for others." He is there for you and me. Experiencing this in prayer, we should appreciate and love our Lord more for it.

All of us have our own calling in life. We must respond to it in the framework of our personal capabilities and the circumstances of time and milieu. Serious and mature people understand that only a life of service is a meaningful life. What do you consider your main calling in life, and how do you fulfull it? "Almighty, eternal God, keep us, your children born of water and the Spirit, faithful to our calling" (Opening Prayer). Today's feast marks the end of the Christmas season.

Reading I   Is 42, 1-4. 6-7
A Call to Service

It is not clear what kind of person the inspired poet had in mind when he depicted an ideal servant of God in the four "Servant Songs," as we have them in Isaiah. Is it the whole nation of Israel? Is it some prophet or king of the past? Is it a Messiah (Anointed King) to come?

Reapplied by the evangelists and the Church, the Servant is identified with Jesus, who is manifested as God's beloved Servant (Son) in baptism. The song depicts what the Lord Jesus' mission is to all of us. Reapplied by the Church, the Responsorial Psalm refers to the voice of God "over the waters" when Jesus was baptized in the Jordan.

Reading II   Acts 10, 34-38
Doing Good Works

Peter sees Jesus as in his baptism "anointed with the Holy Spirit and power" and so equipped for his calling: doing good works and healing all who were in the grip of the devil. A similar calling is ours as baptized Christians. Being a Christian does not mean just avoiding sin. We are anointed to do good and to be concerned about those who are in the grip of evil. And God will be with you!

Gospel
Lk 3, 15-16. 21-22
"You Are My Beloved Son"

"He will baptize you in the Holy Spirit and in fire": fire is a familiar biblical image which points to the presence of God. Here it could indicate the Holy Spirit's purifying and sanctifying activity at baptism. "Like a dove": Israel is often compared with a dove. Here it stands for the new Israel, the community founded by Jesus, and our Lord himself representing it.

Luke has Jesus pray after his baptism, just as he has him pray often before important decisions in his life. This was an important moment in the life of Jesus, namely one in which he received a clear awareness of the great mission he had to accept. Pray often to the Holy Spirit for fidelity to your calling in life!

◆

ORDINARY TIME

See p. 29

2nd SUNDAY IN ORDINARY TIME
"For the Lord Delights in You"

WHEN in a marriage two people have grown into a mature love for one another, one of them can be heard to say in the course of a lively conversation: "But my wife and I think . . ." Such partners have grown into the conjugal oneness mentioned by the Bible: "The two of them become one body" (Gn 2, 24; Mt 19, 6: note that in Biblical language "body-flesh stands for the whole person!). It can also happen that the marital oneness is overly stressed by one of the partners. The man who once loved that charming little woman so much because of certain beautiful qualities of character may become a tyrant and seek to mold his wife into a blueprint of himself. This is love turned into egotism.

C — 2nd Sunday in Ordinary Time

Real love is participation in one another's personality with great respect, never destroying it! In the awareness of the Bible, human beings are related to God in a sacred partnership (covenant), which has conjugal overtones, as today's readings bring out. But in his great love, God does not destroy us as persons. We are and should be different, though the same Spirit of love has been given to all of us. Christians should live in the joy of the wedding (partnership-covenant) between God and human beings.

Reading I   Is 62, 1-5
As a Bridegroom

Once the prophet Hosea (8th century B.C.) had mentioned his own broken marriage as an example of Israel's unfaithfulness to God, later Biblical writers also began to compare the relationship between God and humans with the intimate love of husband and wife. In this reading it is one of Isaiah's disciples who takes up this theme to console the people of his day: "As a bridegroom rejoices in his bride, so shall your God rejoice in you." He assures them that although past infidelity was punished with defeat and exile to Babylon, God forgives and takes his people back as his spouse.

God's word to you in this passage could be a question: How do you see yourself in relation to God? Is the promised reward or love the main incitement of your Christian life-style? God loves you. "Proclaim his marvelous deeds to all the nations" (Responsorial Psalm).

Reading II   1 Cor 12, 4-11
Accepting One Another as Different

The setting is the congregation in Corinth, Greece, with an active charismatic movement. Some of its members have been overemphasizing the importance of the gifts of the Holy Spirit, especially the gift of speaking in tongues. Paul stresses that God loves all of us and gives his same Spirit of love to all members, but he respects our individualities. We are different from one another: "There are different works [ministries, gifts] but the same God who accomplishes all of them in everyone."

Accept people as different! Apply this to your family, friends, parish. Loving people only if they want to think exactly the way you do is narrow-minded. It is something done in "closed societies." Outgrow this!

Gospel   Jn 2, 1-12
Assuming the Groom's Role

In reading the fourth Gospel, we should keep in mind that for the author, who wrote it some 60 years after the death and resurrection of our Lord, the miracles are primarily signs or symbols which unveil the mystery of the Christ event. John refines and molds the living traditions found among the congregations of his day to bring out his point. It requires study to see all the subtle hints and allusions in these narratives. In today's passage, Jesus reveals his glory and gives us a first inkling of who he is. He assumes the role of the groom by giving wine to the wedding guests.

Remember that in the Christian tradition Christ is related to the Church, all of us, as a groom to his bride (Eph 5, 31-32). And every Sunday, we share the cup with him in the Eucharistic Celebration, if we partake under both species. "May all of us who share in the body and blood of Christ be brought together in unity by the Holy Spirit" (Eucharistic Prayer II).

———◆———

3rd SUNDAY IN ORDINARY TIME
God's Living Word in the Bible

THE word has a formidable impact. Campaigning politicians, lawyers in court, and preachers of revivals are aware of its magic power and work miracles with it. The word is conveyed both in its written and and in its spoken form. A book like Hitler's *"Mein Kamp"* ("My Struggle") led millions into the calamity of World War II, while the sermons of Bishop Sheen on television showed the path of righteousness to a multitude of listeners.

C — 3rd Sunday in Ordinary Time

The best-seller par exellence, which remains unsurpassed by any book, is the Bible. Before Christ it was known as the Torah or the Law. In our tradition, with its Christian interpretation added (New Testament), it became known as the Bible, from the Greek, "Biblos"—the inner bark of the papyrus, paper book, hence, the Book! Today's first and third readings could be qualified as "the Bible on the Bible" What does the "Good Book" mean to you? Do you read/listen with faith? Bible reading just for information's sake becomes boring since many passages are already known to us. Bible reading should be done always prayerfully and meditatively, applying God's word to our own situation.

Reading I   Neh 8, 2-4. 5-6. 8-10
Read—Explained—Agreed Upon

This reading deals with a time when the Babylonian exile has ended and many of the captives have returned home—only to be met with the frustrations of the reconstruction. Word filters back to those who remained in Babylon, and two influential Jews return to aid the reconstruction. One is Ezra the priest. The other is Nehemiah the cupbearer of the Persian king, who eventually rebuilds the walls of Jerusalem.

Today's passage describes the reestablishment of religious worship in the restored and repopulated city. Notice that the word is not only *read*, but also *explained* and *agreed upon* by the listeners' "Amen." Ezra, reading and explaining the Bible, prefigures Jesus in the synagogue of his hometown (Gospel).

Reading II   1 Cor 12, 12-30 or 12, 12-14. 27
Diversity in Unity

Paul brings out our diversity in unity. We are one and responsible for one another. Each one of us should do his/her part of the job as well as possible and so contribute to the well-being of all. Apply this to your Christian life-style as you live it with your fellow Christians. You should not try to "go it alone." Such an approach never works. As is true for members in the family and for religious in community life, we need our mutual inspiration. This involves giving and taking.

Apply this also to the committees of your parish council. They can call upon a diversity of talents. In what field are you proficient? Your priest is the teacher (preacher), but you may be particularly adept in area of showing hospitality, making strangers feel at home, or in some other area that is just as important!

Gospel Lk 1, 1-4; 4, 14-21
Glad Tidings to You?

We should make note of a few points in this narrative. Jesus entered the synagogue on the sabbath "as he was in the habit of doing." Hence, besides healing and expelling demons, Jesus took time for regular worship. Those in favor of "Horizontal Christianity" (worship God in your neighbor only/mainly!) should pay attention. Jesus found worship important. Moreover, Jesus *read* Scripture, sat down to *explain* it, and *applied* it to a situation, i.e., to himself: "Today this Scripture passage is fulfilled in your hearing." These are important elements in both private and communal Scripture reading.

Explanation is important, since only through understanding "man's word" first can we understand "God's word" in it. *Application* is equally important. The Bible contains God's word to you and me now! Jesus has been sent to bring glad tidings *to you* and to heal our blindness of mind! The first reading brought out a fourth element: Your "Amen" (or *assent*) to God's word to you.

4th SUNDAY IN ORDINARY TIME
Fulfill the Role of Prophet

WHEN politicians campaingning for office deliver a speech, they may run into various reactions. Some of their listeners agree, others disagree, even violently, while still others shrug their shoulders and do not really care. Why is it that this happens also to honest would-be public servants, who have a good platform and are seriously intending to serve their community? One reason must be our limited human nature. Narrow-mindedness, prejudice, lack of general information, being part of a closed

C — 4th Sunday in Ordinary Time

society and evil threatened by good may contribute to these various reactions.

Christianity as a beautiful philosophy of life is preached all over the globe. Some accept it and find a meaningful life which leads to satisfaction and happiness. Others reject it, possibly because they see it as a threat to their own set of values. Still others really do not care, and among these are persons seeking a short-term meaning in life. Not all who fail to accept the message of Christ are bad people.

Accepting Christ and his outlook on life requires faith, and faith is a free gift of God. It is risky to accuse nonbelievers of guilt and ill-will. We do much better to leave judgment up to God, and by word and example to give witness of a Christian lifestyle which we believe leads to lasting happiness.

Reading I — Jer 1, 4-5. 17-19
"Be Not Crushed!"

The mission of Jeremiah covers a period of some 40 years (from 627 to 587 B.C.). Well aware of the usual fate of a prophet (meaning a person who speaks in the name of someone else, not one who foretells the future!) Jeremiah had no desire whatever to be a prophet but finally and with great reluctance obeyed God's call.

Speaking in the name of God and stating what he commands people to do runs into the opposition of evil, especially when the evil ones belong to the power structure of society. Jeremiah prefigures the prophet Jesus and prophetic figures of all ages, actually all Christians who suffer because they try to do what is right. Take a stand!

Reading II — 1 Cor 12, 31—13, or 13, 4-13
Love Is Patient

The Church must fulfill its role as prophet in our society, hence be willing to experience reactions similar to those Jeremiah and Jesus had to face. As members of that Church (the "body of Christ" about which Paul speaks so eloquently in this reading), we must do likewise. It can be done, provided we are inspired and guided by genuine love.

We should continue to bear witness through word and example, and pray that God may open the minds of those who cannot see the light.

Gospel   Lk 4, 21-30
Christian Witness—Suffering?

This passage is intelligible only if we reread what comes before in the Gospel of last Sunday. The early Church, for whom Luke wrote his Gospel, had to face the fact that Judaism as a whole opposed the Christian message and could not see Jesus as the promised Messiah. By recounting this tradition about what happened to Jesus in his hometown, Luke deals with this problem. Actually, he fuses several visits and several reactions together in this one story. Notice: "They marveled." Others asked: "Is not this Joseph's son?" Who does he think he is? Why does he not work a few miracles here also? And finally they reject him.

Since Judaism as a whole rejected Jesus, the message was directed to the Gentiles. Jesus points out that Elijah and Elisha worked their miracles for non-Jews (see 2 Kgs 5; 1 Kgs 17, 7-16). God's word to all who suffer because of Christian witness: "But he [Jesus] went straight through their midst and walked away." Suffering is part of Christian witness. Final victory belongs to Christ and all who are willing to suffer with him.

◆

5th SUNDAY IN ORDINARY TIME
Awareness of God's Presence

IN the awareness of persons who form part of a technological society it is better to keep the sacred and secular in their lives separated. Phenomena that were considered mysterious in the past can now be explained by science. When we are sick, we do not go to the priest to have him expel a demon; we go to the doctor for our antibiotics. Counselors delve into the psychological structure of youngsters and advise them as to what direction they should choose in life. It seems that the intuitive awe for the sacred and the mysterious presence of God in all of life is disappearing to the degree that psychology steps in.

Can only artists, painters, and poets still have the intuitive awareness of the sacred in the reality of life? All believers have it in their best moments. We should keep it alive. In faith, we should be just as fully aware of God's presence in any scientific process as we are of his presence in the beauty of nature and in all that happens in our lives.

The Bible readings deal with the calls of Isaiah, Paul, and Peter, all three of them overwhelmed by a feeling of utter unworthiness in the presence of the Most High when they experienced him and heard his call.

Reading I   Is 6, 1-2. 3-8
Seeing the King!

In beautiful figurative language, Isaiah tells of his call to be a prophet, a man to speak in God's name: "I saw the Lord seated. . . ." All our speech about God is analogous and conditioned by time and culture. Isaiah portrays God as an ancient Oriental monarch, surrounded by messengers (angels, seraphim).

Isaiah felt unclean, humble, and unworthy in the presence of the Lord His final answer to God's call is important: "Here I am; send me!" God's word to us may be the question: "Where does God fit into your planning?"

Reading II   1 Cor 15, 1-11 or 15, 3-8. 11
"Seen by Me"

We see from this reading that Paul had an experience similar to Isaiah's awareness of God's presence in the temple. "Last of all he [Jesus] was seen by me, as one born out of the normal course." Only "by God's favor I am what I am." Notice again that feeling of unworthiness in the presence of the Lord.

Gospel   Lk 5, 1-11
Amazement!

"Leave me, Lord. I am a sinful man." These words indicate Peter's awareness when our Lord showed a glimpse of his real being by working a miracle. "Amazement seized him."

Amazement could be the beginning of faith! Like Paul, and Isaiah with respect to Yahweh, Peter and his mates left everything and became Jesus' followers. What was there so extraordinary about the call of these three men? We know that God is present to you and me just as he was to Isaiah, Paul, Peter. Hence, we can say that the "extraordinary" element lay simply in an "awareness in faith" on their part.

The signals of all television stations of your area are in your room. But you must "tune in" in order to receive the sound and images emitted by them, that is, in order to be "aware" of them. In faith, we should keep "tuned in" to God. Then we will hear his daily call, and with his help our answer will be: "Here I am."

◆

6th SUNDAY IN ORDINARY TIME
Search for Happiness

THERE is no being in the world who does not want to be happy. There is only a difference of opinion about what happiness is and how to attain it. Happiness implies that certain desires are being satisfied; and since a human being's desires are never fully satisfied, a happy person trusts, has hope, for more to come. Happiness that is present is beautiful, but it always prompts the question: What about tomorrow? Since no person is happy alone, our hope for present and future happiness has to do with others who will not disappoint us.

There are people who want instant happiness. "I am only young once; hence let me live it up!" Others search for happiness in an affluent life. But what about getting old and finally facing the end? Many want happiness if necessary at the cost of destroying the well-being of others. It requires a sound philosophy of life to obtain a happiness that fully satisfies the human heart, which goes on searching restlessly. Christianity is such a philosophy (wisdom) of life. Today's Bible readings offer a few thoughts to those who are searching

C — 6th Sunday in Ordinary Time

Reading I
Jer 17, 5-8
Trust in the Lord

Guided by God, the writer of this poem offers his ideas on lasting happiness, for which human beings are ever restlessly searching. His observation is: Unhappy is the person who trusts in humans alone. Comparing such a person with a shrub in the desert clearly expresses the reason why there can be no lasting happiness.

On the contrary, happy the person who trusts in the Lord! Again, the comparison gives the reason. Such a person is like a fruitful tree planted beside water. The Responsorial Psalm (1, 1-6) continues that same idea of trust in the Lord.

Reading II
1 Cor 15, 12. 16-20
Our Hopes in Christ

As already mentioned (see Introduction) happiness implies hope for more to come. Paul deals with our restless desire for more that reaches even beyond the grave. "If our hopes in Christ are limited to this life only, we are the most pitiable of men." Christianity is that philosophy of life which offers hope to our "restless heart till it rests in God" (St. Augustine).

Gospel
Lk 6, 17. 20-26
Blest Are You

(For Matthew's version of Jesus' sermon, see the Gospel of the 4th Sunday in Ordinary Time—A, p. 34). We should see this sermon as a challenge to perfection directed to all who seriously search for happiness. "Blest are you poor. . . . Woe to you rich." It is true that the poor feel the insufficiency of the human condition, hence the need for God, more keenly than the rich do. Matthew's version speaks of "poor in spirit," which refers to responsible stewardship. If the have's are constantly aware that they do not own anything, but that they are just God's stewards, and that having more means more responsibility (social justice, charity by sharing), then they too will receive their reward in heaven.

God's word to the wealthy Christian is: With your money and talent for management, are you actively involved in any program to make the poor help themselves? If there is none, start one! "More will be asked of a man to whom more has been entrusted" (Lk 12, 48)

7th SUNDAY IN ORDINARY TIME
Growth into the Image of the Heavenly Father

CAREFUL observance of our own instinctive drives and the behavior of fellow human beings especially at moments when they do not control themselves (anger, frustration, fear) teaches how much we have in common with animals, not only in our physical makeup but in our instinctive and subconscious life as well. The motion pictures of Walt Disney show how selfish and cruel animals in the jungle can be. And which of us has not experienced how horribly little children can behave toward one another! It takes a lifetime of constant maturation to outgrow the animal in us. And some hardly make it. Even as old people, their minds are not yet in control of their passions and selfish desires.

Christianity, that beautiful philosopy of life, offers guidelines on how to grow into maturity, but it also gives motivations and reasons for doing so. Christian growth into maturity is growth into maturity in Christ and a challenge to be the kind of person our heavenly Father is. Today's Bible readings invite us to meditate upon a few aspects of Christian growth into the image of God.

Reading I   1 Sm 26, 2. 7-9. 12-13. 22-23
Magnanimity

This Old Testament tradition shows us a beautiful feature of David's character—his magnanimity. He spares his enemy when he could easily kill him with impunity! Note that David's reason for letting Saul live is that he does not dare to lay hands on the Lord's anointed King out of the fear that he might be punished.

C — 7th Sunday in Ordinary Time

With reference to today's Gospel, the point of this reading for us is mainly David's compassion to be followed. Though his motive is good and laudable, we could not expect David (1000 B.C.) already to possess the insight and motivation which the Gospel gives for moral behavior. The Responsorial Psalm's accent on the mercy of God introduces the Gospel exhortation to be compassionate. (See Ps 103, 1-13.)

Reading II 1 Cor 15, 45-49
Our Likeness to Christ

Paul compares our risen Lord Jesus with the Adam of the Book of Genesis. Adam is our origin and model as plain human beings. Jesus Christ is our origin and model as baptized Christians who are reborn from water and the Spirit. As such, we are now already like "the man of heaven," Jesus Christ, to a certain extent. Our likeness to Christ will be realized more perfectly in the resurrection.

During our lifetime we should constantly grow into the likeness to the risen Lord, and in him into the likeness of the heavenly Father. (See Introduction.)

Gospel Lk 6, 27-38
Be Compassionate

This reading continues Jesus' sermon in which he challenges his followers to attain perfection. Throughout the ages countless men and women have tried to follow the recommendations set forth in this sermon and those who have succeeded have become great saints. We also should try to do so. Love of enemies has already been treated in detail (see Gospel of 7th Sunday in Ordinary Time—A).

The exhortation to "lend without expecting repayment" should cause us no wonder if we remember that in Biblical times money did not yet have the commercial function it has now. Moreover, there is a vast difference between a bank granting a business loan and an individual helping a friend as well as possible under the circumstances.

We might also compare the motivation for showing mercy to others found in the words "Be compassionate, as your Father is compassionate" with that of David (Reading I). Both motives are good, but the one of the Gospel is the more perfect. Finally, we must keep in mind that the words "Give, and it shall be given to you" provide just one motive for generosity. It does not have to be our only one. The Gospels offer many reasons for us to be generous.

◆

8th SUNDAY IN ORDINARY TIME
Honesty in Christian Witness

WHETHER we like it or not, our language shows whether we are educated or not. It usually indicates which country we are from and, within the country, even which part. It tells about our age and sex, our temperament, our profession, our honesty, our moral values, and our outlook on life.

However, not all language is honest and reflects the real person. We are constantly exposed, for example, to the multifaceted language of diplomacy and the deceptive language of the slick commercial. Our language, though, should be the language of the heart, honestly reflecting our best selves. Only by being honest with one another can human beings communicate and overcome the ailment of alienation.

Reading I — Sir 27, 4-7
Disclosing the Bent of Your Mind

This reading introduces the theme of the Gospel on human language. Nonbelievers observe Christians, preachers (priests) and lay people alike, very critically. All Christians are called to witness to Jesus Christ and what he stands for. But Christian witness is credible only if it can stand the test. Are we honest?

As the Responsorial Psalm (92) brings out: Only just people, they that are planted in the house of the Lord, shall bear fruit.

Reading II — 1 Cor 15, 54-58
Steadfast and Persevering

Paul deals again with our hope of the resurrection. But faith in a hereafter should not be an excuse to take it easy. "Be steadfast and persevering, . . . fully engaged in the work of the Lord," which includes honest Christian witness.

Gospel
Lk 6, 39-45
Honesty

In their language of preaching, the disciples must check whether their words are genuinely inspired by the standards of the Lord Jesus. His light should shine through their rhetoric. If such is not the case with a preacher, he is like a blind man guiding another blind person. The same should be true when a preacher is correcting sinners. His language is credible only if he is honest with himself.

Finally, since not only priests but all Christians should bear witness, we should be honest with one another. Only if people feel that I am a good person who produces goodness from the good of my heart will my words be accepted by them.

9th SUNDAY IN ORDINARY TIME
Tolerance for All Religious Faiths

TWO extremes which have hurt the Church over the 2,000 years of its existence are indifferentism and fanaticism. Let us look at fanaticism and intolerance. It has done much harm to the establishment of God's reign of love and justice on earth, which is the primary task the Divine Founder has given us. We think immediately of the inquisition and one of its best known victims, Joan of Arc. We think too of the fierce wars in which Catholics and Protestants have senselessly shed one another's blood.

Fanaticism caused many devout Christians to leave their home countries and come to the "land of the free," often to continue their intolerance, though in a milder form, on these shores. Only in the wake of the Second Vatican Council are we outgrowing a "ghetto" Catholicism and trying to see positive values in other Christian Churches. Today's first and third readings encourage Christians to be open-minded as far as people of other faiths are concerned.

C — 9th Sunday in Ordinary Time

Reading I   1 Kgs 8, 41-43
A Foreigner's Prayer

This prayer (figuratively put into the mouth of King Solomon, the traditional patron of wisdom) reflects a remarkable universalism which became part of Judaism possibly around the time of the Babylonian exile when Jews had to live together with people of a different faith.

Its lesson for us could be: Never wavering in our dedication to what we possess, we should be open-minded in our dealings with people who seek God honestly but in a different way.

Reading II   Gal 1, 1-2. 6-10
Guided by the Gospel

Like other congregations founded by Paul, the one in Galatia was also disturbed by Judaizers, i.e., Jewish-Christian preachers, who tried to impose the Law of Moses on Gentiles who had joined the Church. In this reading Paul exhorts the Galatians to hold fast to the Gospel of Christ which he preached to them. Among other things in this preaching he had told them that faith in Jesus, sealed by baptism, was sufficient. Circumcision and other regulations of the Jewish faith did not have to be observed by Gentiles who became Christians.

God's word to us could be: Be guided by the Gospel of our Lord as it is made available to you in your Bible and in the explanations of the Church. Be open-minded; recognize and acknowledge good wherever you experience it (Reading I and Gospel), but do not let others confuse you.

Gospel   Lk 7, 1-10
Be Open-Minded!

Luke relates this tradition in such a way that our attention is drawn first to the open-mindedness of the centurion, who apparently was not of the Jewish faith. He loved the Jewish people and had even built a synagogue for them. He shows himself very considerate and does not want Jesus to become legally unclean by entering the house of a Gentile (i.e., his house). Finally, this good man comes to faith in Jesus through what he has heard about our Lord's preaching and miracles. Secondly, Luke brings out that Jesus sees the good in this Gentile, admires his great faith, and heals his servant.

Luke intended this message for his congregation, which had to contend with a certain "ghetto" mentality in the Judaism of its days. In relating this passage to the first reading, we learn that we should be open-minded. Acknowledging the positive good in other religions in no way endangers our own faith! God works wherever he wishes, as Jesus did.

———◆———

LENTEN SEASON

See p. 43.

1st SUNDAY OF LENT
The Profession of Faith

CANDIDATES for public office and their aides know that the more they are convinced of their beliefs, the greater their enthusiasm and the better their chances of winning. In campaigning they draw up posters that tell in a nutshell what they stand for. Slogans on badges and bumper-stickers as well as "position papers" serve the same purpose. These formal statements of belief strengthen the identity of the group and show others what their party program is all about.

Religion as organized into groups has its "Confessions of Faith." They are brief formal statements of what the collective faithful believe in. These confessions determine the identity of the group or church. They are pronounced at meetings repeatedly and they strengthen mutual belonging, which is so important in religion. Think of our Profession of Faith during our weekly worship services! Today's Liturgy deals with confessions of belief in both the Old and the New Testament. Prayerful reading may help us to profess our faith wherever we are.

C — 1st Sunday of Lent

Reading I
Dt 26, 4-10
A Eucharistic Confession

This reading is a "Eucharistic Confession," a confession of thanksgiving. It is taken from the ritual prescribed for the feast of the harvest thanksgiving. "My father was a wandering Aramean . . ." Jacob (Israel), perpetually seeking pasture for his flock, ended up in Egypt where his clan first enjoyed prosperity and later was enslaved. Notice that the Exodus from Egypt "with terrifying power, with signs and wonders," has for the Jews a meaning similar to what the death and resurrection of our Lord Jesus Christ means to us Christians. Both are mighty acts of God resulting in liberation. Both inspire a Confession of Faith in which these mighty acts are recited. "Say to the Lord, 'My refuge and my fortress, my God in whom I trust' " (Responsorial Psalm).

Reading II
Rom 10, 8-13
A Baptismal Confession

This reading contains a baptismal Confession: "If you confess with your lips that Jesus is Lord, . . . you will be saved." Our Confession of Faith at baptism is now more elaborate, but the very core of it is that God has raised the Lord Jesus Christ from the dead and made him Lord. Pay special attention to your Profession of Faith during the next worship service!

Gospel
Lk 4, 1-13
A Confessing Church

Luke uses this tradition about our Lord to describe the temptations of the early Church. Notice the Confession: "Not on bread alone shall man live. — You shall do homage to the Lord your God; him alone shall you adore. — You shall not put the Lord your God to the test." Jesus was tempted to give up his vocation, the Church is tempted time and and again to be unfaithful to her original calling, and we as individuals are tempted as well. We should be a "confessing" Church. Others should know clearly what we stand for. Could the above Confession of Faith inspire you during the week to come?

C — 2nd Sunday of Lent

2nd SUNDAY OF LENT

In Prayer, Lift Up Your Hearts to God

WE all know the classic story of the dedicated family man who exclaims to his wife: "Honey, please do not ask me anymore whether I love you. I told you so when we got married ten years ago. I provide for the family and pay all the bills, including the notes on the new refrigerator and the mink I gave you for Christmas. . . ." All this *shows* that he loves her. Is that not enough? The fact is that it is not! His wife wants to *hear* that he loves her over and over again, and he needs to say it. If this is not done, these two people will drift apart and jeopardize their marriage.

Your relationship with God is that of a sacred partnership (covenant) which has clearly marital overtones. Of course, no comparison is adequate. God does not feel unhappy when you do not encounter him directly in prayer or fail to say that you love him and appreciate what he is doing for you. But *you* need to do so! And if you do not, you will drift away from him, regardless of your charity to others.

Today's Scripture readings deal with persons conversing with God. Their examples may inspire us. Have a look at yourself during Lent: "Do I find prayer important? How often and when do I pray? Does my daily Bible reading result in meditative prayer to God?"

Reading I   Gn 15, 5-12 17-18
Conversing with God

A living faith in God is the prerequisite for prayer: "Abraham put his faith in the Lord." A trance fell upon Abraham, and in prayer he experienced God who sealed his faith with a covenant. The ancient covenant rite (two people making a covenant) prescribed that the sacrificial animals be divided into two halves and the contracting parties walk in between, stating that they were willing to become like the dismembered animals if they should fail to keep the covenant. In the tradition found in the present reading, it is God who seals the covenant by passing between the "pieces" in the form of a "smoking brazier and a flaming torch" (fire symbolizes God's presence; think of Pentecost, for example).

What is the sacred writer, inspired by God, trying to teach us? Obviously, that we should follow Abraham's example of faith and conversing with God. By doing this, you will experience that the Lord is your "light" and "salvation."

Reading II   Phil 3, 17—4, 1 or 3, 20—4, 1
"Stand Firm in the Lord"

Paul invites the Philippians to follow him as he follows Christ, whom we see in today's Gospel as a man of prayer. At the beginning of the Eucharistic Prayer, the priest invites you to lift up your hearts. Paul does the same by inviting "those who are set upon the things of this world" to look up to heaven. Then God will give a new form to "this lowly body of ours," as we see indicated in the Lord Jesus praying on the mountain (Gospel).

Gospel   "Listen to Him!"   Lk 9, 28-36

In this highly symbolical narrative, Luke brings out an important lesson on prayer. Conversing with God in prayer changes us; it widens our vision, and with God's grace it often makes us experience the transcendent—in other words, it makes us feel that there must be something more than simply what we can observe with our senses.

Jesus was a man of prayer. Luke compares him with Moses and Elijah who often conversed with God in prayer. He wants his disciples to do likewise. Peter said: "Master, how good it is for us to be here." Prayer is something you must learn and by doing it regularly you will find out it has meaning. Only by listening will you hear God's voice in you. "Listen to him."

3rd SUNDAY OF LENT
The Need of Ongoing Reform

AS long as you are in the process of growing, you are alive. As far as our physical condition is concerned, at a certain

C — 3rd Sunday of Lent

moment we feel that the process of decay has set in. True, we can slow it down by keeping ourselves in good shape, and a whole industry is even helping us to do so. But we cannot stop the process of getting old.

It is different, however, with our growth as persons. We are most aware of our personal growth during the years of formation: students in school, engaged partners getting to know and love one another, religious during the novitiate. The key to a happy and meaningful life is to keep growing. Paul speaks of "maturing in Christ." This is a lifetime job.

The Lenten Season is a time of paying renewed attention to our growth as persons. Am I approaching the design God has in mind for me? In the Liturgy we are confronted with Moses who experienced God in the desert, and the Lord Jesus speaking of reforming our lives. Reforming is not an instant happening. It is an ongoing process. Am I growing as a person?

Reading I   Ex 3, 1-8. 13-15
Going Over to Look

In constantly reforming our lives, we must check where God fits into our set of values. The tradition found in this reading teaches that God is not far away. Moses experienced him in the situation of the desert. Last week the image of "a smoking brazier and a flaming torch" was used to teach about God's presence. Today it is again fire which symbolizes God's closeness. By using this imagery, the Old Testament teaches exactly the same thing that Paul taught in concise language: "In him [God] we live and breathe and have our being" (Acts 18, 28).

Moses experienced God as "One who cares," and during his life he grew in intimacy with God. An example to be followed! Meditate on God's closeness and care by reading the Responsorial Psalm (103, 1-11).

Reading II   1 Cor 10, 1-6. 10-12
Written as a Warning to Us

Paul indicates how we should read the Bible. The sacred writers did not relate ancient traditions just to inform us. Neither does the Church want us to listen to them every three years in order to entertain us. The Bible is not a bedside story book! Inspired by God, the authors of the Bible want to teach us religious values by relating traditions of the past.

In this passage, Paul refers to some events, as he knew them from the Old Testament (Gn 13; 14; 16; 17; Nm 20; 14), and observes: "These things happened as an example to keep us from wicked desires such as theirs. . . . They have been written as a warning to us."

In reading the Bible, we should always try to find the point (God's word to us) and apply it prayerfully to our own situation.

Gospel
Lk 13, 1-9
Ongoing Growth and Reform

This Gospel tradition refers to violent reprisals by the Romans who occupied Israel during Jesus' lifetime. There were constant uprisings on the part of the Jewish people which finally culminated in the wholesale destruction of Jerusalem in 70 A.D. According to popular thinking, disaster and suffering were caused by sin. Jesus corrects this way of thinking, but takes these incidents as a stepping-stone to teach about penance and reform using the parable of the fig tree to illustrate his lesson.

This lesson is God's word to you and me. Check your priority of values and ask yourself where God fits in! Stating that everything is all right means stating that you are "old" and not growing anymore as a person. (See Introduction.) We need constantly ongoing reform and growth into what God has designed us to be for all eternity.

◆

4th SUNDAY OF LENT
God Has Reconciled Us to Himself through Christ

A FRENCH king is said to have stated: "The crown of France is worth a Mass a week." In reality, he cared little about religion, but since all of France was Catholic, as king he had to go to church on Sunday. We could liken this to a modern teenager thinking: "The keys to the family car for my date

C — 4th Sunday of Lent

are worth that Mass on Sunday." There are various reasons why the "faithful" observe religious obligations.

Some do so out of fear. One never knows what will happen on the other side of the grave, so they want to play safe. Others calculate like the Pharisees of Jesus' time; they are "righteous" people, diligently observing the laws of their religion, and they expect God to give them salvation in return.

Such scrupulous observers of the legal requirements of Christianity forget that salvation cannot be bought with good works. In the matter of leading a Christian life, it is the reason *why* one does so that counts. Love and gratitude should be the principal motivations, not calculation or fear, and certainly not commercial considerations! Good works should be the result of sanctification. We should do them not to buy salvation, but as a sign of appreciation and gratitude for what God has done on our behalf.

Reading I — Jos 5, 9. 10-12
God Removing the Reproach

In the promised land, the Hebrews celebrated the Passover. Their motivation was not to get something. They offered their lambs as a sign of gratitude to Almighty God. Our Passover Lamb is Jesus Christ, the Lamb of God, who takes away the sin of the world.

Note that the setting of our weekly Passover is the Eucharistic Prayer, a prayer of thanksgiving and praise, and these sentiments should be *your* motivation for taking part in it. "We offer you [God] in thanksgiving this holy and living sacrifice. . . . Through him [Jesus Christ], with him, in him, in the unity of the Holy Spirit, all glory and honor is yours, almighty Father, for ever and ever" (Eucharistic Prayer III).

Reading II — 2 Cor 5, 17-21
The Message of Reconciliation

The message of this reading is that God, in Christ, has reconciled us to himself. Apply this to yourself. Whether you are "the prodigal son" or "the righteous son" of today's Gospel, you need reconciliation, which is not bought with good works, but given freely! (See Introduction.)

Gospel

Lk 15, 1-3. 11-32

Return to Your Father

We note first that the popular name of this parable, "The Prodigal Son," is misleading. The parable of "The Merciful Father" would be a better name. It is all about "a man," called "father" fourteen times and obviously representing Almighty God, who cares for both the son who ran off and the law-abiding son who remained home.

Luke indicates those to whom the parable is directed: the tax collectors and sinners (the son who ran off), and the Pharisees and Scribes, the righteous observers of the law (the son who remained home). The latter observed the law but their motivation was wrong. They tried to buy salvation by scrupulous external observance. Their attitude was like that of the oldest son: "For years I have slaved for you."

Unloving service is not far from servitude. Parents are annoyed when fear and calculation are the only reasons why the children obey them. Both sons were wrong. (See Introduction.) Hence, no matter with which one you must identify yourself, return to your Father who is merciful!

5th SUNDAY OF LENT

"Racing To Grasp the Prize

EVERY day we come into contact with optimists and pessimists, and traits of both are part of our own selves. Pessimists take the gloomiest possible view of the human condition. They are captives of the "good old days," of what is not anymore and never will be again. They are not creative because they regard all efforts as doomed to fail in the first place. This represents anything but the "spirit of '76." Imagine if the Founding Fathers had fostered this kind of thinking! Optimists look to the bright side of things. They are creative and dynamic. They have confidence in life.

Today's Liturgy invites us to be optimistic. Whatever the past, look to the future! Christians are optimists by definition. As far as the past is concerned, they believe in a merciful God who forgives the penitent sinner. As far as the future is concerned, they know that they will overcome misery and evil and build a better future because they have faith in Someone who is stronger than they are.

Life is a constant challenge: the future of your family, your success in business or on your job, your personal growth through human relations. With confidence in God, Christians accept this challenge. Their philosophy of life is that of Paul: "I give no thought to what lies behind but push on to what is ahead" (Reading II).

Reading I God Doing Something New Is 43, 16-21

The exiles in Babylon were depressed, as only displaced persons with no hope of ever returning home could be. They dreamed about the past, "the good old days" of the Exodus from bondage in Egypt, for in their eyes God was really with his people at that time! The prophet warns against this kind of useless daydreaming. "Remember not the events of the past, the things of long ago consider not." Have faith in the future! "See, I [God] am doing something new!"

Life can be depressing. It can even be our own fault that we are in a mess. Are we then to take refuge in the remedies for depression recommended by television commercials—or even turn to the escapisms of alcohol and dope? Try to heed this Bible message! And if your faith is weak, ask God to strengthen it. "Those that sow in tears shall reap rejoicing" (Responsorial Psalm).

Reading II Am I Racing? Phil 3, 8-14

With an unshakable faith in Christ, Paul is full of optimism for the future. Born and raised in a city, he has watched the games, the races, and the fights in the amphitheater. He can thus equate life with a race course: "I am racing to grasp the prize if possible!" And what is the basis for his optimism? "I have been grasped by Christ."

Pray for faith in Jesus Christ and you will have the imagination and courage to "push on to what is ahead" no matter what comes.

Gospel Jn 8, 1-11

Working at a Happy Future

From the outset in this reading, it is clear that the Pharisees who bring the adulteress to Jesus are not honest. Jesus simply bends down and starts tracing on the ground with his finger, indicating that he is bored and not interested in their hypocritical nonsense, very much as we doodle when bored! Finally, they leave. And an unhappy woman who had faced death regains hope by meeting a good person.

God's word to us through this tradition could be: With regard to the past, God is merciful. With faith in him work for a happy future!

◆

PASSION SUNDAY
[PALM SUNDAY]

Death and Life

GREAT people were often controversial figures during their lifetime. It is history, which can look on from a distance and see things in proper perspective, that rectifies the often limited contemporaries. Something like this has happened to the Lord Jesus. His judgment of contemporaries, even his closest coworkers, did not understand him, especially not his strange ideas on suffering and death as a necessary passage to a better life. Only later did all of this become clear them.

Today Christians celebrate Passion (or Palm) Sunday. "Christ entered in triumph into his own city to complete his work as our Messiah to suffer, to die and to rise again" (Procession Rite). The triumphal entry, celebrated at the beginning of the passion-week, emphasizes that the three elements: suffering, death, and resurrection belong together. Jesus' death was not a defeat. It was a victory. It is the genuine insight of Christianity that the events of Jesus' earthly life were the execution of God's saving purpose. This genuine insight should be ours also concerning our own lives when suffering strikes us.

C — Passion Sunday [Palm Sunday]

How do you deal with suffering in your life and when you encounter fellow humans who die in suffering and distress? Paul states: "If we believe that Jesus died and rose, God will bring forth with him from the dead those also who have fallen asleep believing in him" (1 Thes 4, 14). "Lord, the death of your Son gives us hope and strengthens our faith. May his resurrection give us perseverance and lead us to salvation" (Prayer after Communion).

Gospel   Lk 19, 28-40
"Who Is This?"

Like King David and all kings in his culture, Jesus enters the capital riding on the traditional animal. In the midst of the people, he is the Son of David, a Messiah sent by God to give freedom and self-determination to his country. But Jesus is a humble and peaceful king, not in favor of worldly display. He enters Jerusalem, "meek and riding on an ass" (Zec 9, 9).

All the four of the evangelists relate this tradition as an introduction to Jesus' passion and cruel death. Why? To teach us that Jesus is indeed the Messiah, though on a higher level than the people thought. Jesus is sent by God to establish his reign (kingdom) on earth. His impending suffering and death will not thwart this divine plan, but must be seen as the means to fulfill it, as will be clearly understood after the resurrection. "Did not the Messiah have to undergo all this so as to enter into his glory?" (Lk 24, 26).

Participating in the Liturgy of Holy Week, we should keep in mind that suffering pain, and death are also mysteriously part of our passage to a glorious life with our Lord.

Reading I   Is 50, 4-7
"The Lord Is My Help"

This reading is taken from the third song of the Servant of Yahweh. As mentioned at the feast of the Baptism of our Lord, it is not clear whom the inspired writer had in mind when he composed these four songs describing the ideal Servant (Son) of God. Is he a collective person: Israel, God's people? Is he a king of the past or the Messiah (anointed king) to come?

C — Passion Sunday [Palm Sunday]

In any case the Christian community applied these hymns very early to Jesus and they are used throughout Holy Week as a beautiful commentary on the passion narratives. Indeed, "the Son of Man [Jesus] came not to be served but to serve, and to give his life for the ransom of many" (Mt 20, 28). Read the Responsorial Psalm (22) meditatively, applying it to the Lord Jesus dying on the cross.

Reading II "Your Attitude" Phil 2, 6-11

This text is actually a Christ hymn, sung in church. It beautifully describes our Lord's utmost humiliation which he suffered on the cross. By being obedient, he made up for our sinful disobedience. But this hymn also sings of Christ's exaltation by the Father.

Meditating on the Lord's suffering and death, as Christians do during Holy Week, we should keep both sides of the Christ event in mind. It is suffering and death which actually constitutes a passage to exaltation. Good Friday and Easter belong together even in our lives!

Gospel Lk 22, 14—23, 56 or 23, 1-49
No Greater Love

Paul states: "For our sakes God made him [Jesus] who did not know sin, to be sin so that in him we might become the very holiness of God" (2 Cor 5, 21). Jesus identified himself entirely with sinful man, whom he freed from sin and death. Each of the evangelists relates the narrative with only a few different memories of the tragedy. In Matthew and Mark, Jesus' last words are: "My God, my God, why have you forsaken me?" Luke remembers that on the cross Jesus promised paradise to the criminal who repented and that Jesus said: "Father, into your hands I commend my Spirit." All three relate the Lord's Supper, which Jesus gave us to celebrate as a memorial of his passion, death, and resurrection.

Prayerful meditation on Jesus' passion should make us grateful for what Jesus did. He has said: "There is no greater love than this: to lay down one's life for one's friend. You are my friends" (Jn 15, 13-14).

EASTER SEASON

See p. 55.

EASTER VIGIL MIDNIGHT MASS

See p. 56.

EASTER SUNDAY

See p. 57.

2nd SUNDAY OF EASTER
Faith and Fellowship

"BIRDS of a feather flock together." With respect to certain instincts, we humans are no different from cows in a pasture flocking together when a thunderstorm is threatening. We need one another's company and inspiration to keep going. Marital love can survive only if the partners daily foster togetherness with all the means nature and religion suggest. The survival of faith is subject to the same conditions. A Christianity lived "alone," all by oneself, does not last.

The first reading describes the communal life of the early congregation in Jeruslem. "Koinonia" (fellowship, brotherhood, communion) should be an important element in the life of all Christians of ages. Faith, like love, is constantly exposed to the temptation of doubt and indifference. We need one another's support. You are blessed, if you have/belong to a family where Christian fellowship is part of family life; where the members pray/worship together, read the Bible together, practice the Christian values of love, justice, mutual respect, decency, and concern together. In such a case, the members of the family carry one another and that fellowship keeps faith alive.

Fellowship should also be part of every congregation, though this poses a problem in a large parish. We need belonging! Parish Councils should discuss available options. Participate in some activity of your parish. Do not be a loner!

Without being exclusive, have friends who feel the same as you do in matters of faith. And at meetings, contribute to the value of "belonging" for all. Listen, be open to others, exchange ideas and experiences, share time and talents. "The brethren devoted themselves to the apostles' instruction and the communal life." The above may suggest how to realize this in our time and culture.

Reading I — They Used To Meet! — Acts 5, 12-16

Signs accompanied the early Church's preaching. They indicated clearly what the impending reign of God was all about, namely, the defeat of evil, the healing of wounds, and the advent of salvation. People held the early Church in great esteem. Can your community have a great esteem for your congregation? What does your congregation stand for?

Start by showing what Christianity really means in your conduct, and make creative suggestions wherever feasible! "Let the house of Israel [the Church—your congregation—you] say, 'His [God's] mercy endures forever' " (Responsorial Psalm).

Reading II — Witnessing to Jesus — Rv 1, 9-11. 12-13. 17-19

Addressing seven local churches in Asia Minor, John uses the apocalyptic language of vision. (See commentary on Reading I of the Day Mass of the Assumption, August 15, p. 341.)

Since the second reading for the next six Sundays will be taken from the Book of Revelation (or the Apocalypse), we should keep in mind the very esoteric literary form in which this book is written and take special pains to uncover the true meaning underlying it. In the center of his vision, the author describes the Son of Man, Jesus Christ, who shares power with God.

Gospel
Jn 20, 19-31
With the Disciples, Believe!

By relating the well-known tradition concerning the unbelieving Thomas, the writer of John indicates that even seeing, as Thomas did, is no guarantee of faith. Faith comes by hearing the word of the risen Lord who addresses Thomas personally. Christianity knows the golden rule: faith comes from hearing. It is God, personally addressing you in an "I-Thou" situation!

This intangible situation can never be fully explained, just as we cannot explain what exactly happens when someone falls in love! Respond when the Lord says "Shalom—peace" to you in any situation of your life and keep that faith alive!

3rd SUNDAY OF EASTER
What the Lord Jesus Means to Christians

HOW do we remember a beloved person, father or mother, who passed away? We console one another with our common faith that he/she is happy with God. As time heals the wound caused by death, the memory of this person lives on in our minds. We remember sayings: "Father used to say. . . ." Anecdotes that reflect him/her as a lovable person are told time and again: "Mother used to . . . ," followed by a little flash which shows how concerned she could be. Something like this took place after the death of Jesus.

First, there was utter dismay and sadness. But then the disciples experienced the Master as alive. They told others about it. And long after the Lord's last apparition, they shared experiences with others, telling what he had meant to them. These narratives, related time and again in the congregation, reflect the personality of Jesus Christ, his forgiveness, his power, his care, his mercy. Only the most characteristic ones were used by the writers of the New Testament to teach us who the Lord Jesus is and what he means to Christians.

We have some examples in today's Scripture readings. May these traditions help to make us more aware of the significance of the risen Lord in our lives.

C — 3rd Sunday of Easter

Reading I
Acts 5, 27-32. 40-41

Bringing Repentance

The disciples had experienced the Lord Jesus as living after his crushing death on the cross. They shared their joy with others. His death was not a defeat but a victory. Indeed, he had a message for a better future. And since he was alive, his message of repentance and forgiveness of sins was still valid. The power structure of those days told the disciples to stop talking about this man, but, full of his Spirit, they could not comply.

Are we so convinced of Jesus and what he stands for that we share our experiences spontaneously through word and example?

Today's Liturgy puts the Responsorial Psalm (30) into the mouth of Jesus, who thanks God for his resurrection. We could make prayerful use of it to thank God for rescuing us with Christ and insuring that we will not go down into the pit ("sheol"—the nether world) but will live forever.

Reading II
Rv 5, 11-14

"Worthy To Receive Honor"

The writer uses the apocalyptic language of vision. (See last Sunday's second reading, p. 266.) He consoles Christians with our common faith that the Lord Jesus is alive and exalted with God. "Worthy is the Lamb that was slain . . .": Jesus is compared with the sacrificial lambs that were offered as sin offerings in the temple of Jerusalem. He is the Lamb of God who takes away the sins of the world."

"I heard the voices of every creature in heaven and on earth and under the earth": this saying is conditioned by the Hebrews' understanding of the universe. For them, the earth is a plate, heaven is up, and down is "sheol," the nether world, where the dead go. "The one seated on the throne" is God. "The Lamb" is Jesus Christ. "The four living creatures" represent all of life: the lion, mobility; the bull, strength; the man, wisdom; the eagle, swiftness (see Rv 4, 7).

God's word to us could be: Be consoled. Whatever your problems are, the Lord Jesus is alive and powerful. Turn to him in faith!

C — 4th Sunday of Easter

Gospel
Jn 21, 1-19 or 21, 1-14

"It Is the Lord!"

The tradition found in this reading brings out what the risen Lord meant to the disciples in the view of John who relates it, and at the same time what he means to us. The Lord is always with us, though often, like the disciples, we do not recognize him.

A meal is the symbol of togetherness. At the meal described by the author Peter experienced the Lord's mercy. When we share the Eucharistic meal with our Lord, we should get to know and love him evermore.

4th SUNDAY OF EASTER
Perseverance in Trials

WE are told that day by day life can be a joyous experience. The commercials on television assure you that it will be if you buy what they try to sell you. This is also the message of not a few psychologists who assert that the learning process in school, home life, job, and religion/faith should all be one joyous experience! This is fine in theory but what happens if circumstances prevent our lives from being joyous all the time?

What if gradually a school becomes an anti-intellectual fun house? In this respect, teachers who do not dare to challenge their students are not their friends. As for the home, here too there are unpleasant chores to be done. And there are parents who spoil their children—doing them a great disservice for their later life. Even if we love our work, there is no job which does not entail unpleasant aspects as well. And as far as religion is concerned, worship services should be a mutual inspiration, and a Christian life of mutual love is a splendid thing; however, we cannot have that good warm feeling all the time, neither is the church a theater where we go to enjoy "an exciting show!" Loyalty requires sacrifice.

Today's Liturgy deals precisely with those times when life seems to be anything but a joyous experience, when Christians have to undergo disappointment, rejection, trials; and it sets forth the reserves which they can call upon to help them persevere. Can everything we mentioned above continue to be a joyous experience in such circumstances? To a certain extent, yes, if we have learned the joy of sharing and of service, based on a firm faith in Someone who cares. Paul and Barnabas of the first reading are encouraging examples for us.

Reading I   Acts 13, 14. 43-52
When Things Don't Go Your Way!

Paul and Barnabas had the joyful experience of making many converts, but they also had to face the pain of rejection. Though persecuted, they could not but "be filled with joy and the Holy Spirit."

Life is never a continuous success story. When things do not go your way, think of Paul and Barnabas and their disciples, and with great faith make the Responsorial Psalm your prayer to God: "We are his people: the sheep of his flock." God cares!

Reading II   Rv 7, 9. 14-17
After the Period of Trial

In veiled language, the sacred writer encourages his fellow Christians who are "in the great period of trial." The phrase "white in the blood of the Lamb" signifies being cleansed from sin through Jesus' meritorious death on the cross.

God's word to us is that a Christian life does not shield us from disappointments and even suffering. Be conscious of God who will eventually wipe every tear also from your eyes.

Gospel   Jn 10, 27-30
"No Snatching out of His Hand!"

In using the imagery of shepherd and flock, Jesus brings out the same message as that of the second reading. When you are depressed, keep up your courage! Jesus cares. No one shall snatch you out of God's hand unless you yourself turn away from him. Jesus knows you and your problems!

5th SUNDAY OF EASTER
Christian Joy Tempered by Trials

HUMAN beings cannot live without joy. If life consisted only of funerals without weddings, only of work without recreation (a party, a show, a vacation), the burden of human existence would be unbearable for most of us. However, expecting too much joy from life is also dangerous because it easily results in disappointment. Friends may tell us enthusiastically about a new movie in town: "You must see it!" We look forward with great anticipation to it and finally get to see it. In most cases, we come away sorely disappointed by it! Similarly, at every wedding, the mother of the bride sheds a tear of joy but it becomes a tear of sadness when the bride leaves home to follow her husband.

During the fifty days of Easter, the Liturgy of the Church invites us to be joyful because Christ, our Savior, is risen and we as God's adopted children will live with him forever. Christians have reasons for joy, but we should not forget that God's kingdom has only been initiated in us. The full realization will come later. On this side of the grave we will have to live with the tension between "already" and "not yet."

Expecting too much from Church and religion may disillusion you, and it takes maturity and courage to cope with this situation. Today's Bible readings deal with Christian existence which is often joy mingled with tears.

Reading I   Acts 14, 21-27
Undergoing Many Trials

On their way home from their missionary journey, Paul and Barnabas revisit the congregations which they have previously founded. Notice the encouragement "to persevere in the faith with this instruction: 'We must undergo many trials if we are to enter into the reign [kingdom] of God.' "

Indeed the Christian can sing: "[God] Your kingdom is a kingdom for all ages, and your dominion endures through all generations. I will praise your name for ever" (Responsorial Psalm). We have reason for abundant joy, but we must be ready to undergo trials as a condition to enter God's kingdom.

Reading II
Rv 21, 1-5
No More Pain

Utilizing the language of vision, the sacred writer consoles those "who must undergo many trials" (Reading I). According to the ancients, storms at sea were thought to be caused by evil monsters; hence, "sea" stood for threat and peril. Accordingly, the words "the sea was no more" mean that all peril had passed.

The author also sees "a new Jerusalem, the holy city": God had been present in the sanctuary of the old Jerusalem temple; now there will be a new kind of divine presence, enjoyed by all the members of God's people. All these new things are initiated in their lives as Christians, but they will be fully realized only later.

During the Easter Season, meditation on God's saving presence may help us to persevere in the faith.

Gospel
Jn 13, 31-33. 34-35
Mutual Support in Love

In this reading, Jesus is seen looking forward to his glorification, his enthronement as Son of Man, King of God's reign. And God will be glorified in him.

Today Christ is no longer visibly present to his Church. He knows that we are subjected to trials (Reading I). Waiting for his return, the disciples and all of us must support one another with our mutual love and concern. This life-style, mutual support in love, is so characteristic of Christians that others should be able to recognize us by it!

6th SUNDAY OF EASTER
Constant Renewal under Guidance of the Spirit

RENEWAL implies continuity, yet it outgrows the old. The founder of the Ford Motor Company, for example, would hardly recognize his own first assembly line if he could see the Ford plants now. Yet basically it is the same. His successors have renewed the process of producing constantly in the spirit of the founder. They would be unfaithful to his great vision if they were still working as he did so many years ago.

The early leaders of the Church, commissioned by our Lord to continue his work on earth, faced a similar problem of renewal and continuity. Should Christianity be a renewal movement in the framework of existing Judaism? There should indeed be continuity, for Jesus had said that he did not intend to do away with the law and the prophets (Mk 5, 17). Yet, should Gentiles, who joined the Church, be forced to observe so many Jewish laws, especially those conditioned by time and culture?

Guided by the Spirit, the gift of the risen Lord to his people, the Church has renewed itself over the centuries, and is still doing so. Today's Bible readings deal with this issue.

Reading I   Acts 15, 1-2. 22-29
Continuity and Renewal

This passage continues the first reading of last Sunday. Paul and Barnabas had baptized Gentiles without having them first circumcised and telling them to observe the law of Moses. Some Christians from Jewish backgrounds did not agree. Hence, Paul and Barnabas decided to go up to Jerusalem and ask the apostles for a decision. Acts 15, 3-12 (skipped in this reading) and also Galatians 2, 1-14 tell about the procedure.

There was a lengthy discussion on the issue now brought out in the open: Should Christianity be a renewal movement in the framework of Judaism, or should it outgrow it to a certain extent? The consensus was that in the spirit of the founder, Jesus Christ, there should be profound renewal, yet also continuity. A compromise was then reached: Gentiles may join the Church by baptism alone and do not have to be circumcised, but they should follow a few laws in order to facilitate social contact with Christians from Jewish background.

Note the words: "It is a decision of the Holy Spirit, and ours too." Apostolic collegiality is guided by the Spirit! How do you see the renewal of your Church? Notice the three elements: renewal—continuity—guidance of the Holy Spirit! Pray for discernment!

Reading II — Rv 21, 10-14. 22-23
The Church a Renewed Israel

Utilizing the language of vision, the sacred writer describes the splendor of the Church, seeing the earthly and heavenly Church in one perspective. The language is highly symbolic. The Church has a particular brilliance, which is the divine indwelling.

In order to understand the symbolism of this passage one must remember that in New Testament thinking the Church is the "Israel of God," succeeding the "Israel of the flesh." Thus, the author shows that the Church is a renewed Israel by referring to her as "Jerusalem," founded on "the twelve apostles of the Lamb," who succeed the twelve patriarchs of the Israel of old. In so doing the sacred writer clearly indicates that there is *continuity* between the old Israel and the Church as well as a distinct aspect of *renewal*.

Hence, in order to be faithful to its mission in the world the Church should renew itself constantly. As long as this is done under the guidance of the Spirit and the continuity of essentials is safeguarded, we should approve with an open mind.

Gospel — Jn 14, 23-29
Instructed by the Spirit

Continuing the main thought of today's readings, this passage from John wants us to keep in mind that Jesus did not outline all the institutional details of the Church he founded. He left this up to the apostles and their successors.

However, Jesus specified that in organizing the Church they should be true to his words and Spirit, the Paraclete (Advocate, Helper): "The Holy Spirit, whom the Father will send in my name, will instruct you in everything." We should have confidence that Jesus keeps his promise. Preparing for Pentecost, pray often: "Come, Holy Spirit, and enkindle in us the fire of your love."

ASCENSION
Heaven and Earth

NOT all members of our species have the same outlook on life. There are people for whom this life means everything and "heaven" nothing. Naturally good people, they may cherish love as a great value, but when one breathes his last, that is the end. There are others for whom "heaven" is all-important and this life almost completely unimportant. Save your soul! Many Christians have cherished those outlook, especially concerning others and as long as the self was not involved. Finally we have those for whom "heaven" is realized already on earth in love!

If we understand Jesus' philosophy of life well and try to understand the exaltation of his humanity as we celebrate it today, we could give it a try. We may live life, including marital sex and love, as an earthly reality. We may develop our potential as earthlings to its fullest. We may make use of the results of science (sociology, etc.), to achieve a better life on this planet. We may consult marriage counselors and psychiatrists and seek the best medical care available. Yet in our best moments ("disclosure situations"), we know that there must be something more than all of this, a transcending reality.

In faith, following Jesus of Nazareth, we see this "transcending reality" as a loving Father who is waiting for us. He (Jesus) is the beginning. "Where he, our head, has gone, we, his members, hope to follow him" (Preface). "God, our Father, may we follow him [Jesus] into the new creation for his ascension is our glory and our hope" (Opening Prayer).

Reading I
Lifted Up
Acts 1, 1-11

The wording of this tradition on the ascension of our Lord is clearly conditioned by the limited understanding of the universe during the writer's lifetime. The wording is not part of divine revelation. There is no absolute up or down. Heaven is not a place somewhere up in outer space. Heaven is a situation outside our concepts of time and space. What the evangelists have tried to do is describe the final appearance of Jesus and/or the fact that the Lord Jesus is "sitting at God's right hand," which is a Hebrew idiom for sharing power with God. (For both this reading and today's Gospel, see the general introduction to the Easter Season, p. 55.)

Luke's message is: Christ has died ("in the time after his suffering"), Christ has risen ("he showed them that he was alive"), Christ will come again ("this Jesus . . . will return"). That is the way we word it in our second Memorial Acclamation at Mass.

Reading II   In Heaven   Eph 1, 17-23

Paul, a learned Jewish rabbi, relates the same message as Luke and the Evangelist do in the first and third readings, only he does it in difficult theological language. Paul relates the risen and ascended Christ to all that exists. Christ is supreme above all creatures, seated at God's right hand (a Hebraism for "sharing power with God").

Paul prays for the Ephesians and for all of us: "May God grant you a spirit of wisdom and insight to know him [the Lord Jesus] clearly."

Gospel   Lk 24, 46-53
Witnessing "Filled with Joy"

In comparing the way Matthew (A), Mark (B) and Luke (C) describe the last apparition of the Lord Jesus to his disciples, we see some differences. This should not shock us. The sacred authors took existing traditions at face value, and simply used them to proclaim their message—which is that the Lord is alive, is with God, prays for us in heaven, and communicates his Spirit. This message is God's word to us, not all these details. (See general introduction to the Easter Season, p. 55, commentary on the Gospel of the Easter Vigil, p. 56, and Acts, the first reading of the Pentecost Day Mass, p. 77.)

In the tradition used by Luke, Jesus stresses penance as part of the Christian message. Notice that the disciples returned to Jerusalem "filled with joy." In witnessing for Christ, we should be full of joy as well, knowing that the Lord's Spirit dwells in us.

7th SUNDAY OF EASTER
The Image of Jesus Christ Keeps Us Together

CHILDREN of a family are one in the parents. It is the parent image which keeps them together. And when there is a strong and beautiful parent image, there is usually a harmonious oneness of the children. As grown-ups they love to come to see their own parents, and to a certain extent continue their lifestyle in their families. After the parents' deaths, they remember them at family reunions, repeat characteristic sayings, and tell anecdotes which bring out how beautiful, caring, humorous, and energetic they are.

Just as children are one in their parents, so Christians establish a similar oneness in the Lord Jesus Christ. His image keeps us together as a family, and his Spirit, the Holy Spirit, inspires us to go on establishing God's reign in ourselves and in all those entrusted to us. Today's Scripture readings deal with our oneness in Jesus Christ.

Reading I   Acts 7, 55-60
Christ's Image

The early Christians, a tiny minority in the mighty and hostile Roman empire, had the courage to suffer persecution and even death rather than give up their loyalty to Jesus Christ and what he stands for. They possessed a oneness in Christ, which was created and daily fostered by the strong image of a beautiful person. What about your mental picture of the Lord Jesus? Is it alive in you and does it fascinate you so that you "get involved"? Do you keep that image alive by constant and prayerful Bible reading?

This first reading, which describes the martyrdom of St. Stephen who had only recently been converted to the faith, offers a vivid example of what can be done by one who is filled with the Holy Spirit—as all of us are by faith and baptism. Let a prayerful reading of the Responsorial Psalm (97, 1-9) inspire your Christian commitment!

Reading II
Rv 22, 12-14. 16-17. 20
"Come, Lord Jesus!

Still utilizing the language of vision, the sacred writer brings out how a Christian's life is wholly concentrated around the risen Lord Jesus. The words "the Alpha and the Omega" refer to the first and last letters of the Greek alphabet which are used by the Jews to symbolize the fullness and eternity of God; the early Church fittingly applied them to Jesus, the Son of God. The expression "wash their robes" means to cleanse themselves from sin; and the phrase "access to the tree of life" refers to the tree of paradise in Genesis 3, 3.

"Come, Lord Jesus" is the ardent prayer of all genuine Christians. "Coming" results in presence. The Lord Jesus is present to his people; hence, repeated "coming" will result in an ever more intimate presence, a greater oneness in love and mutual understanding of Jesus Christ. Come, Lord Jesus, and share your Spirit, the Holy Spirit, with us at the approaching feast of Pentecost!

Gospel
One in the Lord
Jn 17, 20-26

We learn from this Scripture that the Lord Jesus wanted us to be one with him, and in him with one another. It is a oneness in love, founded on the oneness of Father and Son. Finally, Jesus prays that our oneness may be complete.

Love must be fostered daily. It is like a plant. If you do not water it regularly, it withers. Friends who fail to keep in touch soon drift apart. Keep in touch with the Lord Jesus! The more Christians do this, the more they will establish a beautiful oneness with one another.

PENTECOST
See pp. 73-78.

ORDINARY TIME (cont'd)
See p. 79.

C — Trinity Sunday

Sunday After Pentecost
TRINITY SUNDAY
The Ineffable Mystery of God

THE first thing our parents taught us about our religion was most probably the sign of the cross. The last thing a priest will do at our graveside is make the sign of the cross over our body. A Christian's life is marked "in the name of the Father, and the Son, and of the Holy Spirit." The Sunday Bible readings often speak to us about the Father (as originator of all life related to creation), sending his Son or Word (for our salvation) and communicating the Spirit (related to our rebirth from water and the Spirit.

The revelation of God as Father, Son, and Holy Spirit tells us first of all what God is for us. But as to the mysterious unity of Father, Son and Holy Spirit, we can only stammer with inadequate human concepts, which are not able to express the ineffable mystery of God in himself. We want to know. But we must realize that more important than knowing about God, is knowing God, the way two beloved know one another!

An intimate person-to-person relationship gives a knowledge which cannot possibly be expressed in human terminology. It is that kind of knowledge of God which ultimately satisfies a human being. "How deep are the riches and the wisdom and the knowledge of God! How inscrutable his judgments, how unsearchable his ways" (Rom 11, 33).

Reading I   Prv 8, 22-31
The Wisdom of God

God has created the universe by his infinite Wisdom. The universe is "the work of [his] fingers" (Responsorial Psalm). In this passage God's Wisdom is introduced to us a person. Later John will speak of God's Wisdom as Word of God and Light of God.

We learn how the ancient Hebrews experienced God's Wisdom in creation. We should follow that example. "O Lord, our God, how wonderful your name in all the earth!" (Responsorial Psalm).

Reading II Rom 5, 1-5
Experiencing God

Paul describes how afflicted persons can experience God—Father, Son, and Holy Spirit—in their lives. Whatever happens, in faith we know that we are at peace with God through Jesus Christ, who died for our sins. We have hope in God, and the Holy Spirit, given to us in baptism, is the pledge of God's fidelity.

Gospel Jn 16, 12-15
Father, Son and Holy Spirit

John does not teach the doctrine of the Blessed Trinity explicitly. But he speaks of Father, Son, and Holy Spirit. The Father is the origin of all creation. We experience him through Jesus Christ, who is his Wisdom, Word, Light, and perfect Image. And the Spirit, who proceeds from both, will guide us to all truth.

The apostles did not have a complete understanding of their mission when our Lord left them visibly. But his Spirit was to guide them. Similarly, we need the Holy Spirit to guide us on our path through life.

Sunday After Trinity Sunday
CORPUS CHRISTI
Sharing Life with Christ

IN an affluent society basic food such as bread and water is no problem. However, for many people in the world it still is . Thus they can understand better than we do that it is a real sign of love and care when God intervenes to feed his people. For them, water and bread are a question of life and death. But we are often hungry and thirsty for other values than sustenance of physical life. In a depersonalized society we suffer from absence where there should be presence. We hunger and thirst for companionship, love, concern, mercy, respect, which are no problems in the great family of primitive people. Whose need is greater?

C — Corpus Christi

Where we suffer from absence, the Lord Jesus wants to be present to us with all the concern and love of a friend for a friend. In the signs of plain daily food for Orientals, water, bread, wine, Jesus indicates what he intends by being present to us. He wants to share life. He wants to strengthen. He wants to mean something to you and me.

When we celebrate the Eucharist, we celebrate this mysterious presence of the Lord Jesus with the community. Open up to make "Communion" possible. "Whoever eats my flesh and drinks my blood will live in me and I in him, says the Lord" (Communion Antiphon)

Reading I
Gn 14, 18-20
Bringing Out Bread and Wine

It is not clear why Melchizedek is called "a priest of God Most High." The letter to the Hebrews (Ch. 7) refers to this passage and sees Melchizedek as a priest, foreshadowing Jesus Christ, because he blessed Abraham. Church tradition, as reflected in the first Eucharistic Prayer, refers to the bread and wine offered by this mysterious King Priest.

It may be that Melchizedek had offered the gifts of bread and wine previously to God and gave them to Abraham as a sacrificial repast together with his blessing. As such they could be types of the Eucharistic bread and wine, the Body and Blood of our Lord.

"Look with favor on these offerings and accept them as once you accepted the gifts of your servant Abel, the sacrifice of Abraham, our father in faith, and the bread and wine offered by your priest Melchizedek" (Eucharistic Prayer I). Relate the Responsorial Psalm (110, 1-4) to our High Priest, Jesus Christ!

Reading II
1 Cor 11, 23-26
"In Remembrance of Me"

The early Church celebrated the Eucharist as part of a communal meal, the "agape." Even today parish activities, picnics, and potluck dinners keep the members together and impart that feeling of belonging which we all need to persevere in the Christian way of life. However, in Corinth it had gotten out of hand. The rich brought their own food and did not share it with those who had less or nothing. Hence, the meal, which should result in a closer oneness of Christians, became a means of division.

Referring to this abuse, Paul invites the Christians of Corinth to meditate on the real meaning of the Eucharist. Are you aware that your partaking in the Eucharistic Banquet signifies not only your oneness with the Host, Jesus Christ, but also your oneness with the guests at that banquet, your fellow parishioners?

Gospel   Lk 9, 11-17
Breaking the Bread

The way Luke relates this tradition is clearly colored by the Eucharistic Liturgy of his Churches: Jesus took the bread, looked up to heaven, pronounced a blessing, broke the bread, and gave it to his disciples. The narrative points into a clear direction: People are in the desert and they are hungry; Jesus feeds them through the apostles. It all foreshadows the Eucharist.

On our way through the desert of life, we are in need. The Lord is there with his care and love, feeding us with "the bread of life and the cup of eternal salvation" (Eucharistic Prayer I). "Lord Jesus Christ, you give us your body and blood in the eucharist as a sign that even now we share your life. May we come to possess it completely in the kingdom where you live for ever and ever" (Prayer after Communion).

10th SUNDAY IN ORDINARY TIME
Victory over Death

THE well-known writer Stewart Alsop made headlines some years ago because he was able to speak so frankly and quietly on television about his death which he knew was impending. Physicians had told him, and newsmen were anxious to know how he felt about it. How one looks at death has much to do with one's religious faith.

C — 10th Sunday in Ordinary Time

The Jews before Christ had no clear idea about a hereafter; hence their outlook was somber. "We must indeed die, we are then like water that is poured out on the ground" (2 Sm 14, 14). But there was also a growing awareness that death could not have a part in God's original plan of creation (Gn 2, 17). Hence, death appears as an evil power in opposition to God. It is the envy of the devil which causes it (Wis 2, 24).

We find in the old Testament momentary glimpses of a possible overcoming of death (Prv 14, 32), but full assurance of survival after death came only with the Easter-event. Christ's victory over death, is the Good News of the Gospel (2 Tm 1, 10). Since that time, death though still a sad separation from beloved ones, has lost its sting (1 Cor 15, 55). We Christians possess a living hope (1 Pt 1, 3). There will be no more death in the consummated kingdom of God (Rv 21, 4). Today's Liturgy deals with life and death. What is your stand?

Reading I — A Man of God — 1 Kgs 17, 17-24

Following the common belief of her time, the poor widow sees the early death of her child as a punishment for her sins. In her eyes, the presence of the holy man in her house reveals God's anger about her hidden faults. Hence, she attributes her child's death to the prophet. The ensuing miracle confirms the woman in her belief that Elijah is a man of God.

This narrative teaches that God is the Lord of life and death. "He holds the whole world in his hand!" This miracle together with the widow's reaction foreshadows a similar event found in today's Gospel. Pondering the mystery of death, we may make our own the words of the Responsorial Psalm: "I will extol you, O Lord, for you drew me clear and did not let my enemies [death, sickness, evil] rejoice over me.... I will praise you, Lord, for you have rescued me."

Reading II — No Mere Human Invention — Gal 1, 11-19

As readily as the people of Galatia had accepted the Christian message from Paul, they just as readily listened later on to other preachers, who told them to follow the Law of Moses.

(See 9th Sunday—B, p. 180.) Paul refutes those preachers ana refers to his credentials as an apostle. He states that he is an apostle because he has seen the Lord, who illumined him about his meaning for all men (1 Cor 9, 1; Acts 9, 5). "The gospel I proclaimed to you is no mere human invention."

God's word to us in this tradition could be: In our society, we are in constant danger of being brainwashed by the glamorous sales technique of those who try to sell us instant happiness. We should not let anybody confuse us in our religious faith. Besides watching ball games and soap operas on television, we might try tuning in on some serious educational shows now and then; these could help us maintain a balanced outlook!

Gospel Lk 7, 11-17
A Great Prophet

The reaction of the people to Jesus' miracle was similar to that of the widow in the first reading: "God has visited his people." This is precisely the way we should see these miracle narratives They indicate the hidden reality of God's kingdom, which is victory over death.

Life everlasting was initiated in us when with Christ we died to sin in baptism. It will be fully realized in "the resurrection of the dead, and the life of the world to come" (Profession of Faith during Mass).

―――――◆―――――

11th SUNDAY IN ORDINARY TIME
Love, Understanding, Forgiveness

SELF-IDENTITY is one of the most important qualities we need in order to attain our purpose in life. Who am I? It is important that we accept ourselves as we are including the fact that we are sexual beings. Sex is present in all of us whether we are young or old, married or celibates, males or females. We should see sex as part of our being in its right perspective.

During the annual parish missions, sex was often a topic which was extensively preached upon! At the same time, Jesus' own emphasis on love and justice as most important (Jn 13, 35) remained somewhat in the background. Nowadays, there are healthy reactions—and as always over-reactions as well—to this one-sided emphasis on sex.

Today's Liturgy deals with this topic. Sex is good and beautiful but sinful if not in line with what our Maker designed it to be. Deviation should be avoided. But since all of this has so much to do with human weakness, God is willing to forgive, if there is repentance.

Reading I 2 Sm 12, 7-10. 13
The Lord Has Forgiven Your Sin

King David had sinned by committing adultery with the wife of one of his army commanders who was on duty away from home. When the woman became pregnant, David called the husband back, hoping that a short stay with his wife would cover up his own fatherhood. When this did not work, David ordered the commander to be put in a dangerous position during battle and as a result he was killed. Today's passage shows the prophet Nathan rebuking the King for having sinned grievously after God had been so good to him.

Note the theme of repentance, followed by forgiveness. The point is: Whenever we have been weak, we should repent (which implies that we should try to do better) and ask God for forgiveness. We could do so by using the words of the Responsorial Psalm (32, 1-11), which also introduces the topic of the Gospel.

Reading II Gal 2, 16. 19-21
Justified by Faith

This passage gives a summary of Paul's learned and difficult teaching on faith versus the Law of Moses. The Jews of Paul's time saw observation of this law as resulting in justification. Paul states that human endeavor cannot justify anyone. Rather it is faith, total dedication of self to God in the Lord Jesus, that leads to salvation, and faith in God's gracious gift, which we obtained because of Jesus' meritorious death and resurrection. Is our faith in God genuine dedication?

Gospel
Lk 7, 36—8, 3 or 7, 36-50
Your Sins Are Forgiven

In reading this tradition, as Luke presents it, we wonder who was more guilty in the opinion of our Lord, Simon his host or "the woman known in town to be a sinner." We read that Jesus rebukes Simon for his ungracious behavior, and that he has a warm understanding for the woman.

Jesus does not condone what she has been doing. He forgives. "Your faith has been your salvation. Go now in peace." What do you read as God's word to you in this Scripture?

12th SUNDAY IN ORDINARY TIME
Ongoing Knowledge and Deeper Understanding of the Lord Jesus

WHEN two young people pronounce their marriage vows and promise one another to go on together for the rest of their lives, they have already gotten to know one another previously, and they have mutual faith and love. Both will admit, however, that their mutual knowledge is only an understanding "to a certain extent." Knowing one another is an ongoing process, and it should be in order to remain exciting.

Seeing new aspects of her/his character time and again implies the element of surprise and overwhelming wonder which underlies happiness. This element of discovery should be part of all human friendship. As soon as we stop seeing "something" in the other, a relationship becomes boring and slowly the friends/lovers drift apart.

We should apply this piece of psychology to our faith-commitment to the Lord Jesus. Our knowledge and understanding of his mysterious personality should grow all the time. We keep it growing by prayerful and meditative Bible reading, by discovering him in fellow human beings ("As often as you did it for one of my least brothers, you did it for me": Mt 25, 40), and by celebrating his mysterious presence when we are together as Christians in our church. Today's Gospel deals with this subject ("Who do you say I [Jesus] am?").

C — 12th Sunday in Ordinary Time

Reading I   Zec 12, 10-11
"Mourning for Him"

The prophet writes about someone—a messiah, redeemer of suppressed people—who suffered and was killed, and his death poured a new spirit of grace on Israel. John applied the words "they shall look on him whom they have thrust through" to Jesus, who died on the cross (Jn 19, 37). The passage is used as an introduction to Jesus' statement in today's Gospel that the Messiah must suffer, an idea the disciples were never able to grasp during the Lord's lifetime.

Our life is patterned after that of the suffering Savior. Going through the valley of darkness, we may make the Responsorial Psalm (63, 2-9) our own prayer to God.

Reading II   Gal 3, 26-29
"All One in Christ Jesus"

In a few beautiful lines, Paul defines who we are as Christians. Note his emphasis on the unity of all Christians regardless of nationality, ethnic background, social standing, and sex. Does your congregation not simply tolerate but warmly welcome people of all races? And how about you yourself? For instance, is your handshake of peace during Mass a real sign of fellowship with all?

Gospel   Lk 9, 18-24
An Ongoing Process

If we read the Gospels carefully, we see that the disciples came to understand and know Jesus only gradually. Their initial attitude toward him was one of curiosity: " 'Teacher, where do you stay? 'Come and see,' he answered. So they went to see where he was lodged, and stayed with him that day" (Jn 1, 38-39). Then they received his call and became his disciples: "They became his followers" (Lk 5, 11). As such, they held discussions with him, asked questions, and received answers. Slowly, the disciples became aware of something special about this Teacher.

Today's passage reflects that growth in awareness: "You are the Messiah of God." Yet when Jesus brought up the necessity of suffering, they could not comprehend him (Mk 8, 32-33; Lk 9, 46). Only after the resurrection did their knowledge and understanding grow clearer. We see growth of insight up until the last books of the New Testament.

Who do you say that Jesus is? Do you know him and are you growing in knowledge? (See Introduction.) And keep in mind that more important than *knowing about* Jesus is *knowing him* as a person, as a friend knows a friend.

13th SUNDAY IN ORDINARY TIME
Fit or Unfit for the Reign of God

IN his book *The Cost of Discipleship,* Dietrich Bonhoeffer, a minister of the Confessional Church in Germany during the Hitler regime, wrote: "When Christ calls a man, he bids him come and die." He knew by experience the truth of his statement. Arrested by the Gestapo, he inspired his guards in prison and concentration camps. He obtained permission to minister to his fellow prisoners and his ability to comfort the anxious and depressed was amazing. A few days before the liberation of his concentration camp, he was executed. *The Cost of Discipleship* is a powerful attack on an "easy Christianity."

In reading today's Gospel, one is only amazed that Christians dare to take the easy way. The Founder of Christianity did not mean it to be that way. True, not all Christians are called to give up everything in life, neither must all become martyrs, but a firm commitment to Christ and what he stands for in our own life situation must be a part of every Christian's life.

If God calls you to be a Christian, "he bids you come and die" to your old self, your egotism and all evil, and become a new creature in Christ. There is no easy way for us to do this. Dying is after all a painful process.

C — 13th Sunday in Ordinary Time

Reading I
1 Kgs 19, 16. 19-21

A Challenge Accepted

This narrative tells about a call and the acceptance of the challenge to be a prophet, one who speaks in the name of God. If the prophet speaks up as he should, he knows that evil will resist him—even with a certain degree of violence. The action of throwing one's cloak over another possesses a symbolism similar to that of imposing hands on another. Here it stands for transmitting the charism of prophecy. This tradition is used to introduce a similar challenge of Jesus to his disciples in today's Gospel.

God's word to us in this narrative is clear: Accept the challenge to be a resolute Christian. Make the words of the Responsorial Psalm (16, 1-11) your own and praise God for your call to be a Christian.

Reading II
Gal 5, 1. 13-18

Guided by Love

Paul states that salvation comes through faith and not as a result of observing the Mosaic Law. It is a free gift of God. A Christian is free, but Paul qualifies Christian freedom. It is a freedom for love. One may ask: Do we need the ramifications of love and its applications to life situations known as laws? Yes, because of our limited human condition.

If we were so mature in Christ that the compass of love would point out the direction unfalteringly, we could do without the laws that explain the ramifications of love in various human situations. Usually we are not. Laws are needed, but their observance should always be guided and motivated by love.

Gospel
Lk 9, 51-62

An Easy Christianity

From this passage we learn that Jesus resolutely accepted the consequences of his preaching of God's reign. Renewing society and cleansing it from evil provokes resistance and even violence when the preacher of righteousness attacks an evil power structure. And Jesus requires that same resoluteness from his followers. Putting one's hand to the plow but looking back makes one unfit for the reign of God.

How strong is your commitmnent to Christ, and where are you inclined to take the easy way?

14th SUNDAY IN ORDINARY TIME
The "Already" and "Not Yet" of God's Reign

THE decades after World War II have seen many nations emerging from the mixed blessings of colonialism to self-determination. In such nations the urge for freedom was great. Many of their people risked their lives to oust the colonizers. And jubilant celebrations took place when finally the flag of dominance went down and their own national flag was raised. However, these nations quickly discovered that gaining freedom is one thing while building up an economically strong nation with a reasonable level of well-being for all is another one.

The Jews who returned from exile in Babylon had a similar experience. Reconstruction entailed much frustration. Where were the blessings (Shalom—peace—prosperity) promised them by God's holy men, the prophets?

Christians who take a life of Christian witness seriously may also be frustrated. Time and again they read in their Bible that the reign of God (justice, love, peace) has been initiated in this world. But they look in vain for an abundance of it in their children! For their part, young people are critical of what the Church has failed to do and turn away from it. Even religious are afflicted with the same problem: after years of work in the inner city, a dedicated Sister may feel disappointed! Today's readings preach optimism nevertheless.

Reading I
Is 66, 10-14
Have Hope!

The prophet called "Third Isaiah" addresses his fellow citizens who have returned from exile in Babylon. He urges them to rejoice, for they have regained at least relative freedom.

C — 14th Sunday in Ordinary Time

He compares the holy city, Jerusalem, with a mother who receives the returning exiles back at her breasts. But the prophet is well aware that rebuilding a ruined country is not so simple; it involves much frustration. Hence, he also consoles his people: Have hope! Sometime in the future, God will bestow shalom—prosperity on his chosen people!

We apply this promise to our own situation. We have been freed from the alienation/exile/bondage of evil. But we do not yet share in the shalom and blessings of the heavenly Jerusalem. It is the "already" and "not yet" we have to live with. Make the Responsorial Psalm (66) your prayer of thanksgiving for what you possess as a Christian, and keep your hope alive for perfect happiness to come. "For thus says the Lord: . . . As a mother comforts her son, so I will comfort you."

Reading II — Created Anew — Gal 6, 14-18

Paul refers to what he had to suffer as a missionary. Most of his pain was caused by his fellow Jews who did not accept his vision of the new Israel of God. According to them, Gentiles who joined the Church should be circumcised according to the rule of the Jewish faith. Paul states that it does not matter.

"All that matters is that one is created anew. Peace [shalom] and mercy on all who follow this rule of life." This could be God's message to us! We are created anew, reborn from water and Spirit. This is what gives us real shalom—peace and constitutes the reason for our gratitude.

Gospel — Always an Optimist! — Lk 10, 1-12. 17-20 or 10, 1-9

What Jesus said to the Twelve (9, 1-6), Luke now has him say to the seventy-two. The numbers symbolize respectively the twelve tribes of Israel and the nations of the world. The quintessence of the Christian blessing (God's gift to humankind) is shalom—prosperity. On entering any house, the seventy-two are to say first of all: "Peace to this house." The next part of their message should be: "The reign of God is at hand." The mission of the seventy-two was successful. They expelled demons!

What actually happened? Some good was done to those who received the message. Much evil went on as before. This is the "already" and "not yet" of God's reign in each individual and in the world at large. Shalom—peace—spiritual prosperity is with us. We should be grateful for what God has given us in baptism. But we should realize that God's reign is only *initiated* in this world. Full realization and perfect bliss will come later. A Christian can be an optimist always, as long as he does good to the best of his ability.

15th SUNDAY IN ORDINARY TIME
Christian Love Guided by Faith

IN observing the animal world, we can be touched by the apparent affection a female is able to give to her puppies. But it shocks us, when we see how cruel that same animal can be to other animals which are not her offspring. Seemingly a woman has the same affectionate love for her baby. The instinctive emotional part of love is apparently the same. But there is a great difference. Human love is not merely emotional. It also contains an element of insight. Besides loving her own baby, a mother also loves other children.

This element of insight is even more decisive when love is elevated from the mere human level to the sacred, namely, Christian love, called charity. The insight which guides charity is faith. Today's Liturgy deals with love of God and all human beings regardless of race, creed or color. Paying attention to the insight of faith, which guides it, is important.

READING I   Heeding God's Voice   Dt 30, 10-14

The Book of Deuteronomy (whicn means "Second Law") is a series of sermons or meditations on the Law of Moses. This passage seems to have been composed during the exile in Babylon. The author lets Moses speak figuratively. We should heed the voice of the Lord. It is not far away. It is in your heart. In Christian terminology, follow your informed conscience, through which God speaks to you.

C — 15th Sunday in Ordinary Time

This reading prepares us to listen to the Gospel which deals with God's commandments. Make the Responsorial Psalm (69, 14-37) your prayer when you need guidance in life.

Reading II   Col 1, 15-20
Reconciled in Christ

We have read in the "Wisdom literature" of the Bible that Wisdom in God was personified (see Reading I for 32nd Sunday in Ordinary Time—A p. 122) and seen as an agent through whom God had created the world and preserves it. Paul sees God's Wisdom incarnated in Jesus Christ. God revealing himself and acting in Jesus is the same God who creates and preserves the universe. Hence, creation is basically good though corrupted by evil.

Christ's task was to restore things, "to reconcile everything in his person." In baptized Christians God's design has been restored; we are reconciled with God "through the blood of his cross."

Gospel   Lk 10, 25-37
Loving God *and* Neighbor

Jesus' commandment of love of God and neighbor is actually a combination of Deuteronomy 6, 5 and Leviticus 9, 18 (see 31st Sunday in Ordinary Time—B, p. 219). We cannot love God without loving our neighbor, nor conversely is love of neighbor possible without love of God. The insight of faith helps us to see the reason why. (See Introduction.) Faith tells us that all human beings are God's children. He loves all of them. You cannot possibly love parents and exclude their children from your love. The other way around, faith tells us that what you do for the least of your brothers you do for God (Mt 25, 40).

Love of God must motivate you; otherwise you will confine your love to those you like, and eventually behave like the priest and Levite in the Parable of the Good Samaritan. Being a good Samaritan requires faith, which tells me that all people, regardless of race, creed, or color, are brothers and sisters of one heavenly Father.

16th SUNDAY IN ORDINARY TIME
Hospitality

THE concept of hospitality has had various connotations over the centuries. In the 6th century St. Benedict wrote in his rule that his monks should receive the stranger as Christ himself. The abbeys were havens for the lonesome traveler. For centuries, men and women have dedicated their lives as religious Brothers and Sisters to welcoming the stranger and the suffering in their hospitals, which were centers of charity, real "guest houses."

Now it is different. Though there are still a few sporadic "hospices" run by Sisters, and Christian denominations still operate hospitals which bear their names, as a rule the stranger checks in at a motel and the sick person is taken care of in the community hospital, both paying for the service they receive.

However, hospitality is still a Christian form of charity. Think of the family. How do we receive our guests? A visit of friends can still be an enriching experience for both the guests and the host and hostess, provided that there is mutual openness, real hospitality. Many Christians make their living by welcoming the strangers and the sick: receptionists, waitresses, physicians, nurses. In doing so they can practice service with a smile. That smile could make their service Christian!

Think of the hospitality of your congregation toward strangers regardless of race, color or creed. Many parishes have a committee on hospitality, and hospitality should be practiced at parish socials which give us that feeling of belonging which we all need to keep on living the Christian life. The first and third Bible readings deal with hospitality, and the stranger/guest was indeed God/Christ himself!

Reading I Gn 18, 1-10
An Example of Hospitality

In this tradition, Abraham is introduced to us as an example of hospitality. He follows the rule of hospitality common to his time and culture. The point is that he was gracious. We should see Abraham's hospitality as related to his faith, which is rewarded by God. Sarah, his wife, will have a son. "He who does justice will live in the presence of the Lord" (Responsorial Psalm).

Reading II Col 1, 24-28
The Mystery of Christ in You

We should receive Christ with a mature faith. Paul had preached this mystery to the Colossians. But a mystery is something we should penetrate into ever more by faithful meditation. Just as we grow in understanding a loved one by daily conversation, so should we grow in understanding our Lord by meditatively listening to his words in Scripture and meeting him with an open mind in our fellow humans/guests (Reading I and Gospel).

Gospel Lk 10, 38-42
Openness to the Guest!

Martha and Mary were hospitable toward our Lord—each in her own way. Martha was "busy with all the details of hospitality" and doing "the household tasks." Mary listened to Jesus' words. Both aspects of hospitality are important. But the openness to the guest as a person, in this case to our Lord's message of salvation, is more important.

When we receive Christ in other human beings, we should have an open eye for this mystery. Wherever I experience goodness, God is present!

17th SUNDAY IN ORDINARY TIME
Ask and You Shall Receive

PARENTS often display a remarkable patience in smilingly listening to the talk of their little children. And the little ones not only ask questions, they also ask for favors. Parents listen, but do they always grant what the little ones ask? Of course not! The horizons of children are limited. Often they ask for favors which would hurt them. Prudent parents show their real love by never giving children more freedom or favors than they are able to handle at a particular moment in life.

However, whether one is a teenager or an adult, it takes humility to admit that one's horizon is limited. Yet when we think of the infinite wisdom and love of the heavenly Father, in faith we should be able to admit that he knows better whatever is best for us. It is in this context that we should see our prayer of petition. Does it make sense to pray for a beloved one who has terminal cancer? Should we pray in a seemingly hopeless marriage situation?

Today's first and third Scripture readings teach us to pray with perseverance but also offer some insights on what to expect from our prayer of petition.

Reading I   Gn 18, 20-32
Building Up Strength

By relating this tradition concerning Abraham, the sacred writer wants to teach us about the necessity of praying with perseverance. Abraham even bargains with God and God listens. "Lord, on the day I called for help, you answered me" (Responsorial Psalm).

But does the heavenly Father always grant exactly what we ask? The same psalm continues: "When I called, you answered me; *you built up strength within me.*" This may be the answer. God will hear our prayers and certainly give us the strength to handle any situation in life.

Reading II   Col 2, 12-14
Appreciating Company

Paul resists preachers who want to impose laws of the Old Testament on Christians. We are saved not by observing those laws (such as circumcision), but by God's grace given to us because of Jesus' death on the cross. We have a new life in company with Christ. Do we appreciate that company?

C — 18th Sunday in Ordinary Time

Gospel — Lk 11, 1-13

Giving the Holy Spirit

Jesus taught us how to pray. We should address God as Father. We should pray with perseverance. But will we obtain exactly what we ask? Comparing God with our father here on earth, Jesus says: "How much more will the heavenly Father *give the Holy Spirit* to those who ask him." Remember, the Responsorial Psalm says: "You answered me; you built up *strength within me.*"

God knows best what we really need! Perhaps we need "his spirit of wisdom and understanding, his spirit of counsel and of strength, his spirit of knowledge and of fear [filial respect] of the Lord" (Is 11, 2). If we become filled with God's Spirit and can cope effectively with some difficult situation or obtain the insight to solve a problem, then God has answered our prayer! (See Introduction.)

18th SUNDAY IN ORDINARY TIME

What Makes Life Meaningful?

LIFE makes sense only if we can relate it to lasting values. If persons seek only values that perish, they will never be satisfied. Money and all that it can buy cannot impart lasting happiness. Think of the high suicide rate among the wealthy!

Life is meaningful so far as it is related to others: fellow human beings and ultimately God in Christ Jesus. Think of people who have meant something to you in the past. These people, parents, teachers, sisters, brothers, friends, partner in marriage and finally Jesus Christ himself, have all contributed to whatever you are now as a person! Remove one person from this list and you would be different, perhaps less fortunate.

The lesson for the future is obvious. Go on building communication with others. In love, friendship, and dedication relate to others, and do not overlook your direct relationship with God—Jesus Christ through prayerful Bible reading and regular worship with fellow Christians.

C — 18th Sunday in Ordinary Time

Reading I   Eccl 1, 2; 2, 21-23
Without God All Is Vanity

When we read the Bible, we expect "Gospel," which means "good news." On first reading this passage, we would be inclined to characterize it as bad news. "All things are vanity." If life is an absurdity, why go on living it in the first place?

Actually, this passage is a very strong statement of what human life is without God. Only if we relate life to God directly in prayer and worship and indirectly in meeting him in other human beings does existence makes sense. "If today you hear his [God's] voice, harden not your hearts" (Responsorial Psalm).

Reading II   Col 3, 1-5. 9-11
Remaining in Company with Christ

Our friends and those with whom we socialize can have a great effect on us—either for good or for evil. Thus, we advise youngsters to get out of the wrong gang. Good friends, however, have an uplifting impact. Paul expects a similar effect from our being in company with Christ: "Set your hearts on what pertains to higher realms!"

In baptism, you have died to selfishness and sin. But this dying to evil is an ongoing process which results in growing into the image of the Creator. Remaining in Christ's company makes life meaningful (Reading I and Gospel).

Gospel   Lk 12, 13-21
"You Fool!"

The rich fool of this passage lived his life without reference to God. And, indeed, a life without reference to God is an absurdity. Where does God fit into your money-making process?

Concern for the future is good stewardship. But if concern becomes greed, egotism, keeping up with the neighbors, inspired by the philosophy that "we live only once," you are in trouble. You are only God's steward of all that you possess! Do you feel responsible for those less fortunate?

19th SUNDAY IN ORDINARY TIME
Faith in God Gives Hope for a Destiny To Come

"LISTEN here, Joe. / Don't you know / That tomorrow / You got to go / Out yonder where / The steel winds blow? / ... Don't ask me why. / Just go ahead and die." These lines are from Langston Hughes' poem "Without Benefit of Declaration." Apparently, life is just such a journey "without benefit of declaration." Simply live it and die! The ancient Hebrew sages searched for "declaration" and, guided by God, they came up not with all the answers but certainly with some remarkable insights. They reasoned that if God is good, he must have a plan of salvation. Life cannot be a journey without destiny!

This outlook on life requires faith in God, and though it does not offer all the answers it gives enough of them to enable us to see meaning in our lives. It is like the faith in a parent that makes a child feel safe even when the child does not know where they are going.

To a certain extent, limited as our human horizon is, we are like children. Trust in a loving God takes away absurdity and gives hope for a destiny to come. Today's Bible readings deal with the journey of life and preparedness.

Reading I   Wis 18, 6-9
God Will Step In

"That night . . .": the author refers to the night of the Exodus from bondage in Egypt. It was known centuries earlier by "our fathers," Abraham, Isaac, Jacob. How? By their faith in a saving God. Whatever happens to human beings, faith in God assures them that somehow God will step in with his loving care.

This passage is a poem on faith. As believers, we feel happy with the sure knowledge of a loving God who cares. "See, the eyes of the Lord are upon those who fear [have filial respect for] him, upon those who hope for his kindness" (Responsorial Psalm).

C — 20th Sunday in Ordinary Time

Reading II **Heb 11, 1-2, 8-19 or 11, 1-2. 8-12**
Faith in a Destiny

"By faith Abraham obeyed . . . ; he went forth, moreover, not knowing where he was going." His journey was apparently "without declaration." (See Introduction.) However, faith in God made his journey meaningful. The sacred writer himself suggests the application of this ancient tradition to our own life situation: "They were searching for a better, a heavenly home."

We are pilgrims who go through the valley of darkness. Faith in a destiny makes the journey meaningful. Abraham's faith was tested. So will yours be! Faith implies an element of doubt, just as love does. You cannot always possess it peacefully. Like love, faith must be fostered by communication, i.e., meditative prayer!

Gospel **Lk 12, 32-48 or 12, 35-40**
Be on Guard!

Jesus encourages us to go "searching for . . . a heavenly home" (Reading II). "Do not live in fear. . . . It has pleased your Father to give you the kingdom."

But be prepared! "Let your belts be fastened around your waists," like the Jews about to leave Egypt! The moment you least expect it, you could be summoned to make "that loath journey," from which there is no return ("Everyman").

20th SUNDAY IN ORDINARY TIME
Can We Stand Correction?

"LEAVE me alone! Mind your own business!" is the usual reaction when others interfere with our way of life. We want to be happy in our own little world, with our good and perhaps also bad habits!

C — 20th Sunday in Ordinary Time

Children do not like to be corrected by parents or teachers. Grown-ups unduly resent their employers' attempts to enhance their working methods. Parishioners may concede that priests should preach on sin, but they do not want them to go into details in which the audience may be involved! And in the "closed society" of the South in the sixties, people who came in to encourage blacks to stand up for their rights were termed "outside agitators." They were told: "Go home and leave us alone!"

Today's second Bible reading compares life with a race course. We should persevere in running the race of life. But no team is going to succeed without a coach who observes every player and corrects the technique of each. Can we stand honest correction? The first and third readings tell us about Jeremiah and Jesus of Nazareth, who did not leave people alone. In the name of God, they had to speak. Their sermons were corrective and aimed at restoring life as it should be!

Reading I — Jer 38, 4-6. 8-10
Demoralizing the People?

Jeremiah the prophet ("mouthpiece of God") corrected the power structure of his society. Israel was God's chosen people, living with him in a sacred partnership (covenant). He wanted those in power to realize this, but they did not like to be corrected by the man of God.

This reading prepares us to understand today's Gospel in which Jesus predicts his passion and death. Suffering and endurance is part of each serious Christian's life, and faith in God should help us to stand it. "Though I am afflicted and poor, yet the Lord thinks of me" (Responsorial Psalm).

Reading II — Heb 12, 1-4
Jesus, a Good Coach

Wherever the ancient Romans built cities, one finds the ruins of an amphitheater. They loved the games. This passage uses sporting language to encourage us not to follow the easy way as Christians but rather to make even painful decisions, if necessary (Gospel). Life is the arena of the local amphitheater.

A cloud of witnesses/spectators watches us. Sins are hindering clothes. Take them off when you are running.

Keep your eyes fixed on Jesus. As a good coach, he inspires and perfects your faith and self-confidence. And he gives the reason for your efforts, namely, the joy of heaven. He himself endured the opposition of sinners (Gospel). The lesson for you and me is: Do not abandon the struggle!

Gospel Lk 12, 49-53
Jesus Came To Light a Fire

"I have a baptism to receive." Jesus refers to "baptism by immersion." In other words, he says: "I will be immersed in pain and death." And he shows that he is human by feeling anguish!

Jesus could not conceive of himself as running a popularity contest. Those who follow him must be willing to make even painful decisions. "Avoiding the occasion of sin" could be such a decision!

21st SUNDAY IN ORDINARY TIME
Shall All Be Saved and You Be Rejected?

"SAFETY first." "Better safe than sorry." Nowadays, safety is almost an obsession. We have our savings. We pay our social security. We insure our cars, our homes, our lives, and we buckle our safety belts faithfully. But what about our ultimate safety, our eternal salvation?

It gives you an unpleasant feeling if you miss the bus, train or airplane. Your feeling is even more miserable if you know that it was your own fault because you wasted time doing unnecessary things which could have been done later. Should we not then seriously consider the possibility that we might come too late for the kingdom of God? Could it happen that though we have been paying our church dues and taking part in the Eucharistic Banquet, we will not be saved? Shall all be saved and you yourselves be rejected? (See Reading I.)

C — 21str Sunday in Ordinary Time 303

This is a serious question in a time when the confessionals are not frequented very much anymore. Perhaps your parish has communal penitential services. Do you take part in them? Penance, conversion, a realistic and humble look at oneself—this is an integral part of the Biblical message. We are not allowed to do away with it in the name of contemporary psychology.

Reading I   Is 66, 18-21
Salvation for All

This reading from Third Isaiah rejects all clannishness on the part of the Jewish people. Although they are God's chosen people, this does not mean that others cannot be saved. When the Messiah will establish God's kingdom on earth, people from all over the world will come to Jerusalem to worship. The early Christians saw this vision fulfilled when the Gentiles joined the Church. And it will be fully realized when the Son of Man, Jesus, will gather all nations into his own.

It often happens that people who joined the Church at a late age make those born and raised in the family ashamed by being more serious than they are. We should be appreciative, "for steadfast is his kindness toward us, and the fidelity of the Lord endures forever" (Responsorial Psalm).

Reading II   Heb 12, 5-7. 11-13
Well-Accepted Suffering

"Whom the Lord loves, he disciplines": suffering and pain are part of human condition. Guided by God, the Hebrew sages searched for some insight into the mystery of both mental and physical pain. "The discipline of God" might be one. It is better to be punished now than later. Suffering, if well accepted, may open our eyes to the real values of life and lead to repentance (Reading I).

Gospel   Lk 13, 22-30
Repentance and Salvation

Luke puts a question into the mouth of "someone": "Are they few in number who are to be saved?" He answers by placing three parables of our Lord in a row. The first parable is the one about the narrow door. There are a few conditions if we want to be saved. We know them! "Oh, when the Saints go marchin' in. . . ."

The second parable is directed to those who are late. They have not repented in time and miss the boat by their own fault: "Away from me, you evildoers!"

The third parable warns Israel not to have pretensions as God's chosen people. Only those who repent, both Jews and Gentiles, will be saved. Constant conversion is part of a Christian life-style!

───────◆───────

22nd SUNDAY IN ORDINARY TIME
He Who Humbles Himself Shall Be Exalted

ONLY those who are really great can afford to be humble. Humility stands actually for truth. There is a story about an actor who wanted a famous photographer-friend to shoot him and instinctively assumed the pose of a character in one of his movies. The photographer had to remind him: "I want a picture of *you!*" The actor had trouble being himself in front of a camera. He was always acting.

It is well-adjusted persons who can honestly be themselves always and everywhere. Such persons do not need status symbols, neither do they have any desire to keep up with their neighbors. They have no need to prove themselves, for "good wine needs no bush."

Humble parents have no pretensions. They know that they are loved and respected by their children for what they are. They can afford to apologize for mistakes, since it is human to make them. Humble persons give in easily when the other proves that he or she is right. One cannot be an expert in all fields. As a Christian virtue, humility is rooted in God. Christians know that all they are and have constitute a gift of God. Hence, they are in constant need of God. Jesus is the sublime example of humility and that is why he can speak about it, as he does in today's Gospel.

C — 22nd Sunday in Ordinary Time

Reading I
Sir 3, 17-18. 20. 28-29
Humble Yourself

"Humble yourself . . . , and you will find favor with the Lord." The writer of Sirach is a keen observer of his fellow humans. People addicted to pride, full of pretensions, are like actors who constantly play the roles of other characters but never their own. They cannot be great in God's eyes.

Humble persons know that they depend entirely on God. "God, in your goodness, you have made a home for the poor [me]" (Responsorial Psalm).

Reading II
Heb 12, 18-19. 22-24
"The Heavenly Jerusalem"

The Old Testament imagery for the greatness of God consists of clouds, fire, storm, angels, blasting trumpets, thunder, and lightning. This imagery is lavishly used at the manifestation of God on Mount Sinai. People were warned not to break through toward the Lord in order to see him (Ex 19, 16-25). They might be struck down.

The author of Hebrews refers to this theophany (manifestation of God) and compares it with the theophany on Mount Zion, located in heaven, where we will see God without trembling and fear. But coming to this mountain in heaven, meeting God there face to face and partaking in his banquet is granted only to the humble, as today's Gospel teaches us.

Gospel
Lk 14, 1. 7-14
Come Up Higher!

Jesus relates a parable and an exhortation to his host. The parable is not just a lesson in good table manners. Rather, it refers to the Messianic Banquet of the end-time. Attendance depends on the invitation of God. And only those who are humble and in need of salvation will be there.

Are you self-sufficient or in need of God? The exhortation to the host suggests that our acceptance of fellow humans now has something to do with our own acceptance at the Messianic Banquet later.

23rd SUNDAY IN ORDINARY TIME
Wisdom and the Demands of Discipleship

IN a computerized society we stress the value of planning and calculation. The computer helps the human mind to make quick and prudent decisions. Does calculation have a place in interhuman relationships, or, on a higher level, in the way human beings decide to style their lives as related to God and religion?

Biblical persons did not know the computer, but they did know about wisdom and prudence. Even if we speak of love, dedication, and faith, the element of prudence must be there! Intuitive and emotional decisions are sometimes feasible and even heroic. But, as a rule, we must sit down, apply wisdom and prudence, and even calculate our resources. The first and third Scripture readings deal with prudence and even calculation.

Reading I — Wis 9, 13-18
The Deliberations of Mortals

The Book of Wisdom addresses Jews living in Egypt (1st century B.C.). As a minority group, they were exposed to the Greek culture and philosophy of their time. Greek wisdom, which survives even in modern universities, endangered the Biblical wisdom Jews were supposed to follow.

The author is convinced that we need wisdom and prudence, and as such this reading refers to today's Gospel. But he also stresses that real wisdom is a gift of God. It cannot be obtained by professional philosophers. We must beg God to give it. Do we pray for guidance when we are about to make an important decision? "Teach us to number our days aright, that we may gain wisdom of heart" (Responsorial Psalm).

Reading II — Phlm 9-10. 12-17
Practicing Clemency

In this letter, Paul, though himself in jail, intercedes for a runaway slave. Was this slave, Onesimus, a young teenager? Paul calls him "my child." Apparently, he had stolen some-

C — 24th Sunday in Ordinary Time

thing from his master. In any case, existence would be hard for this young man; if caught, he would receive the most severe punishment. Under the circumstances, in Paul's opinion, it was best to send him back.

At the same time, Paul wrote this letter in which he pleads that Philemon, the master, will take him back, "no longer as a slave but more than a slave, a beloved brother . . . since now you will know him both as a man and in the Lord." God's word in this tradition could be that we should practice clemency!

Gospel — Calculate Your Resources
Lk 14, 25-33

The first part of this passage consists of Jesus' statement on the demands of discipleship. It is followed by two parables which relate to these demands. "Turning his back on his father and mother" (in other translations, "hating") is a Semitic way of saying "giving his father and mother second place in his affection"; Matthew's version has: "He who loves father or mother *more than* me. . . ." Jesus requires detachment from family ties and the willingness to carry a cross.

If our Lord suggests giving up marriage and possessions, he does so for the reason of following him. Celibacy is not a value in itself, neither is it the same as bachelorhood! Hence, we speak of "celibacy for the kingdom of God." Those who feel called should calculate their resources, as the parables of the tower-builder and the king going to war indicate (see also 13th Sunday in Ordinary Time—cycle C).

The Church has always known young men and women who accept Jesus' challenge. Let us pray that we may always have them. And when you are young, calculate your resources, and pray for wisdom (Reading I).

◆

24th SUNDAY IN ORDINARY TIME
This Man Welcomes Sinners

PARENTS of teenagers know about mistakes being made and the need for understanding and forgiveness. It is part of the process of growing up for children to make mistakes. The real problem arises when teenagers do not feel sorry for their mistakes and want to do things their way, right or wrong. We can envision youngsters dropping out of school, being on dope, running away from home. Although parents suffer, they are always ready to forgive; but what can they do as long as a child is recalcitrant and unwilling?

Relating this to our relationship with the heavenly Father, we often have the same situation. If we determine what is sinful, and do not go by what God thinks, we are in trouble. Sin has not disappeared! Have I given up the diligent search for perfection? Am I failing to be the kind of person I should be in God's eyes? Am I just indifferent? Today's Bible readings deal with God's clemency and our willingness to admit that we were wrong as a condition for restoring a broken relationship.

Reading I   Ex 32, 7-11. 13-14
Moses Interceding

This reading shows us that because of Moses' intercession God agrees not to punish the sinful people. As mediator, Moses foreshadows Jesus Christ, who prayed on the cross for sinners: "Father, forgive them," and who is still praying for us in heaven (Heb 7, 25).

Because of Jesus' pleading for us, God will not destroy the sinner. The condition is that we make the Responsorial Psalm (51) our constant prayer to God.

Reading II   1 Tm 1, 12-17
Coming To Save Sinners

Paul refers to himself as a former sinner (Acts 8, 1-3). God forgave him because of Jesus' meritorious death on the cross. Paul is grateful for God's mercy, as all sinners should be.

Gospel   Lk 15, 1-32, or 15,1-10
The Lord Welcoming Sinners

This passage is a perfect example of the fact that the writer of this Gospel did not intend to provide a biography of Jesus. What he intended to do was write a catechism, a digest of what

Christians ought to know. However, Luke did not write a question-and-answer type of catechism which was used for the last few centuries in the Church and with which most of the older Catholics were taught their religion. He did it his way.

In this passage, Luke makes a thought-provoking statement which he puts into the mouth of the Pharisees: "This man welcomes sinners and eats with them." Then he responds to it with three parables of Jesus: "the lost sheep" and "the lost silver piece" (both concerning God's care for the sinner), and "the prodigal son" (concerning the condition for forgiveness: "I will . . . return to my father," and God's willingness to forgive the penitent sinner.

God's word to us today is clear (see also Introduction). It is through Jesus Christ, his meritorious death on the cross and his constant pleading for us in heaven, that God forgives our sins. "I will . . . return to my [heavenly] father"—this is what the sinner should do, and God will show mercy. Jesus is still welcoming sinners!

──────────◆──────────

25th SUNDAY IN ORDINARY TIME

"To Each His/Her Own"

SUCCESS in business can easily lead to a presumptuous feeling of absolute ownership and the desire for more, often regardless of the right and needs of others. The Bible reminds us that there is no such a thing as absolute ownership. Humankind is God's partner and with God is responsible for a better world. In partnership with God, humankind has the right to use the resources of the planet. Therefore, everyone must be guaranteed a fair share in their ownership. Historical and sociological considerations indicate that the most practical means of insuring everyone's access to the goods of the earth is some system of private property.

The right of private property is derived from the collective right of the human race to use the goods of the earth. "To each his/her own" is the golden rule of justice. Workers are entitled to earn a just wage and to receive humane treatment, and they must do a good job. We have our unions to protect these rights.

C — 25th Sunday in Ordinary Time

Both employers and employees must be careful that their associations and unions do not commit collective injustice! To each his/her own! Today's first and third Bible readings deal with the issue of just management.

Reading I — Trampling upon the Needy — Am 8, 4-7

Amos of Tekoa (750 B.C.) is the well-known prophet of social justice. Though living in the Southern Kingdom, he went to the Northern Kingdom of Israel, the sanctuary of Bethel, where he delivered his message. Imagine that during the worship service in your church, a stranger would stand up and address the congregation as Amos did! ("New moon" and "sabbath": the first day of each lunar month and the sabbath were days of rest; the "ephah" was a standard of measure.) Small wonder that the priest of the sanctuary told Amos to leave.

God's word is that we should be concerned about the rights and needs of fellow humans. God is! "He raises up the lowly from the dust; from the dunghill he lifts the poor" (Responsorial Psalm).

Reading II — Prayer for All — I Tm 2, 1-8

Our petitions during Mass should be universal, not only for the needs of the congregation. We pray that all human beings may be saved. We pray for our politicians and those in authority, that they may do an honest job. Do you try to make the petitions your prayer?

Gospel — Being Trustworthy — Lk 16, 1-13 or 16, 10-13

The Long Form of today's Gospel consists first of the parable of the wily manager. Notice that the owner, Jesus, does not praise the dishonesty of the manager, but rather his cleverness in acting decisively in a moment of crisis. The second part consists of statements on the right use of money. Since this is the topic of the first reading, and the Short Form restricts itself to these statements, obviously the Church wants us to focus attention on the these statements concerning trustworthiness.

"You cannot give yourself to God and money"; the meaning is obvious. If you sever the management of your possessions from your religious faith, you will soon be going by a double standard. The motto "To each his/her own" should be our guide whenever we handle money and do business. Only then can God trust us!

26th SUNDAY IN ORDINARY TIME
"They Have Moses and the Prophets. Let Them Hear Them."

SHOULD bishops and priest speak up for social justice? Should priests and nuns be involved in the civil rights movements of our deprived minorities, blacks, Chicanos, Indians, poor whites in Appalachia? Or should the priest be just the man of the sanctuary and nuns merely remain as teachers in the parochial school?

After all, have we not sent our missionaries abroad? Have we not contributed to the support of these minorities whenever a second collection was taken up for the poor missions? Indeed we have, but since the Second Vatican Council there is a renewed awareness in the Church that we cannot easily do enough for the deprived and the poor!

The Bible today warns against luxury-loving and not being concerned about our unfortunate fellow humans. A rich lady once had occasion to drive the nuns of her parish to the slum area of town to deliver Christmas baskets. Her eyes were opened: "I did not know that such a poverty existed right here!" In the Gospel, we read, the rich man's eyes were opened too late! Abraham tells all who live luxuriously: "You have Moses and the prophets," i.e., your Bible. Why do you not read it, and apply its message honestly to your own life situation?

Reading I Woe! Am 6, 1. 4-7

(See also the commentary of last Sunday's first reading.) Amos describes the luxurious living of his time and blames the wealthy for not caring about the collapse of Joseph. Like Israel [Jacob] and Judah, Joseph is one of the Jewish patriarchs. Their names are often used just to indicate God's people.

The "woe" of this message is addressed as God's word to the wealthy of all times and cultures. "The Lord gives food to the hungry," but he needs our hands to distribute it (Responsorial Psalm).

Reading II 1 Tm 6, 11-16
Your Noble Profession of Faith

Paul reminds his disciple and coworker Timothy of the day of his baptism, when "in the presence of many witnesses" he made his noble profession of faith. "I charge you to keep God's command." "Fight the good fight of faith." (As a born-and-bred city boy, Paul loved the games!) We renew our profession of faith every year at Easter, and as often as we are godparents at a baptism. We do it even every Sunday. Make it meaningful!

Gospel Lk 16, 19-31
Listening to Moses!

In relating this parable of the rich man and poor Lazarus, Luke brings out a message similar to that of Amos in the first reading. It is a "woe" to the have's! And those who have enough should not say that they did not know about poverty and misery in their area! (See Introduction.) You have your Bible. Read it prayerfully!

◆

27th SUNDAY IN ORDINARY TIME
Increase Our Faith!

WHEN we are in real distress, we find out who are our real friends. They are the ones who stay with us even at the cost of sacrifice. They have time for us. They have the patience to listen and the nobility to keep secrets. They are the people we can trust and have confidence in. Unfortunately, there are

C — 27th Sunday in Ordinary Time

not many friends who can stand the test. Patients who have to stay in the hospital for a long time know this.

However, Christians who maintain a living relationship with God are fortunate. They know by experience that God never disappoints those who have faith in him. Such a faith is a gift of God, which must grow with us when we mature. Like love, faith knows its doubts. There are dark periods, but never despair or desolation. Loneliness must be overcome by friendship and confidence in "the other." If this "other" can be God as well, that person is happy! Today's Bible readings deal with faith.

Reading I
Hb 1, 2-3; 2, 2-4
"Because of His Faith"

The setting is Jerusalem, besieged by the Babylonians (600 B.C.). The prophet tries to console his fellow citizens. They must have faith in God. "The just man, because of his faith, shall live." We may be besieged by sorrow and distress. Our faith in God should be our stronghold.

In such moments a Christian kneels down and prays: "Come, let us bow down in worship, let us kneel before the Lord who made us. For he is our God, and we are the people he shepherds, the flock he guides" (Responsorial Psalm).

Reading II
2 Tm 1, 6-8. 13-14
Keep the Faith

Paul, himself in jail, reminds Timothy of his ordination to the ministry. There are dark days of persecution ahead. Leadership in such a situation requires courage and faith. It could be that Timothy was somewhat timid. "Never be ashamed of your testimony to our Lord." And as a bishop, "guard the rich deposit of faith with the help of the Holy Spirit who dwells within us."

When you are depressed, or things do not go your way, keep your faith in God alive with the help of the Holy Spirit who dwells within you!

Gospel　　　　　　　　　　　　　Lk 17, 5-10
"Increase Our Faith!"

Like the apostles, all Christians must pray often that God may increase their faith. Either your faith in God grows or it withers! Since children are baptized into the faith of their parents, father and mother must help them grow in the faith. This is a serious duty.

But we are warned to keep commercialism out of faith, just as we must keep it out of love. Faith and the service of God that it entails cannot *earn* the reward of heaven. God does not owe us anything. When gratefully we have done our duty, we are still useless servants who hope for God's graciousness.

28th SUNDAY IN ORDINARY TIME
Was There No One To Return and Give Thanks?

ALTHOUGH medical science has advanced tremendously, there are still cases where physicians "do not know." This is frightening for patients and relatives involved. Eventually one can adjust to the inevitable. But when there is no certainty as to the diagnosis, the treatment, and final result, one hopes, one prays, one worries.

From these cases we can understand how in prescientific times people worried when they had to face diseases. They regarded sickness, epilepsy, leprosy, fever as caused by demons and evil spirits. Hence, they turned to the holy man, the prophet, for help. He was asked to pray and expel the demons. God had to intervene and show his mighty strength. Actually, these people did right away what we do after the doctors have exhausted all their means—they directed themselves to God.

It is against this background that we must see the numerous healing narratives in the Bible. Healing stood for expelling evil spirits; hence, it was an apt sign of God being present to his people with his loving care and defeating evil. In reading the healing narratives we should not be more inquisitive than the

C — 28th Sunday in Ordinary Time

Biblical authors themselves were. They took those ancient traditions at face value and fashioned them to bring out their religious teachings.

Jesus did indeed work miracles but the healing narratives of the Bible are not medical reports. They are stories that convey a religious message, which is God's word to the reader. Understand today's healing narratives with this information in mind!

Reading I   2 Kgs 5, 14-17
He Returned To Give Thanks

It is worth our while to read the whole story on Naaman the Syrian in 2 Kings 5. Notice that Naaman was a foreigner, not a member of God's chosen people. This foreigner received salvation and was very grateful. He pledged to worship the God of Israel from that moment on. In line with the opinion of his time, Naaman needs two mule-loads of earth, since the God of the land of Israel can be worshiped only on his own land.

Our Lord's comment on this narrative is also noteworthy: "Recall, too, the many lepers in Israel in the time of Elisha the prophet; yet not one was cured except Naaman the Syrian" (Lk 4, 27). The point of this story is clearly that salvation from evil (see Introduction) will be given to all. God's salvific will is universal! "The Lord has revealed to the nations his saving power" (Responsorial Psalm). This narrative prepares us to read the Gospel.

Reading II   2 Tm 2, 8-13
Living with Him

We who are redeemed from evil (Reading I and Gospel) should heed Paul's words to Timothy: "If we have died with him [i.e., died to evil by faith and baptism], we shall also live with him." A Christian life is a sign of gratitude and appreciation for the salvation from evil which God has bestowed upon us.

Gospel   Lk 17, 11-19
Let Us Give Thanks!

(See 6th and 23rd Sundays in Ordinary Time—B.) Notice that the only one who came back to thank our Lord was a

Samaritan. "Recall that Jews have nothing to do with Samaritans" (Jn 4, 9). The point is similar to that of the first reading. All of us are contaminated by evil (leprosy—sin), but redeemed from evil by faith sealed by baptism.

Salvation from evil is given not only to us, but to all nations. And converts are often more appreciative and grateful than those of the household of faith. Ingratitude is a common human failing. We should be grateful for God's saving presence to us. "Let us give thanks to the Lord our God. It is right to give him thanks and praise" (Introductory dialogue to the Preface).

29th SUNDAY IN ORDINARY TIME
The Sacred Scriptures, Source of Wisdom

THROUGH the media we have contact with people. Since association with people helps make us the kind of persons we are, we should be selective. Youngsters whose parents do not care with whom they are associated through the media (television, movies, books) inevitably hurt themselves. The books you read and the shows you watch reveal a great deal about yourself. There is an unsurpassed best-seller, known not as "a book" but as "The Book," the Bible. It is best-sold though probably not best-read, and certainly not best-understood.

As believers, we know that through this medium, the Bible, we associate with God. But we should realize that the Bible is first a human word, which was written in a time and culture alien to us. Hence it requires some exertion on our part to be understood. Is it worthwhile to put out that effort? Yes! Because through a human word in the Bible, we discover God's word. God inspired and guided the sacred writers!

In reading the Bible, we associate with God, if we do it as it should be done, namely, prayerfully and meditatively. Reading the Bible makes you a different person. Today's Liturgy deals with prayer and Bible reading.

C — 29th Sunday in Ordinary Time

Reading I — Ex 17, 8-13
The Lesson Applied

On their way to the promised land, the Jews pass through territory controlled by another nomadic tribe, Amalek. A tribal war breaks out. Moses picks out a high spot and like the other army commanders of his day holds the staff in his hand. From there he guides the battle. But note that Moses' staff is called "the staff of God." In verse 16 (see your Bible), the victory is expressly attributed to God. What did the sacred writer want to bring out by relating this ancient tradition? His lesson is: God fought on our fathers' side in the past, and he will help us now.

Why do we read this episode about two warring bedouin tribes in a desert some 3,200 years ago? We do not read it just for information. As believers, we pray and meditate on the point which God wants to bring out through this narrative. It could be: "In the battle of life, I am with you!" With this in mind, we make the words of the Responsorial Psalm (121, 1-8) our prayer to God.

Reading II — 2 Tm 3, 14—4, 2
"Scripture Useful for Teaching"

Paul insists that preachers should know the Bible and use it as the source of the wisdom they preach. With Scripture the man of God (priest-preacher) is well-equipped for his job. This implies that we should listen with faith when the Bible is explained in church. But why did Paul not recommend Bible reading by all? Simply because Bibles were not printed in his day and the vast majority of the faithful were illiterates. In our literate age with Bibles available, we should read prayerfully for ourselves (Vatican II: Constitution on Divine Revelation, 22).

Like the "Biblia Pauperum" (Bible stories, painted on the walls of medieval cathedrals for the illiterate poor), paraphrased and pictorial Bibles are all right for children and people with a low reading ability. Literate Christians read God's word in a translation as close as possible to the original, try to understand it with the help of introductions and footnotes, and apply it as God's word to their own life situation, as we do with today's Bible readings.

318   C — 30th Sunday in Ordinary Time

Gospel   The Point Considered   Lk 18, 1-8

It is important to pay attention to the point of this parable. Jesus does not compare God with the unjust judge insofar as he is lazy and unconcerned, nor insofar as the reason why he finally gives swift justice is concerned. The point is that like the widow we should persevere in prayer with a great faith! If we do so, God will be with us in the battle of life (Reading I).

◆

30th SUNDAY IN ORDINARY TIME
The Prayer of the Lowly Pierces the Clouds

THERE is no doubt that "how to pray" is a problem for many Christians. To begin with, one must get rid of the secret suspicion that prayer is nothing else but a good psychological means of comfort by talking persuasively to oneself, as it is for the person who cannot see God transcending creation as an Absolute You. Following the inspired experience of the Hebrews and especially Jesus' example in faith, we know that the ground of our being, the Ultimate Reality, God, is a "You," really related to us as a person.

The great philosopher and devout Jew, Martin Buber, has said: "All real life is meeting." When you meet a good person and become that person's friend, your meeting will enrich your life. Whenever you experience person-to-person contact, a dialogue, you live more fully. This is very evident in the encounter of two persons in love. "Prayer" is that encounter or meeting between you and God. Prayer is a dialogue between you and the "Absolute You," Almighty God. You speak and you listen when you meet God in your Bible, in a good sermon, in the Eucharistic celebration, in any good person, in any event of your life.

If real life is "meeting," this certainly applies to your meeting God in prayer. Prayer is something we must learn by doing. Prayer formulas may help us. They are useful for community prayer. They are a guide and inspiration for private prayer. Daily Bible reading in the family could be concluded by a spontaneous prayer by one member of the family. Try it!

C — 30th Sunday in Ordinary Time

Reading I
Sir 35, 12-14. 16-18
"Piercing the Clouds"

It seems that a regular life of prayer and worship is more difficult when the sun is shining in our lives than when we get our share of life's troubles. We forget God so easily! Nevertheless, praying makes human beings great at the very moment that they confess their insignificance before God! Their prayer, that of the lowly, "pierces the clouds." "The Lord hears the cry of the poor. He is close to the brokenhearted" (Responsorial Psalm).

Reading II
2 Tm 4, 6-8. 16-18
Strength in Prayer

Paul is in jail, and feels that the end is drawing near: "I have fought the good fight." He feels lonesome: "In court, no one took my part. Everyone abandoned me." Yet he harbors no hard feelings: "May it not be held against them!" Faith in God is his strength: "The Lord will continue to rescue me." Paul found strength in prayer.

God's word to us through this tradition could be: When you are depressed, try to follow Paul's example. Do not nurse hard feelings toward those who hurt you. Find strength in prayer!

Gospel
Lk 18, 9-14
Praying with Humility

In the eyes of his contemporaries, the Pharisee of this passage was a righteous man and the tax collector the traditional crook. Yet Jesus points to the latter as the just! Why? The Pharisee was wrong because he trusted in his righteousness and thought that God owed him something for it. God does not owe us a thing. The tax collector knew this. He had no merits to set before God. He could only plead for mercy.

Prayer is encounter between you and God. Meeting the Most High God, we should humbly realize who we are.

31st SUNDAY IN ORDINARY TIME
The Lord Is Gracious and Merciful

"PRODUCE or perish" is a rule in the business world. Applied to university professors, it reads, "Publish or perish!" The guiding principle behind these sayings is that managers should produce. If they fail, they are ruthlessly pushed aside. When they get older and their productivity decreases, they face the same fate if they have not protected themselves somehow. Big business, capitalism, is often as ruthless and ugly as communism. A person is like a machine which either operates or is dumped on a trash heap. This is what humankind often makes of God's wonderful world!

How does the maker of the universe look at his creation? He has designed human beings as his coworkers. In a sacred partnership, called covenant, we must work on a better society together with God. We are God's managers on this planet. But how does God look at those who ostensibly fail: the dope addicts, hobos, prostitutes, criminals, dropouts of society? If he regarded them as "good for nothing," why would he not get rid of them!

Today's Scripture readings deal with this issue. We should learn patience and mercy and try to preserve a person-to-person relationship also in business.

Reading I   Wis 11, 22—12, 1
Loving All Thinsgs

God's loving care manifests itself in the preservation of all things and in the forgiveness of sin. "But you spare all things, because they are yours, O Lord and lover of souls." God's business of maintaining the universe is larger than any of the multinational corporations, yet more human!

This pasage prepares us for the Gospel reading, where God, appearing in Jesus Christ, shows his loving care for the outcast Zacchaeus. "The Lord lifts up all who are falling and raises up all who are bowed down" (Responsorial Psalm).

Reading II — 2 Thes 1, 11—2, 2
Worthy of Your Call?

Because of rumors, the congregation of Thessalonica thought that the second coming of Christ was imminent. Paul tells the faithful not to be so easily agitated, but to be worthy of God's call and do their work!

We pray that God will make us worthy of our call. The name of the Lord Jesus must be glorified in us. We must be like him who showed patience and mercy (Gospel).

Gospel — Lk 19, 1-10
Concern for "Failures"

The tax collectors were the quislings of Jesus' society. They collaborated with the Roman occupation forces by collecting the taxes for them. Tax collectors were hated and shunned by genuine Jews and regarded as "sinners." Zacchaeus' goodwill is clear. But Jesus takes the initiative. He shows concern for this apparent "failure" in his society.

How do we handle "failures" in our community? Do we exhaust *all* means to help them?

32nd SUNDAY IN ORDINARY TIME
Living On as Beautiful Persons

HOW tenacious is that inborn instinct in all of us to go on living even after this life comes to an end. Parents want to live on in their children. A father wants at least one of his sons to continue the business which he has founded. Ex-presidents and former prime ministers found memorial libraries and write memoirs. We do not want oblivion. How do we survive? In the memory of my beloved ones, I will live on as the person they have known. In God, I will live on as the person I am. For God there are no hidden aspects of my character, as there possibly could have been for those who loved me.

We know great men and women who live in our memories: Pope John, St. Frances Xavier Cabrini, foundress of many schools, hospitals, and orphanages in this country, St. Elizabeth Ann Seton, who established a religious congregation of Sisters. These people were great not so much for what they accomplished as for what they were in themselves and the meaning and mission they had in their own eyes. That is why there are millions of housewives who did not accomplish spectacular things but are great because they were faithful to themselves and their call in life. They live on as beautiful persons. Mary, the mother of Jesus, is certainly one of them.

If God would call me today, am I the kind of person I should be? Today's Bible readings deal with our everlasting life in God.

Reading I　　　　　　　　　　　　　　2 Mc 7, 1-2. 9-14
"Being Restored to Life

The First and Second Books of Maccabees relate the persecution of Antiochus Epiphanes, the Syrian ruler of Palestine who tried to impose Greek culture and religion on all subjects of his empire. The orthodox Jews resisted violently. The First Book of Maccabees relates the Jewish revolt. The Second Book offers theological reflections on all that had happened. It has a timeless message for all who suffer for God's sake.

Note the element of hope in the tragedy of the martyrs in this passage: "It is my choice to die at the hands of men with the God-given hope of being restored to life by him." What about *your* fidelity to the vows of your baptism?

Reading II　　　　　　　　　　　　　2 Thes 2, 16—3, 5
Praying for One Another

One of the beautiful elements in the Christian faith is *hope* for a better future, if not in this life then in the hereafter (Reading I and Gospel). In this passage, Paul first offers a prayer for the young church of Thessalonica: that it be given hope and strength. Then he requires the congregation to pray for him. Finally, he prays for them again, that God may bestow love and constancy.

Pastor and congregation should pray for one another. We all need hope, strength, love, and constancy.

C — 33rd Sunday in Ordinary Time

Gospel   Lk 20, 27-38 or 20, 27. 34-38
"The God of the Living"

"Moses prescribed . . . ": the Sadducees refer to Deuteronomy 25, 5-10, the law of the "Levirate" marriage. The reasons for this law were to provide for the widow, the family name, and the inheritance. But Jesus' opponents are not interested in the legality of this law as such; they simply want to ridicule Jesus' teaching concerning the resurrection and life everlasting.

Jesus shows himself master of the situation. Those in the hereafter do not marry because they are no longer liable to death. The Sadducees did not believe in the resurrection because they could not find anything about it in the Books of Moses. That is why Jesus refers to Exodus (3, 6) which was one of the Books of Moses. The God of the living cares also for you.

◆

33rd SUNDAY IN ORDINARY TIME
The Lord Comes To Rule the Earth with Justice

ANY time we read that our armed forces are in a state of alert somewhere in the world, we know that there is a threat to our security. Alertness is good and necessary. When the Internal Revenue Service is about to check our files, we are alert and check first! Quite a few disasters, explosions, and fires could have been prevented if those in charge would have been as alert as they should have. Persons chosen to high office must submit themselves to scrutiny. If they have been honest, they can open their books fearlessly. Such people have been on the alert all their lives and they have no need to fear the day of scrutiny.

A concept found in the Bible time and again is that of "Day of the Lord," often called "The Day" or "That Day." It is a day of darkness and fear, a day of wrath and destruction. God will intervene in favor of the righteous, and punish the wicked. Gradually, "That Day" in the perspective of the prophets is delayed to the end-time. In the New Testament "That Day" is connected with Jesus Christ's second coming to judge the living and the dead. When the "Day of the Lord" is mentioned, a warning to be alert goes with it. The Lord could come at a moment you least expect!

During the fall of the year, the time of harvest, "an end-time" for farmers, the Church has us read about "That Day." Be on the alert! "The Lord comes to rule the earth with justice" (Responsorial Psalm).

Reading I   Mal 3, 19-20
The Sun's Healing Rays

"Lo, the day is coming." (See Introduction.) The concepts of "fire" and "blazing like an oven" constitute a familiar imagery in the Bible, used to express God's wrath which punishes evil-doers. The prophet issues a warning to the proud and the wicked, and he directs a word of encouragement to those who fear (have a filial respect for) God's name. The figure "Sun of justice" is applied in later literature to our Lord Jesus Christ.

The Responsorial Psalm (98) brings out that when you have been on the alert all your life, "The Day of the Lord" will be a day of joy.

Reading II   Thes 3, 7-12
The "Already" and "Not Yet"

Paul had founded the Church of Thessalonica. But other preachers had come along later and emphasized that "The Day of the Lord" (see Introduction) with the second coming of Christ was at hand. Hence, many of the Thessalonians had stopped working. If everything will soon be over, why should they exert themselves? Paul tells the congregation not to be alarmed but go on working quietly.

Christians live with the tension of the "already" and "not yet." We believe in a hereafter, but meanwhile this planet is our home, and as God's partners we must make it as habitable as possible for ourselves and our fellow humans.

Gospel   Lk 21, 5-19
The Day Will Come

Jesus had certainly predicted the destruction of the temple in Jerusalem, for this prediction was used against him during his final trial before the Sanhedrin. Later, however, the sayings of our Lord were expanded. As this passage now stands in Luke, it is an example of apocalyptic literature. The author interprets a present crisis (persecution, calamity, war, suffering of the innocent) with the use of symbolical language (fearful omens and great signs!). Have courage; soon God will definitely intervene!

Note again: "*The day* will come . . . The time is at hand." (See Introduction.) It is a timeless message for all of us. Be on the alert. Be honest! And when you have to suffer, remember that "by endurance you will save your lives."

───────◆───────

Last Ordinary Sunday

CHRIST THE KING

The God-Given Leadership of Our Lord

IT is vital for any organization to have capable leadership. We experience it on the parish level, and on the local and national level as well. That is why we test candidates on their leadership capabilities. We listen to their speeches. Their past is checked. And only if they are honest people and do a good job, do we elect and reelect them.

Leadership as far as God's reign is concerned is God-given, not elected by a constituency. However, since Jesus of Nazareth is the man in whom God dwells in such way that he is called the "Son of God" and even simply "God," we do not have to worry about his honesty and capability. "He [Jesus] is the image of the invisible God" (Reading II). Jesus now living and "sitting at God's right hand" (Hebrew idiom for "sharing power with God") is the leader of all who try to realize the reign of God in themselves and their fellow humans.

The way the Bible describes Jesus as leader is necessarily bound up with a particular time and culture. It speaks of Jesus as the King of God's kingdom! Meditating on the Christ event, the New Testament writers described our Lord after the image they had of their great King David, who was God's vicegerent ruling "the kingdom of God" on earth. In Jesus they saw all

C — Christ the King

Hebrew aspirations fulfilled: the kingdom (reign) of God established in our history. "The Lord God will give him the throne of David his father" (Lk 1, 32). Jesus is King/Leader of God's kingdom. Do you see the Lord Jesus as capable of giving direction to your life?

Reading I
Commander of Israel 2 Sm 5, 1-3

"Your bone and your flesh": In a tribal setting, the king has a strict father image. Moreover, the Hebrews saw the king as a sign of God's kingship. He is God's vicegerent on earth. He leads the people as a shepherd tends his flock. He is anointed, hence called "Messiah," which means "anointed King." The New Testament writers applied these characteristics to Jesus. Jesus is one with his body the Church (Reading II). He is the good shepherd and the Messiah—anointed King

The Responsorial Psalm (122, 1-5) was sung by the pilgrims, coming from all over the country, when full of excitement they entered the temple precincts. We apply it to the heavenly temple where Jesus as King sits at God's right hand.

Reading II
Col 1, 12-20
"He Rescued Us"

Paul describes who Jesus, dying on the cross (Gospel), really is. He identifies Jesus with "Wisdom" in Proverbs 8, 22-31. Jesus, as Son of God, is from God and absolutely prior to the visible universe. He is head of his body the Church (see Reading I). He has reconciled us with God. We thank the Father that he has rescued us from darkness and brought us to the kingdom of his beloved Son.

Gospel
Lk 23, 35-43
"Aren't You the Messiah?"

Jesus is King. But his kingship is something different: Jesus is reigning from a cross. He promises the "good thief": "This day you will be with me in paradise." Apparent defeat is actual victory in the resurrection.

We Christians must learn to see through the paradox of cross and suffering. Our final destiny is eternal happiness with Christ in paradise.

HOLYDAYS and MAJOR FEASTS

February 2

PRESENTATION OF THE LORD

Jesus Christ, a Sign That Is Opposed

SHOULD controversy be avoided at any cost? It seems impossible to do so if one wants to go by values that are not negotiable in good conscience. The person who tries to be nice all the time usually ends up losing friends and incurs the serious troubles associated with constant compromising. If we stand for values like love, justice, and truth, we are controversial and might even hurt feelings. Jesus Christ was controversial. A careful reading of the Gospels shows that he was in conflict with opponents all the time.

Inspired by Luke's narrative on Jesus' presentation in the temple, the Church celebrates another manifestation of the Lord. Who is he? He is a revealing light to the Gentiles (see Blessing of Candles and Procession), the glory of God's people Israel, but also a sign that will be opposed. Luke's point is very clear.

Like our Lord, we Christians are supposed to be a light in our dim and confused human condition. But being honest in business and public office and advocating values like fidelity, justice, and truth must result in controversy every so often. We should have the courage to face it, and follow our conscience whenever it dictates action or requires an absolute "no."

Reading I Mal 3, 1-4
"Like a Refiner's Fire"

The prophet consoles his fellow citizens who are undergoing the disappointments of the reconstruction of their country after the Babylonian exile. The Lord will come! "My messenger," "the Lord," and "the messenger of the covenant" stand for God. He comes to the temple. This passage introduces us to the theme of the Gospel, in which God, in the Lord Jesus, comes to the temple. The Lord will come refining and purifying, as the Lord Jesus destined to be the downfall and the rise of many in Israel, a sign that will be opposed.

Note that Malachi is not against sacrifices as such. He points out that a purified heart is the condition for offering a sacrifice (symbol of self) which pleases God. We should be aware of this when we participate in the sacrificial rites of the Eucharist.

Reading II — Heb 2, 14-18
Jesus Is Able To Help

The author points to the fact that Jesus was fully man and as such able to be our high priest, mediator between God and humankind. He had to become like his brothers and sisters "in every way," and in his parents he observed the Jewish law of purification as described in today's Gospel.

Gospel — Lk 2, 22-40 or 2, 22-32
Our Lord Controversial!

Luke describes the Jewish purification rite which the Holy Family observed as another manifestation of our Lord. He is introduced as "the Anointed of the Lord," the Anointed King or Messiah, who meets two representatives of his people, Simeon and Anna. The words "he took him in his arms" denote the customary ritual for blessing children, while "you yourself [Mary] shall be pierced with a sword" indicates the pain experienced by Mary as the mother of the Redeemer.

Are you willing to accept our Lord as controversial? His values, dos and don'ts, are not always those of your friends and associates! Take a stand!

———◆———

March 19

ST. JOSEPH, HUSBAND OF MARY
An Upright Man

IN order to have one's name on the "Who's Who" list, or to be mentioned in the obituary of the national magazines, one must have accomplished something substantial by worldly standards. One must be at least a kind of hero, or in the negative a very controversial figure, if one wants to be remembered in an encyclopedia. St. Joseph, the husband of Mary, would never have qualified.

All we know about Joseph is that he was an upright man, unwilling to expose his fiancée in a very embarrassing situation; that, in faith, he was obedient to God (1st Gospel); and that he searched for his lost child—something every parent would have done (2nd Gospel). Nevertheless, Joseph is remembered by a special solemnity. He had a very special call in life and was faithful to it.

God's standard of greatness is different from ours. Fidelity to our call in life and fairness in judgment of others, innocent till proven guilty, could be God's lesson to us in this day's Bible readings.

Reading I   2 Sm 7, 4-5. 12-14. 16
Your House Shall Endure Forever

Today's Bible readings want to present to us Joseph, the husband of Mary, in the framwork of the history of our salvation. And that history was first of all national Hebrew history, for Christianity was born from Judaism. (See Rom 11, 25-29.) Joseph is in the line of the great Hebrew patriarchs, David and Abraham (Reading II).

The throne of David stands firm forever because it has been given to the Savior of the world (Lk 1, 32), whose legal foster father was Joseph, according to the Gospel of today. That is why we Christians pray the Responsorial Psalm (89) by applying it to our Savior.

Reading II
Rom 4, 13. 16-18. 22

All Depends on Faith

This reading offers the framework for the Gospel. Abraham and Joseph have in common that both played an important role in the history of our salvation, and attained greatness through their faith. Abraham was faithful to his call in life by hoping against hope. Joseph's faith was similar.

We can learn important lessons from these simple but great personages.

Gospel
Joseph's Faith
Mt 1, 16. 18-21. 24

Note that in this tradition Joseph is central; it is he who receives the revelation from God. "Mary was engaged to Joseph": the marriage contract was drawn up between the parents of the couple. The marriage ceremony was accomplished when the groom took the bride into his house.

Joseph shows great self-restraint in this situation. We could learn something from him. "He is that just man, that wise and loyal servant, whom you placed at the head of your family" (Preface to the Eucharistic Prayer).

Gospel
OR
Lk 2, 41-51

This tradition points to what the Eucharistic Prayer says about Joseph: "With a husband's love he cherished Mary, the Virgin Mother of God. With fatherly care he watched over Jesus Christ your Son, conceived by the power of the Holy Spirit." We could pray: "Father, you entrusted our Savior to the care of St. Joseph. By the help of his prayers may your Church continue to serve its Lord, Jesus Christ" (Opening Prayer).

March 25

ANNUNCIATION

And the Word Was Made Flesh

ALL of the larger art museums of the world that exhibit paintings of both primitive and classic European culture are proud of masterpieces which depict the Annunciation of our Lord.

A-B-C — Mar. 25: Annunciation

The Incarnation of God's Word has captured popular piety as no other event of our salvation history. Church bells of towns and monasteries were tolled three times a day to encourage the faithful to pray: "The Angel of the Lord declared to Mary. And she conceived of the Holy Spirit. The Word was made flesh. And dwelt among us." And this still holds true in many places that hold on to tradition.

This Solemnity, nine months before Christmas, reminds us of this great intervention of God in human history. It is the origin of a human being in the womb of his mother. And this human being was so intimately united with God that the Bible calls him "Son of God—Word of God, made flesh." This should elicit admiring gratitude for God's care. "In Christ, the hope of all peoples, man's hope was realized beyond all expectations" (Preface to the Eucharistic Prayer).

Reading I — Is 7, 10-14
Naming Him Immanuel

(For commentary, see 4th Sunday of Advent—A. Isaiah spoke this oracle around 800 B.C. Jerusalem was threatened by mighty enemies. King Ahaz, of the House of David, did not want to be bothered by the man of God, Isaiah. "The virgin" refers initially to "your maiden," the king's wife. Luke (see Gospel)—and with him the Church—sees this oracle fully fulfilled in Mary bearing her Son, the Anointed King who will establish God's kingdom on earth.

The Responsorial Psalm (40, 7-11), applied to Jesus Christ, stresses that God's Son became man in order to do God's will, and by his obedience to make up for our sins.

Reading II — Heb 10, 4-10
"To Do Your Will"

(For commentary, see 4th Sunday of Advent—C.) Referring to the sacrificial activities of the Jewish high priest in the temple of Jerusalem, the author lets Jesus explain his mission. He became man in order to do God's will, to make up for man's evil and to establish a new covenant (partnership) between God and humankind. And it is for this that we Christians are grateful to the Lord Jesus.

Gospel
Rejoice!   Lk 1, 26-38

(For commentary, see 4th Sunday of Advent—B and the Feast of the Immaculate Conception, December 8.) Luke describes the mission of Jesus Christ: "The Lord will give him the throne of David his father." This thinking is fully in line with the Hebrew concept of salvation history. An Anointed King (Messiah) of the line of David will be God's vicegerent on earth, and bring about salvation.

But this salvation transcends the Jewish concept. It is for all human beings, both in this life and in the life to come. We Christians learn from Mary that we should cooperate with God's plan of salvation. "Let it be done to me as you [God] say" should be also our attitude in life.

June 24
BIRTH OF ST. JOHN THE BAPTIST
VIGIL MASS
Real Greatness

WHAT do the truly great think about their "greatness? We know that many such persons were frightened by it, since greatness implies a mission that frightens. Great men like Jeremiah (Jer 1, 6) and Isaiah (Is 6, 5) were frightened when they were called to a great task. John the Baptizer (or Baptist), whose birthday we celebrate today, was such a man. Jesus himself has said of him: "History has not known a man born of woman greater than John the Baptizer" (Mt 11, 11). Quite an honor!

John was so great that he could afford to state about Jesus Christ: "I am not even fit to carry his sandals" (Mt 3, 11). Only great personages can say such a thing! Was he frightened? The Bible is quite factual with reference to John, and does not say much about his inner life. But we know he had the courage to tell King Herod that it was sinful for him to live with his brother's wife. And after being jailed for that courage, he had the selflessness to send his own disciples to Jesus to follow him.

A-B-C — June 24: Birth of St. John (Vigil)

John was the forerunner of our Lord,. He prepared the way for him. He is great because of his fidelity to the call God gave him. What are your ideas of greatness?

Reading I
Jeremiah's Call
Jer 1, 4-10

In poetic language, Jeremiah describes his call as a prophet. He was afraid to accept it and tried to avoid it. Being a prophet, God's "mouthpiece," implies taking risks. The message to be preached is not always pleasant. Every preacher is well aware of this and of the fact that he will face angry reactions. Jeremiah's greatness is that he finally accepted and was faithful to his call.

Greatness consists in accepting your call in life and being faithful to it. But our strength to be faithful comes from God. Make the Responsorial Psalm (71) your prayer for strength.

Reading II
The Prophets' Searching
1 Pt 1, 8-12

The author refers to the prophets of the Old Testament (of whom John the Baptizer was the last), and declares that God's Spirit was guiding them. The Church has adopted that opinion, and sees the Old Testament as inspired by God. These prophets foresaw a Messiah to come. He would have to suffer in order to gain victory.

All of this became clear in the light of the New Testament. Catching sight of Jesus, John could say: "Look! There is the Lamb of God who takes away the sin of the world" (Jn 1, 29).

Gospel
Filled with the Holy Spirit
Lk 1, 5-17

The infancy narratives of both the forerunner and the Messiah himself are very similar. They already indicate "Gospel," which means "good tidings." Describing the circumstances of John's conception and birth, Luke is influenced by a similar narrative concerning the prophet Samuel (1 Sm 1). He wants to teach that John will be great and dedicated to a magnificent task in life, namely, "to prepare for the Lord a people well-disposed."

A-B-C — June 24: Birth of St. John (Day)
MASS DURING THE DAY

Reading I   Called from Birth   Is 49, 1-6

This passage marks the beginning of the Second Song of the suffering Servant of Yahweh. It is not clear who this suffering Servant is. Is he a person or a collective group of faithful Israelites? In any case, he has a mission as a prophet. Like many great men—Jeremiah, John the Baptizer, Jesus, Paul—he is called by God from his mother's womb. He is disappointed about the success of his preaching, yet, in faith, he knows that his reward is with the Lord.

All of this points to John the Baptizer and to our own call in life. When you are disappointed with what you achieve in life, you should think of your "reward with the Lord," and make the Responsorial Psalm (139) your prayer.

Reading II   John, Christ's Herald   Acts 13, 22-26

Paul sees King David both as a type of Jesus and as his ancestor. According to Hebrew thinking, the Messiah, who would reestablish God's kingdom on earth (after the Hebrews had lost self-determination), would be another David. With Paul we should see the Church as the "Israel of God," which grew out of the ancient "Israel of the flesh."

The New Testament authors see Jesus Christ as that new King David with John the Baptizer as his herald.

Gospel   "What Will This Child Be?"   Lk 1, 57-66. 80

Like the other great men of the Bible, John got his name from God. "John" means "God is graceful," and it indicates his call. John preached to sinners that God is graceful, provided that they turn to him. He preached this even to King Herod, who was living in sin. John had to pay for his fidelity to his call with suffering and violent death.

John challenges you and me to repentance. "[God] open our ears to John's message, and free our hearts to turn from our sins and receive the life of the Gospel" (Alternate Opening Prayer).

June 29
ST. PETER AND PAUL, APOSTLES
VIGIL MASS
Peter and Paul, Examples To Be Followed

EACH country has its national heroes. They are usually the Founding Fathers or heroic leaders in the struggle for freedom and self-determination. These heroes stand for values the country cherishes. They keep the people together. That is why children learn about them in school and we celebrate their birthdays. Hero worship also entails dangers, especially when the heroes are questionable characters. Worshiping only sports heroes or movie stars tells us something about those who worship them! In the heroes we worship values that they stand/stood for.

Two heroes who have captured the popular imagination of the faithful in the Catholic tradition for centuries are the founders of the Church in Rome, the apostles Peter and Paul. Their feasts were celebrated of course first in Rome, and from there devotion to these great saints spread all over the Church. Pilgrimages to their graves in Rome are organized up to the present day.

Hundreds of churches have chosen Peter and Paul as their patron-saints. Celebrating their memorials today, we are reminded of their dedication and heroism, and challenged to follow their example of heroic Christianity.

Reading I   Acts 3, 1-10
In Christ's Name

This tradition shows that Christian heroes or saints are great only insofar as they are related to Jesus Christ. Peter showed care for a crippled man, as the Lord had taught him to do. When he helped him, it was done in the name of Jesus Christ. Keeping this in mind will keep our devotion to the saints in a right perspective. It is God who is great in his saints.

But it is still a remarkable thing that simple folk could have succeeded in spreading the Christian message all over the Roman Empire (Responsorial Psalm 19).

Reading II — Gal 1, 11-20
Called by Christ

Paul is honest to state he had at first persecuted the Church of God (Acts 8, 1-3). He owes his call to Christ, who also revealed his Gospel to him. Paul meditated on it and once it became his, there was no force that could stop him from preaching it all over the cities around the Mediterranean.

Paul kept contact with Cephas (Peter). He found it important to keep himself associated with the body of authority-bearers in the Church.

Gospel — Jn 21, 15-19
Peter, the Leader

(See commentary on 3rd Sunday of Easter—C.) We learn that the Lord Jesus gave Peter the task of chief shepherd in his Church. Peter's triple denial of the Lord is done away with by a triple assurance of dedication. And Peter was faithful to it, though he knew that the demand of discipleship would be suffering and even violent death.

MASS DURING THE DAY

Reading I — Acts 12, 1-11
Peter's Courage

When Peter was in jail because of his courageous witnessing, the Church prayed for him. God showed his care for both the early Church and Peter. Both Peter and Paul were arrested time and again. But opposition never stopped them from doing what they thought they should do.

We can learn from these two men. Being a Christian means that you are a witness of Christian values. You may be in for ridicule. Can you take it? Have faith like Peter and Paul, and make the Responsorial Psalm (34) your prayer.

Reading II
2 Tm 4, 6-8. 17-18

Paul Has Finished the Race

Paul is in jail, and this time he knows that the end draws near. He looks back on his life. Paul must have been quite often in amphitheaters when the fights and races drew many spectators. He compares life so often with fights and races. If he has done well, he attributes it to the Lord, who gave him strength. And looking forward to the end, he trusts that the Lord will be with him till he is safe in his heavenly kingdom.

This is Christianity at its best. Let us hope and pray that when our end draws near, we can have a similarly well-balanced attitude of gratitude for the past and faith for the final passage from this life to a better one.

Gospel
Mt 16, 13-19

Peter's Profession of Faith

Today, we read the beautiful profession of faith by Peter in the name of his colleagues: "You are the Son of the living God." But Jesus puts it in its right perspective. It is God who took the initiative, and if the Church continues to establish God's reign on this planet up to the present it is able to do so only with God's help.

The Preface of today's Eucharistic Prayer says of Peter and Paul: "Peter raised up the Church from the faithful flock of Israel. Paul brought your call to the nations and became the teacher of the world." Both were great in their dedication, which we should follow by our dedication to our call in life.

August 6

TRANSFIGURATION

He Was Transfigured before Their Eyes

WALKING through nature in wintertime and observing the seemingly dead trees and bushes, one can hardly believe what all of it will look like in the spring of the year. When black clouds are building up and a tornado is threatening, we still know that every cloud has a silver lining, but our limited faculty of perception prevents a living awareness of it. In our best moments we are conscious that there must be something more about all we can observe. In faith, we know even that there is a beautiful reality behind the visible universe. Yet faith like love is not always as clear as we would wish it to be.

In celebrating our Lord's transfiguration (Gospel) we actually celebrate his kingship over creation and especially the divinization of human nature in the exalted Christ. In this mystery we anticipate our own exaltation to come. Meditatively participating in today's Liturgy should give us a renewed awareness of the invisible reality which will be ours in the future.

Reading I Dn 7, 9-10 13-14
The Son of Man Coming

(For commentary on apocalyptic visions and symbols, see 2nd to 7th Sundays of Easter—C.) The author wants to console his fellow faithful who are persecuted for their faith by King Antiochus Epiphanes. "The ancient one" is God, and the "son of man" is the Messianic King, applied to Jesus Christ.

We should read this passage and also the Responsorial Psalm (97, 1-9) against the background of our Lord's transfiguration, as described in the Gospel.

Reading II 2 Pt 1, 16-19
My Beloved Son

The author teaches about the exalted Lord Jesus Christ. For those who might refuse to believe in Jesus' second coming, he refers to the transfiguration, as witnessed by the apostles. In other words, the author states that Jesus has already the essential qualities which will be revealed when he comes again.

At the end, the writer explains what meditating on the exalted Christ should mean for us, namely, a renewed awareness of our own exaltation to come.

Gospel   YEAR A: Mt 17, 1-9; B: Mk 9, 2-10; C: Lk 9, 28-36
The Exalted Christ

(For commentary see 2nd Sundays of Lent—A, B, C.) In the transfiguration, we are invited to see the Lord Jesus as he really is. He is the king of creation. And in the exalted Christ, we see ourselves as we will be when our time comes. This faith awareness should encourage us when we are going through a time of depression and darkness.

August 15

ASSUMPTION
VIGIL MASS
Mary Is Taken Up to Heaven

EVERY one of us feels a sense of satisfaction after having done a good job whether it be a mother who has given birth to a healthy baby, a man who has pleased his wife with the gift she had secretly desired for a long time, or a teenager who has mowed the lawn and feels his father's hand on his shoulder: "Son, you have done a good job." We all have a job to do in life. We must make it meaningful for ourselves and those around us. In order to do so, we need images to go by, and we have a beautiful image in Mary—simply because she did nothing spectacular and nevertheless had a very meaningful life.

Mary experienced the darkness of faith, as all of us have. She endured the anxiety of a mother who does not understand a Son who has great ideals and takes frightening risks. She was a woman of sorrow following her Son, harassed and humiliated on his way to Calvary. We learn that suffering is part of life.

But Mary is also an image for our future. In a very eminent way she already shares in her Son's triumph over death, anxiety, darkness, and pain. As a beautiful human being, she is with God and as such constitutes an image for us who hope that when our time comes God will say: "Well done! . . . Come, share your master's joy!" (Mt 25, 21).

Reading I 1 Chr 15, 3-4. 15. 16; 16, 1-2
The Ark of God

According to the oldest tradition, the ark of the covenant contained the word of God (the two stone tablets on which the finger of God had written the ten commandments). During the journey in the desert, God went on revealing himself from the ark, and later the faithful come "before" the ark to meet God. The Responsorial Psalm (132) describes this as a procession of the ark. The history of the ark culminated and came to its end when David transferred it solemnly to Jerusalem where it found its definite place among God's people.

Tradition sees Mary as the ark of the New Covenant. Just as the ark of the Old Covenant contained God's word on stone tablets, so Mary bore the Word of God, Jesus Christ, in her womb. And her assumption into heaven is seen as prefigured in the solemn transferal of the ark into Jerusalem, the city of God where it found its final place among God's people.

Reading II 1 Cor 15, 54-57
Death Swallowed Up in Victory

Paul sees immortality, victory over death, as a victory over sin. God has given us that victory through our Lord Jesus Christ. In Christian tradition, Mary is seen as sinless from her conception on. Hence, the wages of sin (Rom 6, 23) can have no power over her. With soul and body, as a perfect human being, she shares in her Son's victory over death.

Gospel Lk 11, 27-28
Keeping the Word of God

Mary must have felt proud of her Son. But Jesus refers the woman's statement about his mother in this passage to the real greatness of Mary. She was the ark of the New Covenant (Reading I), who bore God's Word (Jesus) and by faithful dedication has listened to it. We should keep God's word in mind and, following Mary, listen to it!

A-B-C — Aug. 15: Assumption (Day)

MASS DURING THE DAY

Reading I
Rv 11, 19; 12, 1-6. 10

The Woman-Mary

The writer of Revelation speaks in symbols which were understandable only to "insiders"! Hence, his symbolic language requires patient explanation for us who read the book some 2,000 years later. (See also 33rd Sunday in Ordinary Time—B, 2nd paragraph of Introduction.)

The woman of this passage is the true, ideal, heavenly Israel of both the Old and the New Testaments, God's people, from which the Messiah who would defeat the dragon (all evil) was born. The arrival of the new Messianic era entails pain, which is compared to childbirth. Evil opposes the woman (God's people) and the child, "destined to shepherd all the nations" (Jesus the Messiah), but he was taken up to heaven. "The woman herself" (the church—God's people) harassed by persecution must flee to the desert, that is, go into hiding. But ultimately the reign of God will prevail. "The woman" is a figure of Mary, the member of Israel who gave birth to the Messiah. We must read this passage with that in mind. As Queen of Heaven, Mary stands at the right hand of her Son, arrayed in gold (Responsorial Psalm 45).

Reading II
1 Cor 15, 20-26

Coming to Life in Christ

Paul writes about the glorious end-time when Christ will have overcome all evil. We who have died to evil with him will also reign with him. Among God's redeemed people, Mary takes a special place, as Mother of the Redeemer. "The queen stands at your [the Messiah's] right hand, arrayed in gold" (Responsorial Psalm).

Gospel
Lk 1, 39-56

Blessed Are You

In this passage, Luke describes Mary as a pious Jewish woman. Mary is great not primarily in what she does (helping out a pregnant kinswoman is done daily!) but in why she does it, namely, out of great love and gratitude toward God, as Luke illustrates by figuratively putting a series of psalm verses (a Jewish song?) into Mary's mouth.

"His servant" is God's people, of which Mary is the most outstanding member. United with Mary in spirit, we too may pray this hymn since we are also God's people, servants, on whose lowliness God looks.

September 14

TRIUMPH OF THE CROSS

We Should Glory in the Cross of Our Lord Jesus Christ

CHRISTIANS in the Catholic tradition are often recognized by their sign of the cross. Christians of other traditions may say their blessing before meals without this sign. We make it. Our Church buildings are marked with a cross. A crucifix on the wall identifies the occupants of a home as Christians. A golden or silver cross on a person tells about his or her faith in Jesus Christ crucified. And finally a cross will mark our grave site.

Today, we celebrate the feast of the Triumph of the Cross. The Latin name of this feast is "Exaltatio Crucis," exaltation of the cross, indicating that the cross was shown to the people as a sign of salvation and victory over evil. The cross has a profound meaning to our lives as faithful. The suffering and death of the Lord Jesus are related to it. In faith we know that on the cross our Lord overcame the power of evil. Hence, the cross is no longer a sign of shame or defeat, but a sign of victory and salvation.

Reading I   Nm 21, 4-9
A Symbol of Salvation

This tradition tells us about the Jews in the desert who were bitten by snakes and looked to the bronze serpent lifted up or "exalted" as a symbol of salvation (Wis 16, 6). By doing so with faith in God, they recovered.

The reading introduces us to Jesus' saying to Nicodemus in today's Gospel. When we are wounded by evil, in faith we should look at the sign of our salvation, Jesus crucified. God, in the Lord Jesus, is willing to forgive. With this in mind, read the Responsorial Psalm (78, 1-2. 34-38).

Reading II   Phil 2, 6-11
Christ Highly Exalted

In this reading too there is reference to "lifting up" or "exaltation" (see Reading I). Because of Jesus' humble obedience, God highly exalted him. And as lifted up or exalted, our Lord grants salvation. We kneel down in respect, for Jesus Christ is Lord. "We acknowledge the mystery of the cross on earth. May we receive the gift of redemption in heaven" (Opening Prayer).

Gospel   Jn 3, 13-17
Jesus Christ Lifted Up

(For commentary see 4th Sunday of Lent—B and Trinity Sunday—A.) Jesus refers to the incident of the first reading, where we read about Moses mounting a bronze serpent, symbol of salvation, on a pole. In both cases, there is a lifting up. In this passage "lifting up" is deliberately given a double meaning. It refers to Jesus Christ as lifted up in the resurrection and ascension into heaven whence he confers salvation on all of us.

If there is reference to looking at the cross as symbol of salvation (Reading I), it is of course to be understood as "looking at in faith." When sinners turn to the "lifted up" Lord Jesus, their sins will be forgiven.

———◆———

November 1
ALL SAINTS
Our Communion with the Saints

WE are acquainted with the Negro spiritual that goes: "When the saints go marchin' in . . . , I want to be in their number." The song reflects popular piety but it is to the point.

So often we see human values out of perspective. Does the constant glittering of neon lights make us myopic? Christians are supposed to go by the light of faith. Why should we hurt ourselves by moving about in darkness when the real light is available? Christ tells us where to put priorities. Yet so often we go by the candlelight of human wisdom and make mistakes.

Many great Christians, unsung heroes of outstanding love and dedication to their commitment in life, have gone before us. Let us follow them, rather than those who are successful in sports, beauty, or money-making! In the Preface to the Eucharistic Prayer, we will pray: "Father, all powerful and ever-living God, their [the saints'] glory fills us with joy, and their communion with us in your Church gives us inspiration and thought, as we hasten on our pilgrimage of faith, eager to meet them."

Do not go it alone! You are part of a great family. A feeling of belonging is something all of us need.

Reading I Rv 7, 2-4. 9-14
Who Are These Dressed in White?

Using visionary language, the author encourages Christians who are suffering persecution. "An angel coming from the east" [the source of light, rising Sun, place of paradise, Gn 2, 8] holds "the seal of the living God": Just as Oriental kings customarily impressed their seal on their belongings, so all who are "marked" by the seal of God belong to him and are saved. The number 144,000 is symbolic (12 x 12 x 1000—12 is the symbol of perfection!). "The throne and the Lamb": Jesus Christ, the Lamb of God.

This Bible word, God's word, should also encourage us, who still walk in the valley of darkness and go perhaps through a period of real trial and hardship. From our lowliness, we could pray with the psalmist: "Lord, this is the people that long to see your face" (Responsorial Psalm).

Reading II 1 Jn 3, 1-3
We Shall See God As He Is

When in despair many turn to the escapisms of dope, alcohol, and even suicide, Christians somehow do not give in because they have hope. God loves us. With his help, many Christians before us (some of them outstanding figures) have achieved their goal. With God's help we hope to do the same.

Gospel   Mt 5, 1-12
Blest Are Those—You?

(For commentary on this passage, see 4th Sunday in Ordinary Time—A.) Jesus shows us ideals we should pursue! Outstanding Christians of all ages have done so and are now happy with God. Inspired by their example, we should try also! Take one of these sayings that appeals to you, and work on that one today!

November 2
ALL SOULS
FIRST MASS
For Faithful People Life is Changed, Not Ended

NOTHING is more sure than that all of us are born to die. We have to face death first quite often, when it strikes our beloved ones, and finally when we ourselves are involved. We have to leave everything behind us. We may try not to think of it. Some consider death as an absurdity. Others learn to handle this reality as an integral part of our condition.

Am I, who came into being and grew into a person through my relationship with other human beings, doomed to break for always the very ties that made me the person I am? Am I, who believe that God called me to live with him in a sacred partnership (covenant), rewarded with mere nothingness the moment I breathe my last?

We Christians are aware in faith that beyond death we will be with God. We are also aware that at the moment of death, we are not always the kind of persons we should be for all eternity; hence, a process of purification follows death before we will share life with God, as promised. On this awareness Christians base their ancient custom of praying for the deceased, that

A-B-C — Nov. 2. All Souls (First Mass)

God may grant them the vision of his glory. All Souls Day is a special day of prayer for all our brothers who have gone ahead of us.

Reading I   Jb 19, 1. 23-37
I Shall See God

If you are not familiar with the Book of Job, you should read Job 1—2, 13 and 42, 7-17. It is a folktale used by the author as a framework for a series of speeches or dialogues dealing with the problem of human suffering. Why do I have to suffer and ultimately die?

In this passage, we have a beautiful specimen of God-inspired Hebrew insight. It should help us, when we have to face suffering and death. Whatever happens, "the Lord is my good shepherd; there is nothing I shall want" (Responsorial Psalm).

Reading II   1 Cor 15, 51-57
Victory Over Death!

(For commentary see also 8th Sunday in Ordinary Time—C, and the Vigil of the Assumption, August 15.) "Not all of us . . .": the just living at Christ's second coming will not die, but they will be transformed. Paul still expected Christ's second coming during his own lifetime. "The trumpet will sound" is Biblical imagery to describe the awe-inspiring greatness of the Judge of the living and the dead.

Gospel   Jn 6, 37-40
Having Eternal Life

God wants all human beings to be saved. Nobody who turns to our Lord will be rejected. And because of his meritorious death and resurrection, the Lord Jesus has the power to raise up all, so that all will have everlasting life with him.

Hence, we pray: "Lord God, may the death and resurrection of Christ which we celebrate in this eucharist bring the departed faithful to the peace of your eternal home" (Prayer after Communion).

ALL SOULS
SECOND MASS

Reading I   Wis 3, 1-9 or 3, 1-6. 9
In the Hand of God

The author wrote his book for the Jewish community in Alexandria of Egypt. He wants to strengthen the faith of his fellow Jews who, as a minority group, are continually exposed to sophisticated Greek thinking. They should be guided by the inspired wisdom of God and not let themselves be confused by secular philosophy.

In this passage the author deals with the great issue of life and death. "Hope full of immortality" is expressed in the Responsorial Psalm: "I will walk in the presence of the Lord in the land of the living."

Reading II   Phil 3, 20-21
Our Citizenship in Heaven

(For commentary, see also 2nd Sunday of Lent—C.) As Christians, we are citizens of two cities. It is our task to make this world a better place for all of us. But we should never forget that our ultimate goal is life everlasting, "our citizenship in heaven." Then we will be somehow like the risen Lord Jesus.

Gospel   Jn 11, 17-27 or 11, 21-27
"Do You Believe This?"

Like Martha and Mary, we believe that Jesus is the resurrection and the life. And it is important for us to keep alive our faith in him. "Whoever believes in me" should be a living thing! And if our faith is alive, it is a source of consolation whenever we face the mystery of death.

ALL SOULS
THIRD MASS

Reading I   2 Mc 12, 43-46

In this passage we have a clear reference to faith in the resurrection, and an indication that those who at death are not yet as pure as they should be will go through a process of cleansing. Christian theologians would eventually develop this into the teaching on purgatory.

Actually, we do not know how this takes place. But we should remember that we are in line with a great tradition when we pray for those who have gone ahead of us. The Responsorial Psalm (130, 1-8) may be a prayer in union with all who wait for redemption.

Reading II   Rv 14, 13
Dying In The Lord

The author says that God authorized him to teach that the dead who die in the Lord are with God. According to Jewish teaching, a person's good works follow him or her as witnesses in God's court. Christians believe that we are saved because of our faith in God, but that good works must accompany faith.

Gospel   Jn 14, 1-6
A Place Prepared for Us

Jesus speaks words of consolation. Have faith! All who have to face death and think about deceased loved ones should remember these words. "In my Father's house" means heaven to which Jesus is returning. We will go there, but through the Lord Jesus in whom we firmly believe: "Merciful Father, . . . as we renew our faith in your Son, whom you raised from the dead, strengthen our hope that all our departed brothers and sisters will share in his resurrection" (Opening Prayer of 1st Mass).

◆

November 9
DEDICATION OF ST. JOHN LATERAN
Christians Are God's Living Temple

EACH congregation celebrates the annual memorial of the dedication of its church. Sometime in the past, the parish church was consecrated to God and dedicated for worship. However, the church building can only be an effective sign of

God's presence to his people, and as such a type or image of the heavenly city Jerusalem, if the members of the congregation let themselves be built like living stones into a spiritual temple with Christ as the foundation.

Today, Christians celebrate the dedication of the basilica of St. John Lateran, the Cathedral of the Holy Father, in Rome. Today, we should be aware that we are God's temple not only as a local congregation, but also as God's people at large all over the globe. In union with all Christians of the world, we should be like a temple in which are offered sacrifices of good works that are pleasing to God (1 Pt 2, 5).

Reading I　　　　　　　　　　　　2 Chr 5, 6-10. 13—6, 2
God Dwelling Among Us

The author describes the dedication ceremony of the Jerusalem temple, built by King Solomon. "The building of the Lord's temple was filled with a cloud" from the incense they were burning. In his dedication speech, King Solomon sees this cloud as a sign of God's presence to his people.

Your church should remind you that God is present to us who are figuratively called his temple, or dwelling place. With this in mind, pray the Responsorial Psalm (84, 3-11).

Reading II　　　　　　　　　　　　　1 Cor 3, 9-13. 16-17
We Are the Temple of God

Paul elaborates on the temple figure, of which your parish church is a sign. God's people can be a solid building, in which the Spirit of God dwells, only if it is built on the solid foundation that is Christ. "Fire will test the quality of each man's work": fire is the usual symbol the Bible uses to mention God's judgment. Poor material will burn up; good material (works) lasts.

Paul reminds us to be aware of God's closeness to each of us, and not to destroy God's temple by aversion, indifference, sin. The Opening Prayer states: "God our Father, from living stones, your chosen people, you built an eternal temple to your glory."

Gospel
Lk 19, 1-10
Staying at Your House

We must read this passage with the symbolism of the former readings in mind. "You are God's building" (Reading II). Jesus intends to stay at the house of Zacchaeus, marked as a sinner. But this sinner repented and therefore Jesus could say: "Today, salvation has come to this house."

God will come to our "house," he will be close to us and be the principle of our salvation, provided that we repent and remain hospitable.

December 8
IMMACULATE CONCEPTION
Mary's Faith and Love That Never Knew Sin

A CHILD born and reared in an irreligious family of evildoers and thieves is seriously handicapped in becoming and remaining a good person. Similar to this is the human condition into which we are born. In the human race we experience a mysterious collectivity in evil which we cannot understand completely. Evil will always be obscure. And one thing is sure: it would require a special favor of God for us not to be infected by evil in and around us.

This special favor was given to Mary, the Mother of our Lord Jesus Christ. In today's Gospel, God addresses Mary through his angel: "Rejoice, O highly favored daughter! The Lord is with you. Blessed are you among women." We are not so favored! Hence, from the lowliness of our sinful condition, we pray: "Father, Mary had a faith that your Spirit prepared and a love that never knew sin, for you kept her sinless from the first moment of her conception. Trace in our actions the lines of her love, in our hearts her readiness of faith" (Alternative Opening Prayer).

Reading I
Gn 3, 9-15. 20
Victory over Evil

Adam ("Everyman") and Eve (the "Woman") have sinned and remain entangled in sin, since they do not show even the slightest sign of repentance. The man projects his guilt onto the woman, and the woman onto the serpent. The writer of Genesis, though a keen observer of the omnipresence of evil, believes in God's mercy! God must give a way out. "I will put enmity between you [the evil one] and the woman, and between your offspring and hers."

Later revelation will confirm this optimism and tell how victory over evil is attained. The woman's offspring then is primarily Christ. With the words of the psalmist we may praise God for overcoming evil through a woman (Mary) and her son: "Sing to the Lord a new song, for he has done marvelous deeds."

Reading II Eph 1, 3-6. 11-12
To Be Full of Love

We are invited to thank God for all the blessings he has bestowed upon us. From all eternity you and I exist in the mind of God. And somehow, somewhere we fit in his great plan of salvation. This is true in a very special sense for Mary, since she was chosen to be the mother of the Redeemer.

Gospel Lk 1, 26-38
Mary "Full of Grace"

We are taught about Mary, highly favored by God and blessed among women. Christian tradition sees in the greeting of the angel and Mary's unique destiny that she was given grace in a special measure and united with God in such a way that she is "full of grace," hence sinless from the moment of her conception.

Mary was deeply troubled and overwhelmed by the words of the angel. Things were not very clear in her mind from the beginning. It was her great faith in God that made her respond: "I am the maidservant of the Lord. Let it be done to me as you say." We are invited "to follow Mary's faith that God's Spirit prepared and her love that never know sin" (Alternative Opening Prayer).

◆

INDEX OF MASS THEMES

Acceptance and rejection .. 191
Affliction 99
Annunciation 330
Appreciation 112
Ascension 69, 175, 275
Assumption 339
Bible 168, 240, 316
Bishop, support for 102
Blindness of mind 218
Call and response 45, 138, 140
Christ: Ascension .. 69, 175, 275
  authority of 142
  baptism of 27, 137, 236
  Bread from heaven 196
  and Christians 267
  eternal life in 159
  eternal reign of 132
  feeds us 195
  Good Shepherd 64
  healing activity of .. 144, 205
  in our midst 47
  kingship of 125, 225, 325, 337
  Knowledge of 286
  leadership of 9
  lifted up to give all life . 159
  manifestation of 327
  our knowledge of 30
  our light 56
  our Viaticum 198
  Resurrection of 57
  royal Messiahship of all . 26
  salvation in 170
  sharing life of .. 81, 181, 280
  and sinners 307
  union with in the Church 171
  unity in 277
Christian heroes 325
Christian maturity 248
Christian optimism 260
Christianity 242
Church management in service 207
Correction 106, 300
Covenant of love 150
Creative fidelity 123
Cross 207, 342
Day of the Lord 323
Death ... 52, 121, 161, 282, 345
Discipleship 31, 306
Diversity in unity 67
Eucharistic celebration 200
Evil to be conquered 183
Faith 12, 48, 253, 312
Faith and fellowship 45, 166, 265
Family life 21, 134, 234

Fidelity, creative 123, 212
Forgiveness 148, 284
Freedom 37, 151
Future life 323, 345
God: call and response 45
  cares for us 15
  generosity of 109
  and history 116
  ineffable mystery of 80
  is for us 155
  is love 173
  joy in 130
  judgment of 323
  kindness of endures forever 85
  living word of 240
  love for 118
  mercy of 320
  our Savior 231
  patience of 93
  presence of 244
  providence of 40
  reign of to be established . 90
  reign of, here and to come 290
  reign of, in the making .. 225
  salvation of, for all . 129, 229
  temple of 348
  word of 92
Good News and great joy ... 16
Good Shepherd 64
Gratitude 314
Greatness, real 332
Happiness, search for 246
Heaven and earth . 69, 175, 275
Holiness 38
Honesty 41, 250
Hope 184, 223, 299
Hospitality 294
Humility 33, 304
Image of God, growth in .. 248
Immaculate Conception 350
Impatience 227
John the Baptist 332
Joseph, an upright man 329
Joy and hope 11, 130, 271
Justice for all 309
Kindness 85, 107
Knowledge, ongoing process 286
Law 37, 157
Life 50, 52, 81, 161, 162, 181,
    188, 262, 280, 297, 321
Light 18, 56
Love ... 83, 104, 118, 150, 151,
  173, 210, 219, 238, 284, 292
Mary, ... 23, 232, 339

Meaning to life 297
Mercy 107, 320
Messianic Banquet 97, 114
Mystery of God 80, 179, 279
Neighbor, love of . 118, 173, 219
Pain 144
Patience 93, 227, 320
Penance and forgiveness ... 148
Perseverance in trials 269
Peter and Paul 335
Petition 295
Poor, Christian concern for . 311
Prayer ... 72, 99, 186, 255, 318
Priests 119, 190
Profession of faith 253
Prophet 242
Providence 40
Reconciliation to God in Christ 258
Reform 256
Rejection 191
Religion, human and divine . 204
Renewal under the Spirit ... 272
Renunciation of self .. 214, 288
Repentance 140
Respect for all 210
Responsibility 111
Sacrifice and love 104
Sadness and joy 271
Saints, communion of 343
Self-giving to God 221
Sermon 88
Servant of Yahweh . 27, 137, 236
Service 209, 216
Sin and temptation 44
Spirit at work 73, 76
Suffering 144
Symbolism 196
Table fellowship in the Lord . 195
Time of favor 66
Tolerance 251
Transfiguration 338
Unclean spiritually 145
Understanding 284
Unity 67, 177
Universalism 100
Values, priority 35, 95
Vigilance 8, 72, 127
Wisdom 121, 306
Witness and fear 87
Word of God 19, 24, 62, 92, 240, 316
Worship 83, 157